HOW TO REVIEW
SCHOLARLY BOOKS

SKILLS FOR SCHOLARS

For a full list of titles in the series, go to https://press.princeton.edu/series/skills-for-scholars.

The Entrepreneurial Scholar: A New Mindset for Success in Academia and Beyond, Ilana M. Horwitz

How to Mentor Anyone in Academia, Maria LaMonaca Wisdom

On the Art and Craft of Doing Science, Kenneth Catania

Academic Writing as if Readers Matter, Leonard Cassuto

Thinking through Writing: A Guide to Becoming a Better Writer and Thinker, John Kaag and Jonathan van Belle

The Pocket Instructor: Writing: 50 Exercises for the College Classroom, Edited by Amanda Irwin Wilkins and Keith Shaw

Stellar English: A Down-to-Earth Guide to Grammar and Style, Frank L. Cioffi

Try to Love the Questions: From Debate to Dialogue in Classrooms and Life, Lara Schwartz

The Elements of Visual Grammar: A Designer's Guide for Writers, Scholars, and Professionals, Angela Riechers

Writing with Pleasure, Helen Sword

The Grant Writing Guide: A Road Map for Scholars, Betty S. Lai

The Secret Syllabus: A Guide to the Unwritten Rules of College Success, Jay Phelan and Terry Burnham

Writing on the Job: Best Practices for Communicating in the Digital Age, Martha B. Coven

The Economist's Craft: An Introduction to Research, Publishing, and Professional Development, Michael S. Weisbach

How to Review Scholarly Books

READING, WRITING, RELISHING

STEVEN E. GUMP

PRINCETON UNIVERSITY PRESS
PRINCETON & OXFORD

Copyright © 2025 by Princeton University Press

Princeton University Press is committed to the protection of copyright and the intellectual property our authors entrust to us. Copyright promotes the progress and integrity of knowledge created by humans. Thank you for supporting free speech and the global exchange of ideas by purchasing an authorized edition of this book. If you wish to reproduce or distribute any part of it in any form, please obtain permission.

Requests for permission to reproduce material from this work should be sent to permissions@press.princeton.edu

Published by Princeton University Press
41 William Street, Princeton, New Jersey 08540
99 Banbury Road, Oxford OX2 6JX

press.princeton.edu

All Rights Reserved

GPSR Authorized Representative: Easy Access System Europe - Mustamäe tee 50, 10621 Tallinn, Estonia, gpsr.requests@easproject.com

Library of Congress Cataloging-in-Publication Data

Names: Gump, Steven, 1975- author.
Title: How to review scholarly books : reading, writing, relishing / Steven Gump.
Description: Princeton : Princeton University Press, 2025. | Series: Skills for scholars | Includes bibliographical references and index.
Identifiers: LCCN 2024036063 (print) | LCCN 2024036064 (ebook) | ISBN 9780691270494 (paperback) | ISBN 9780691270487 (hardback) | ISBN 9780691270500 (ebook)
Subjects: LCSH: Book reviewing—Handbooks, manuals, etc. | Scholarly publishing—Handbooks, manuals, etc. | Academic writing—Handbooks, manuals, etc. | BISAC: LANGUAGE ARTS & DISCIPLINES / Writing / Academic & Scholarly | EDUCATION / Teaching / Subjects / Arts & Humanities
Classification: LCC PN98.B7 G86 2025 (print) | LCC PN98.B7 (ebook) | DDC 808.06/6028—dc23/eng/20241223
LC record available at https://lccn.loc.gov/2024036063
LC ebook record available at https://lccn.loc.gov/2024036064

British Library Cataloging-in-Publication Data is available

Editorial: Matt Rohal and Alena Chekanov
Production Editorial: Jaden Young
Jacket and Cover Design: Heather Hansen
Production: Lauren Reese
Publicity: Alyssa Sanford and Kathryn Stevens
Copyeditor: Karen Verde

This book has been composed in Arno

10 9 8 7 6 5 4 3 2 1

For reviewers everywhere,
new and seasoned

CONTENTS

Prelude: Previewing Reviewing   1

1   Getting Started as a Scholarly Book Reviewer   9

Interlude 1: Thinking Like a Reviewer   49

2   Reading for Reviewing   54

Interlude 2: Finding Your Way In   81

3   Writing a Scholarly Book Review   85

Interlude 3: Celebrating Completion   119

4   Considering Special Cases   125

Interlude 4: Transferring Your Skills   159

5   Improving the Craft and Context of Reviewing   164

Postlude: Teaching Scholarly Reviewing   189

Acknowledgments 199

Appendix: Questions for Scholarly Reviewers 203

Notes 209

Works Cited 227

Index 243

HOW TO REVIEW
SCHOLARLY BOOKS

PRELUDE

PREVIEWING REVIEWING

Who Needs This Book?

You've come to the right place if you're looking for a guide that will help you understand the genre of the scholarly book review and learn how to write engaging reviews yourself. You are likely aligned with the humanities or narrative social sciences: the "book" disciplines, where monographs, either single-authored or coauthored, are key vehicles for disseminating scholarly ideas. You know that scholarly reviews of published books, when done well, can apprise you of such ideas, guiding you to books that you should read or steering you away from books that do not complement your intellectual or professional needs. You are also likely a graduate student or someone with an advanced degree who wishes to address, in some small way, the ongoing conversation in your academic field. Perfect! I've written this book with you in mind. Even if you're more advanced in your career or have written a review or two already, I trust you'll still find some useful perspectives and ideas herein.

I wrote this guide, in part, because I've read a lot of unengaging, unhelpful reviews—those that are more akin to summaries or book reports. Perhaps you've seen such reviews in scholarly journals yourself: They tend to march through a book serially, chapter by chapter, and offer little to no analysis beyond a concluding assessment, often cliché, with minimal justification. "This book is a welcome addition to the literature," or "Everyone should read this book." Right. The limited message such reviews send is that the reviewer can read, sure. And the reviewer can follow a (boring) template to produce a text that minimally qualifies as a review. But did the reviewer engage with the ideas presented in the book being described? Did the reviewer sufficiently honor the labors of the author and publishing team by taking the act of reviewing seriously instead of superficially, mechanically, peremptorily? And did the reviewer imagine you, the reader of the review, and try to anticipate your curiosities and needs, one of which is generating and maintaining your interest in the material being presented?

Yes, some books are, by virtue of their subject matter or author, "must reads" for you or for me. But most, by far, are not. Perhaps I'll glean everything I need (or think I want) to learn about a book from reading an especially insightful review. When a reviewer teaches me something about a book I otherwise might not have picked up, though, I am often liberated from the norm, from the known. In short, my horizons expand. The books that have most transformed me as a thinker, as a writer, and as a human being are those that I otherwise might not have encountered, save for a helpful nudge from a helpful reviewer. If you care about your field, you should aspire to be that reviewer yourself.

Have no regrets if you've already written an "unengaging" review yourself. The first book review I wrote, more than two decades ago, in fact takes a chapter-by-chapter approach. I'll have more to say about it later. We all must learn through doing. And we can all continually be improving our craft. Read on, consider my advice, and your next review will surely engage.

As you'll see throughout these pages, I propose that the scholarly book review can make an intellectual contribution of its own. This idea is not new, but it seems to have been forgotten, at least in some circles. Certain evaluative contexts, too, especially those that encourage—or require—individuals to focus on publications of a certain type, usually journal articles in "approved" outlets, have also diminished the value of the scholarly book review. By offering a contextualized summary, clear analysis, and cogent assessment, the scholarly book review embodies a type of creative work that taps into the reviewer's intellectual and associative capabilities. I avow that the scholarly book review can come closer to the literary book review in the way it accomplishes its primary goals. (What is a "literary" book review? Think of what you would encounter in the *Los Angeles Review of Books*, the *New Yorker*, or the *Times Literary Supplement*, if you're familiar with these venues. Such reviews are also known as "critical" reviews.) Beyond the fact that literary book reviews may address works of fiction, a primary difference between a scholarly book review and a literary book review is the presumption that the literary book review should be enjoyable to read. Why shouldn't the scholarly book review be enjoyable, as well? This book offers ideas and suggestions for making it so.

The genre of the scholarly book review is evaluative yet is itself not commonly evaluated: With few exceptions, nobody regularly reviews the reviewers. Scholarly journals occasionally acknowledge stellar peer reviewers of submitted manuscripts, but if any journals award prizes to their book reviewers, that's news to me. The National Book Critics Circle, a professional organization, annually awards the Nona Balakian Citation for Excellence in Reviewing to one of its members. (The 2023 recipient was Becca Rothfeld, nonfiction book critic for the *Washington Post*.) And in journalism, where literary book reviews fall, Pulitzer Prizes in Criticism were first awarded in 1970. (The 2024 recipient was

Justin Chang, film critic of the *Los Angeles Times*, now of the *New Yorker*.) Categorically, criticism encompasses a much broader field than scholarly book reviewing. Yet scholarly book reviewing is fundamentally a form of criticism that crosses into the terrain of scholarly service.

In the general absence of such accolades in the scholarly realm, how can you tell what makes a scholarly book review "effective" or "successful"? One goal of this book is to describe the values, aims, and purposes of scholarly book reviews to help reviewers cultivate a certain connoisseurship—and to push the concept into territory where the review takes on greater meaning as a creative, intellectual product. Some of my ideas for scholarly book reviews may seem aspirational, but I offer them because I see promise and potential in the genre. Of course, different fields have different expectations. If, in my presentation, I fail to touch on a point that is fundamental to scholarship in your field, be sure to consider that point in your evaluation. I expect you to be the disciplinary expert. This book does not teach *how* to assess the intellectual content or contributions of scholarly books. (That is a task of upper-level undergraduate coursework and, fundamentally, graduate school.) But this book does point out *what*, in general, you should be considering while you read and formulate your opinions about scholarly books in your field. And it offers strategies for presenting your reviews in a thoughtful, engaging manner.

Another reason I wrote this guide is because, after more than two decades of book reviewing, I have refined a practice that makes reviewing—dare I say it?—a generally enjoyable activity. Engaged reviewers are more likely to write engaging reviews. When I encounter a promising new title, I am excited about the possibilities that lie between the covers, since I believe every scholarly book has something to teach me. *First*: Who is this author, and what message does this book intend? *Then*: How is the book structured, substantiated, presented? *Finally*: Is the book successful in accomplishing its stated goals? How has my worldview shifted by engaging with the contents? And how could your worldview be similarly enlarged, if you were to pick up and read this book yourself? Scholarly books offer readers this tacit promise: In return for your time, you will be rewarded with new knowledge, new perspectives, new insights for applying to your work and your world. Scholarly books—and their reviews—are a serious business.

I presently serve as book review editor of the *Journal of Scholarly Publishing*, so one additional reason I wrote this book is to be able to have something to share with potential reviewers who reach out for guidance. Self-serving? Perhaps. But my eagerness to solicit, receive, develop, and publish engaging reviews cannot be extraordinary.

The least enjoyable reviews to write are those for books where the contents or the delivery does not live up to my initial excitement. (Contemporary American slang has the perfect term for being underwhelmed: Those books are "mid.") If I feel disappointed upon finishing a book, I usually want to cut my losses and move on to something more promising. But I will address how to write challenging reviews—those that tend to be more critical—in a way that is fair to the authors and helpful to their fields. Sometimes the better choice is just not to review a particularly problematic book, of course. This book, though, presupposes that your intended goal will be to write a review: positive, mixed, or "mid."

Despite the rumors that have been circulating for years, books are not going away anytime soon. As long as scholarly books are being published, disciplines will need scholarly book reviews. Together we can strive to improve the value of scholarly book reviews for readers, for reviewers, for book authors, for publishers, for academic communities—for all parties involved.

What Does This Book Offer?

Authors can structure and organize their ideas to signal their themes and theses. This book progresses linearly, to a point. I begin, in chapter 1, by introducing the genre of the scholarly book review, explaining why you should write (and read) reviews, and helping you identify publication outlets and titles for review. The remainder of the book will prove most useful once you have a book in hand that you are planning to review and a venue that has expressed interest in your review. Still, you are certainly welcome to read through the entire book to give yourself a sense of what to expect before embarking on your first scholarly review. I make this point later, yet it's worth mentioning here: Because you want to tailor your review to a specific audience and want to know that a specific venue would welcome your review, you shouldn't write a scholarly book review on speculation. Always line up a venue for a review before you begin writing.

This book emphasizes writing, but a core and often overlooked element of reviewing is the real work of reading. Yes, work. Chapter 2 explains how your goals as a reviewer translate into the elements of attentiveness and inquisitiveness as a reader. The secret to enjoyable book reviewing, if there is one, lies in how effectively you read and take notes. Then, chapter 3 describes how to convert your valuable reading notes into a framework for a contextualized, clear, and cogent review. You'll find ideas, strategies, and suggestions throughout. For examples, however, I expect you to turn to published reviews in your discipline.

Not all scholarly books worthy of review are monographs. In chapter 4, I introduce strategies for reviewing edited volumes, writing review essays (of multiple, complementary titles), and coauthoring reviews. And because one of my broader pedagogical goals is to convince you of the benefits of honing your scholarly voice as a reviewer, the final chapter offers additional ideas for increasing your engagement with reviewing and enhancing the enjoyment factor of your reviews. You will see in chapter 5 that I also revisit, by way of reinforcing the importance of reflective practice, some of the principles introduced in chapter 1. My aspirational goal with chapter 5 is that you may find some material that will transfer to your writing projects beyond reviews.

Between each chapter you'll find an interlude that serves as a pause for reflection or action and as a bridge to the following chapter. A postlude offers ideas for teaching scholarly book reviewing in the college or university classroom—to counter the contemporary "book malaise" apparently afflicting undergraduates worldwide. And the appendix provides a list of key questions to consider addressing as you prepare a scholarly book review. My approach throughout *How to Review Scholarly Books* is to present both how-to material and why-to material. I want you to develop an orientation and a skill set that will help reinvigorate, reposition, and revalue scholarly book reviews in your field.

Scholarship is creative work, and reviewing any creative work involves judgment, a foundational element of critique. Judgment involves trust, knowledge, standards, ideals, aesthetics. If the aesthetic I project is not to your liking, remember: There's no one right way to review a scholarly book. But the core components of a review—contextualized summary, clear analysis, and cogent assessment—are nonnegotiable. The key to an engaging scholarly review ultimately lies in how you, the reviewer, invoke those elements. Both the act and the product can be relished. Ready? Let's get reviewing.

1

Getting Started as a Scholarly Book Reviewer

THIS CHAPTER PREPARES you for the task of scholarly book reviewing by introducing you to the genre and its expectations, itemizing motivations for reviewing, helping you recognize your qualifications, suggesting ways to find venues for your review, and helping you identify and procure a book to review. If you already know why scholarly book reviews matter and have a book in hand that you are committed to reviewing—and know the journal or other outlet to which you will be submitting your review—you are welcome to skim or skip this contextualizing chapter.

Preparing for the Task of Scholarly Book Reviewing

What is a scholarly book review? Who writes them? Why are they written? Where are they published? Who reads them? Why do they matter?

Categorizing Scholarly Book Reviews

You're likely reading this book because you know that different norms and expectations accompany different genres of writing. In short, that reality helps explain why this book exists. Another reason for this book? According to social psychologist Robert Milardo, "book reviews in all their variations are among the most underdeveloped and underappreciated forms of scholarship."[1] Well, together we can do something about that. If we accept that scholarly book reviews manifest a specific genre of academic writing, we must be able to identify their generic characteristics and modes of expression.[2] Before doing so, let me briefly describe the general types of scholarly book reviews. Different venues may have their own names and length guidelines for these and other types of scholarly reviews.[3]

- *Book note.* More common in journalistic outlets than in scholarly venues, this short piece (generally 150–750 words) focuses on summarizing the contents of a recently published book. The apotheosis of compression and concision, the shortest forms of these super-short "reviews" often feel impressionistic and leave little room for substantiated critique. Also known as a *capsule review*.
- *Book review.* A review of a single scholarly book, recently published, generally in 1,000–1,500 words (or fewer, or more, depending on the venue). Books requiring special considerations for review include edited collections, anthologies, scholarly editions, and reference works.
- *Review essay.* A review of two or more recently published, complementary books, generally in 1,500–3,000 words (or longer). Also known as a *comparative review*.

- *Retrospective review essay.* More akin to a scholarly journal article, and thus often involving 5,000–8,000 words (or more), this type of essay reviews the impact of an important scholarly work—often one published two or more decades earlier—on a field.
- *Omnibus review.* Two or more reviews of the same book presented together. Each component review, written by a different reviewer who is usually solicited by the venue to ensure perspectival diversity, falls in the range accepted by the venue (typically 1,000–1,500 words). Also known as a *review forum*, a *review roundtable*, or an *integrated book review*.[4]
- *Book symposium.* A rare sort of omnibus review that concludes with invited comments by the author or editor of the book under review. The commenter reads all of the reviews prior to publication and responds to the reviewers either individually or collectively.

Exploring the Characteristics of Scholarly Book Reviews

Because straight-up "book reviews" of single titles are the most common types to appear in scholarly journals, I focus on those types of reviews in the first three chapters of this book. In chapter 4, I address special cases: edited volumes (including edited collections, anthologies, scholarly editions, and reference works), review essays (including retrospective review essays), and—not a type but a method—coauthored reviews. The foundational concepts I present here, upon which I elaborate in subsequent sections of this book, apply across all types of scholarly books.

Scholarly book reviews focus on scholarly books. This first point, tautological though it may seem, emphasizes that scholarly book reviews form only a segment of a much broader reviewing ecosystem. The scholarly books considered here are nonfiction books that contribute to knowledge by advancing intellectual arguments through disciplinarily grounded methods of inquiry befitting the problems or questions at hand. Such works are most commonly issued by university presses, professional academic associations, nonprofit research institutes or other similar organizations (including museums and archives), and for-profit scholarly publishers. Upstanding publishers of these sorts typically subject submitted manuscripts to peer review, helping to ensure that scholarly books are indeed "scholarly." What happens in peer review? Editors and subject-matter experts weigh in on submitted book proposals and manuscripts, offering their comments, criticisms, and suggestions to the authors with the expectation of revision before the works are finalized and released as books.[5] Reviews written after their subjects have been published—those that form the focus of this book—therefore manifest another form of peer review, one with an outward-focused audience. The reviews described in this book are technically "post-publication" reviews, but I simply refer to them as "scholarly book reviews" or "scholarly reviews" throughout. You'll also find me interchanging the words "book" and "monograph," but when I write about edited volumes (chapter 4) I have a distinct form of scholarly work in mind.

Scholarly book reviews both describe and assess. The two primary functions of a scholarly book review are the descriptive and the evaluative. A scholarly review describes and assesses the scholarly merits of a book and addresses how the book and its contributions fit into the existing literature. A review that merely summarizes a book is just that: a summary. Summaries have their places, of course. But because assessment offers a value-added perspective that is not innate to the book under review, the evaluative element of a scholarly book review elevates the contribution of the review itself. A third function of a scholarly book review is the annunciative: to let the world—or at least the members of a particular disciplinary community—know of an addition to the scholarly literature. Francess Halpenny, longtime editor at the University of Toronto Press, describes the value of scholarly book reviews as follows: "Reviewing, conscientiously carried out, is an important means of entering an author's addition to knowledge into the scholarly stream of consciousness." She then notes that reviews "bear information to help research in the present and future."[6]

Scholarly book reviews are written by individuals who know something about the topic at hand. Literate individuals can express opinions about anything they read. As you've likely noticed, the internet hosts countless opinions about published books. But a scholarly book review is more than a vehicle for expressing opinions. Scholarly book reviews should be written by individuals who can suitably contextualize and evaluate the contributions of the books under review. Reviewers are typically members of the intended readership. When done well, scholarly book reviews express confidence, awareness, and authority. Literary journalist Gail Pool notes that "readers take reviewers' words on trust."[7] And readers should come away from such scholarly book reviews having learned something.

Scholarly book reviews are primarily read by students or other scholars. Writers—including reviewers—must be cognizant of their audiences. Because students who read scholarly reviews may be newcomers to the field, reviewers must include appropriate context. (What is "appropriate," of course, varies widely by field and venue. Jargon, that efficient intellectual shorthand, can certainly have its place in scholarly reviews. But reviews intended for less specialized audiences should include definitions of key terms, especially if the terms are contestable.) The more you know as a reviewer, the more difficult it becomes to remember what it was like when you were first dipping your toes into a field. Advanced graduate students, who are often an intended audience of scholarly books, can therefore make ideal reviewers. Other regular readers of scholarly book reviews include research and acquisitions librarians, academic administrators (in the realm of assessment), and scholarly publishers (by way of quality control, another use for assessment).

Scholarly book reviews tend to be short. Given the length of scholarly books—70,000–110,000 words is typical for scholarly monographs these days—scholarly book reviews can just scratch the surface, with reviews often limited to 1,000–1,500 words.[8] Do not presume that this brevity makes scholarly reviews easy to write. Instead, brevity forces focused selectivity and creativity on the part of the reviewers, who must strike appropriate balances between description and evaluation.

Scholarly book reviews take time to materialize. The blurbs that may accompany scholarly books upon publication have been solicited by the publishers and are normally based on the final submitted manuscripts (often prior to copyediting). These brief, positive statements are intended to encourage sales, not to be objective. Full-blown reviews, serving a host of other purposes, commence after scholarly books have been published and formally released into the world. Even for individuals who are incredibly efficient, reading and reviewing can't transpire overnight. Scholarly journals, which serve as primary outlets for scholarly book reviews, tend to have fixed publication frequencies and page limits, contributing to the lag—often a year or more—between the publication of a scholarly book and the publication of initial reviews of that book.[9]

Scholarly book reviews are published in a variety of outlets. Scholarly journals, including dedicated reviews journals, are traditional outlets for scholarly book reviews. The overlap makes sense in terms of audience (of scholarly books) and readership (of scholarly journals): Scholars who read articles in disciplinary journals are likely to be interested in scholarly books in those disciplines. Online journals and online review sites are not hindered by page limits, can embrace digital technologies (such as podcast reviews and author interviews), and can dramatically shorten the time to publication for scholarly reviews.[10] Even print journals with online versions commonly make articles and reviews available once accepted, helping to reduce publication lag.

If you're wondering about writing and posting reviews to personal blogs or social media sites like Goodreads or LibraryThing, you'll note that I'm not emphasizing such reviews here, though the advice in this book is certainly transferable to such reviews. I focus on reviews with at least one layer of vetting, since, well, the scholarly world is a hierarchical place. Vetted reviews carry more weight, count as publications, are often indexed in online directories and databases, are imagined to require more time and attention to produce, and thus tend to be taken more seriously. Nor am I referring to unsigned—that is, anonymous—reviews, which are more popular in some fields (and for some readerships) than others.[11]

Scholarly book reviews help other scholars save time. By summarizing, synthesizing, and assessing new publications so that the ideas in these works can reach an even wider audience, scholarly reviewers do favors for their colleagues. In *The Art of the Book Review*, a booklet issued by the University of Wisconsin Extension Division in 1963, writer Ralph Alan McCanse notes the "timesaving guidance" afforded by book reviews.[12] And scholar of African literature Wendy Laura Belcher highlights this assessment in Nicholson Baker's *U and I*: "Book reviews, not books, [are] the principal engines of change in the history of thought."[13] The joke—and it is at least somewhat of a joke—is that more people base their understandings of influential works on reviews of those works than on the works themselves. (Here, since you must be curious, Baker is referring to how he acquired his own knowledge of the theories of literary critic Harold Bloom.)

Scholarly book reviews have a more illustrious past. Sociologist David Beer points out that, as recently as the second half of the twentieth century, "the book review was central to the practice of knowledge formation, dissemination and debate."[14] (Ah, so Baker was being somewhat serious, after all.) Beer encourages us to reclaim the dialogic, boundary-pushing role of book reviews in order to defend debate and dialogue and to protect our disciplines from "turning into spaces of monologic cacophony and speaking without response."[15] When book reviews move beyond mere summaries, as I encourage in this book, their role—and their very power—expands. Book review editor (and prolific reviewer) Stephen Donovan posits that "a well-crafted review is a work of scholarship in its own right."[16] And he is absolutely correct.[17]

Scholarly book reviews signal importance, benefiting fields, ideas, movements, publishers, and authors. In bibliocentric disciplines, scholarly book reviews serve multiple purposes. Scholarly book reviews evaluate and assess the merits of a contribution within a discipline. Reviews curate and filter, emphasizing the relative value of a contribution. They bring attention to topics or voices that deserve it, underscoring the political and ideological dimension of reviewing. Because citations to books take time to accrue—scholarly books reach their citation peaks after an average of eight years—book reviews can serve as earlier indicators of potential impact and contribution.[18]

Reviews also serve publishers and authors, indicating that a work has been noticed and read.[19] Publishers with positively reviewed books in a field attract quality submissions from future authors. Positive reviews bode well for book prizes and awards.

Authors whose works are reviewed positively can more easily land interviews, speaking engagements, additional publicity, and subsequent book contracts.[20] Authors with faculty appointments benefit from positive reviews when seeking promotions. Authors of well-received works become sought after as peer reviewers themselves. (In peer review, reviewers, often more so than editors, wield tremendous gatekeeping power.)

In short, fields can benefit, ideas and movements can benefit, publishers can benefit, and authors can benefit from reviews. And your colleagues benefit: Reading a review is much less of a commitment than reading the book in question. But what about the reviewers? Why are individuals willing to write reviews in the first place? Let's consider some reasons for investing time and energy into writing scholarly book reviews.

Positioning Yourself as a Viable Reviewer

What are reasonable motivations for writing a scholarly book review? How am I qualified to do so? If I'm a graduate student, do I need my adviser's "permission" before writing a review?

Understanding the Roles of Scholarly Book Reviews

So much is published these days that it's easy to be overwhelmed by the sheer volume of new material. As bookseller Jeff Deutsch aptly puts it, "There are just *so many* books."[21] Oxford University Press and Cambridge University Press, two respected behemoths in the world of scholarly publishing, together publish more than 7,500 books annually: That's more than twenty new titles per day between just two presses! Although I like to conceptualize scholarly book reviews as a service to the profession—that is, as benefits to others—I realize that altruism and goodwill stretch only so far when demands on our time seem incessant. So what's in it for you, the reviewer? Let me articulate some practical (and instrumental) purposes for reviewing scholarly books. Some of these rationales may resonate with you. Others may expand your understandings of the potential value of scholarly reviews, exciting you even more about the prospect.

Scholarly book reviewing allows you to draw attention to a work you feel strongly about (usually for the better). Have you ever read a recently published scholarly book that transformed the way you understand your field, your relationship to your field, or your relationship to the world itself? Have you wanted to tell everyone in your scholarly circle to drop everything and read that book? Reviewing offers you a vehicle for your enthusiasm. It allows you to identify and address precisely how a book edifies, illuminates, and transforms its readers. Conversely, have you ever read a scholarly book that unsettled you in ways that demanded a reply, a response, a correction? Reviewing offers you a means of entering into dialogue with authors for the purposes of rectifying substantive or potentially damaging oversights, thus going on the record to amend the scholarly narrative in an area of importance to your work, your identity, or your worldview.

Scholarly book reviewing allows you to keep in touch with developments in a field. Although retrospective reviews or retrospective review essays, described in chapter 4, address how a work or collection of works has affected a field or a methodology, most scholarly reviews focus on recently published books. One customary goal is to draw attention to new books so they are not overlooked. Reviewers thus must imagine how a new publication may propel a field forward. As I will explain later in this book, the work of reading and reviewing cultivates faculties of reflection and expression that can take scholars outside their normal modes of operation. By seeking new works and reading them before we know how or why they matter, we are contributing to the forward momentum of our fields. Sure, we may choose to review books only in our narrow subfields, allowing us to demonstrate our expertise. But even when we are well within our comfort zones, the act of reviewing—of turning inside out our preconceptions and our expectations—shines a spotlight on a future that we are helping to realize.

Scholarly book reviewing offers a way for you to focus and reflect. Scholarly reviewers take nothing at face value; they must question everything. Since reviewers go on the record with their evaluations, reviewers must be supremely attentive to the texts at hand, and they must think beyond their own needs. When we consider what a scholarly book means to us or to our work, we are necessarily selective. But when we think about what a scholarly book may mean to others, we are forced to place the work in a broader context. Being reminded of, and therefore remaining mindful of, that context helps us activate connections that we may, in our routine haste to cherry-pick, have otherwise overlooked.

Scholarly book reviewing helps make you a better scholar and writer. I've slipped this rather bold claim—perhaps the most important benefit to reviewing—toward the middle of this list not so that you would overlook it but so that you pause here and remember that reviewing, as a creative, intellectual act, is a scholarly activity in its own right. Ralph Alan McCanse notes that "a book review is properly a critical essay, a discriminating report. It is carefully perceptive and is wrought with deliberation."[22] And historian Karin Wulf writes that "book reviewing is the best kind of thinking work."[23] By critiquing the work of others, you learn ways to strengthen your own work. By tightening and refining your prose to describe and assess others' contributions in a limited amount of space, you hone your use of language to support your views. I am far from the first person to make such claims.[24] You'd likely not be reading this book if you needed convincing that scholarly book reviewing offers such rich dividends.

Scholarly book reviewing allows you to exert your presence and belonging in a field. By reviewing a scholarly book, you are signaling to others that this book resonates with your scholarly identity. You are saying, in effect, "I am here, and I care." You are demonstrating your willingness to offer your expertise and your critical commentary on a topic in a space that respects "the spirit and nature of interactive academic discourse."[25] And you are cementing your identity as a contributor to your field.[26] When you are a relative newcomer to a field—graduate students, I'm looking at you—you can revel in greatness by association when a review of yours is published in one of the top journals in your field.[27] If nothing else, such an accomplishment should yield a confidence boost and help to counter imposterism, even when you realize (as I explain in chapter 3) that the standards for book reviews are distinct from standards for peer-reviewed journal articles.[28] For newcomers to a field, scholarly book reviewing can offer an ideal entrée into an academic space.[29]

Scholarly book reviewing can be conceptualized as a form of academic service. Critic Anna Leahy notes how "academia positions the book review as something good for someone else to have written," in part because of how reviews can ultimately benefit *others'* impact.[30] Let them be beneficial to others. The world could use more freudenfreude. Reviewers, in this sense, serve as model academic citizens.[31] And, in the words of literary scholar David Ross, "whatever might be said about the specific book, the reviewer affirms the collective aspiration that underwrites all such books."[32]

Scholarly book reviewing allows you to contribute to the broader scholarly ecosystem. Sociologist Casey Brienza, in a convincing essay published by *Inside Higher Ed* in 2014, argues that book reviews contribute to the "collective good." They are, she writes, "important voluntary inputs into the wider system of academic book publishing upon which the contemporary academic profession is symbiotically dependent."[33] Book reviews are an important though uncompensated form of service to the profession.

Scholarly book reviewing gives you insights into the world of scholarly publishing. Anyone new to writing for scholarly publication understandably has scores of questions. (Academic mentors are invaluable at such times. How-to books can also help.) Writing scholarly book reviews helps pull back the curtain on otherwise occluded practices. Reviewers may learn how online-submission systems work; they practice how to respond to editorial feedback (if offered); and they learn about copyright and about the time-sensitive nature of reviewing page proofs. While learning how a submission eventually ends up in print or published online, reviewers develop their skills in professionalism and professional writing by reaching out to and working with book review editors, copyeditors, and production editors. Altogether, reviewers learn about the collective efforts that underscore the publishing enterprise. The experience bolsters confidence when reviewers embark on the writing and submission of their own manuscripts and book proposals, projects for which the stakes feel much higher. Sociologists Kevin Haggerty and Aaron Doyle describe writing scholarly book reviews, in brief, as "a useful initiation into academic publishing."[34]

Scholarly book reviewing can help propel your other, larger projects. You might not believe me, but it's true. Working simultaneously on different types of writing projects can result in greater progress on all fronts. Since time is finite, how is such a thing possible? It's all about shifting gears when you feel that you are spinning your wheels. Or, for a better metaphor, consider this sage advice from media scholar Joli Jensen:

> Logs burn better side by side, so if you have a big log that you want to burn well, you put a smaller log beside it. When you are discouraged or bored by your single big log project, you can use a back-burner project as a buddy log to get it blazing again. A back-burner project can be used strategically to motivate your front-burner project.[35]

The implications for scholars should be clear. The "big log" is your thesis or dissertation (or journal article or book chapter or book manuscript); the "buddy log" is the scholarly book review (or conference proposal or grant proposal or other complementary though sufficiently distinct and typically smaller-scale project).

Scholarly book reviewing gives external, outward-facing value to how you inwardly spend your time. If you're a scholar, you likely busy yourself with tending to at least some of the new literature in your field. (Perhaps you even read scholarly book reviews yourself in service of that mission. If you don't, you should start today.) I've seen the argument that if you've read or are going to read a book anyway, you "might as well" review it.[36] This suggestion always strikes me as odd, since it sublimates the active work of reviewing, as if writing the review itself were just an afterthought. But it nevertheless allows us to reconsider productivity and its various measures. For example, dissertators for whom a new book proves especially central to their work might very well wish to undertake a review of that book, since they have read it carefully and attentively for their dissertation. The same can be said of doctoral students preparing for their qualifying exams or of scholars embarking on research projects or monographs of their own: When new texts are central to these enterprises, consider capturing and recording some of your commitment to the works via scholarly reviews.

Scholarly book reviewing is equally well suited to senior scholars or nonfaculty academics. Reviewing is a means of gaining experience, yes. But it is also a way of sharing experience. I am always happy to see senior researchers or faculty members activating or reactivating their reviewing habits. Once you reach a certain point in your career (or in life), what other people think about how you spend your time becomes irrelevant. Similarly, academic professionals with advanced degrees and at least some modicum of discretionary time—even if only during nights, weekends, and holidays—can make ideal reviewers.[37] (This category is the one to which I belong.) Reviewing keeps individuals both junior and senior connected with ideas, disciplines, developments.

Scholarly book reviewing offers a way to develop or round out your CV. This rationale is particularly instrumental, so it's not one of my favorites. But the truth is that, comparatively, book reviews are among the most straightforward publications: They are the low-hanging fruit of scholarly publishing. And because they signal your expertise and your willingness to contribute to your profession, a small number of well-placed reviews can add depth and diversity to your CV. But be careful, especially if you presently serve or aspire to serve as a faculty member. A large number of reviews on a CV, when not offset by a larger number of peer-reviewed articles or other scholarly contributions, can suggest misplaced priorities.[38]

Scholarly book reviewing affords a way to add titles to your personal library. Reviewers typically receive—and get to keep—gratis copies of the books they review. But I discourage you from embarking on reviewing purely for economic reasons. Why? The amount of time you put into reviewing a book will not be a fair trade, if measured by the list price of the book under review.[39] Yes, I recognize that some scholarly books, especially those published by for-profit scholarly presses, carry hefty list prices. And, yes, I remember what living from stipend check to stipend check as a graduate student was like. If you must have your own copy of a scholarly book and have no other legal way to procure one, reviewing the book affords you a copy of the work. No harm done, as long as writing the review itself does not deter you from accomplishing more important tasks. And always remember the other benefits, those for which the pecuniary values remain abstract: the line on your CV, the gratification of seeing your assessment in print, the sense of contribution to a disciplinary conversation and to the broader scholarly ecosystem. I return to these and additional benefits in chapter 5, where I layer atop these benefits the perspective of having completed a scholarly book review.

Understanding Qualifications for Scholarly Reviewing

Let's now consider that "disciplinary conversation" by way of identifying qualifications for scholarly reviewing. Although we may conduct research and write interdisciplinarily, we cannot escape our disciplines. They are foundational to how we understand the world; they provide the very frameworks and epistemologies our work inhabits. So no scholar is truly alone. As critic Stanley Fish explains, we are part of "interpretive communities."[40] You know where and how you are positioned: You may identify yourself as an anthropologist, an economist, a historian, a linguist, a philosopher, a scholar of religion. Our scholarly identities, then, are disciplinarily contingent. Such contexts transfer to the scholarly book review in terms of defining who is qualified to serve as a reviewer.

Although venues for scholarly reviews may have their own eligibility requirements for reviewers (and those requirements, typically nonnegotiable, supersede my comments here), my message is simple: If you hold or are working toward a graduate degree in an academic or professional discipline, you are qualified to review books in or aligned with that discipline. If you conceptualize—and therefore introduce—yourself as "just a graduate student," I urge you to reframe your relation to your field. Yes, I understand the oppressiveness of hierarchy, the stress of academic rites of passage, the feelings of ignorance and insignificance. I also understand the suppression of voices and perspectives within the academy. For the purposes of scholarly book reviewing, at least, put aside any insecurities. Remember the rationales for scholarly book reviewing. Reviews can become mouthpieces, megaphones, magnetizers. Embrace the potential, and use reviews as a vehicle to help draw attention to the values and ideas that will enhance and enrich your field.

To serve as an effective scholarly reviewer, the qualification that matters more than status or rank or public accomplishments is your familiarity with your field.[41] Chances are, if you're working on—or have recently completed—a thesis or dissertation, you'll have read a substantial portion of the literature most relevant to your specialization. You will therefore have adequate contextual knowledge for commenting on new scholarship in your field, especially scholarship that speaks to your specific topical interests or addresses your particular methodological expertise. Trust me here.[42] You might not feel like an expert just yet, but you know more than you think.

"Hold it," you may be thinking, especially if you're a graduate student. Is writing a scholarly book review something you should clear with your adviser? Do you need to seek "permission" to write a scholarly review? You be the judge. If your adviser has a favorable impression of reviews (having a record of written some, say), you should be given a green light—and could be lauded for your entrepreneurial spirit. Your graduate program might expect or even require that you write at least one scholarly review as a prerequisite for conferral of your degree. Even better: Your adviser might offer to review what you write or to mentor you along the way.[43] (This book presumes that not everyone lives in such an ideal world.) Just assure your adviser that writing the review will not delay your completion of the requirements for your degree. I encourage you to appropriate Joli Jensen's metaphor of the "buddy log" for such reassurance.

Seth Perry, a scholar of religion, wrote his first scholarly book review while completing his graduate studies. Although at the time he felt out of place publicly critiquing a much more advanced scholar's work, he came to understand that advanced graduate students can make ideal scholarly reviewers. Why? Simply because graduate students, whether they realize it or not, often have the luxury of time: time to engage deeply, thoroughly, attentively with scholarship in their field.[44] Linguist Saskia Van Viegen concurs: "Although I thought I was busy during my doctoral and postdoctoral work, my available time for writing during those years had, in fact, been a luxury."[45] I offer these reflections especially for full-time graduate students in the humanities and social sciences by way of encouragement. I, too, wrote my first scholarly book review while in graduate school, and I'll share that story—and the key lesson it taught me—in the next section.

Identifying Review Venues and Books for Reviewing

What journals in my field publish scholarly book reviews? What do I need to know to be able to publish reviews in these venues? How can I identify a potential title for review?

Understanding the Publishing Landscape

If you're not skipping over the section-opening questions, you likely noticed that here I begin with identifying the review venue before identifying a book for review. Does this approach seem counterintuitive? The reason is fundamental to how scholarly book reviewing works, and it's something I wish I'd known when I wrote my first review in summer 2003. Let me explain.

At the library, I came across a copy of this book in the recent acquisitions: *Professional Communication in International Settings*, by linguists Yuling Pan, Suzanne Wong Scollon, and Ron Scollon (Blackwell, 2002). I checked it out, read it, and wrote a review that addressed my concerns about how the coauthors had apparently oversimplified the role of language in international communication. (I had previously lived in Japan and the United Kingdom; I had previously worked as a Japanese translator at an automotive firm in the United States; and I had completed a pair of master's degrees in business and Asian studies.) My target journal was *Business Communication Quarterly*, a journal of the Association for Business Communication that is now published as *Business and Professional Communication Quarterly*. My mistake? I presumed that book reviews work in the same manner as article manuscripts for scholarly journals. That is, I presumed that unsolicited submissions were the norm. So instead of querying the editor *before* writing the review, I sent the completed review to the editor "over the transom," as it were, with no prior contact. Surprise! Fortunately, the editors forgave my ignorance, the journal was able to use the review, and a revised version of the review was published in June 2004. (Thank you, Jim Dubinsky and Debby Andrews.)

I certainly now know that unsolicited submissions are *never* the best practice in scholarly publishing, even though some of what I've written on the subject seems to imply otherwise.[46] For article manuscripts, for book proposals, for anything, really, you can gain from reaching out to an editor first. Although nothing can ever be guaranteed until you've delivered the product, you have nothing to lose by querying about fit or interest or publication backlogs or the like. I'll explain how this system works in the realm of scholarly book reviews below.

In short, do not write scholarly reviews on speculation, assuming you'll easily find a home for your efforts after the fact. Before you invest the time and energy necessary for reviewing a scholarly book, you should identify a venue willing to consider your offering. Doing so will allow you to proceed with confidence as you write your review. And, most importantly, doing so will allow you to tailor your review to a specific target readership.

Casey Brienza, in another excellent piece on scholarly book reviewing, differentiates between two modes used by journal editors to acquire book reviews: *proactive* commissioning and *reactive* commissioning.[47] If an editor reaches out to you to inquire whether you would be willing to review a particular book, you are being proactively commissioned. (As book review editor of the *Journal of Scholarly Publishing*, I proactively commission the majority of book reviews.) Receiving such requests generally requires stature or visibility within your field. When you reach out to a book review editor yourself and propose reviewing a book, your pitch could be reactively commissioned. The remainder of this chapter presumes you will be seeking reactive commissioning. (If, however, you have already been contacted by an editor to review a book: fabulous! You may jump ahead to interlude 1.)

Identifying Review Venues

If you know you want to review a scholarly book—and perhaps you have already identified the book you wish to review—where do you begin? How do you identify potential venues? Here are a few ideas.

Ask your advisers and mentors. One of the best ways to learn anything about the world of scholarly publishing is to talk to someone more experienced than you. Advisers and mentors in your field should know at least some of the various outlets that publish scholarly book reviews. They may even know which outlets are the most prestigious and reputable, the most likely to welcome a book review from you, or the most generous with respect to feedback and editorial support. (To discern for prestige and reputation on your own, pay special attention to the flagship journals of the major scholarly associations, to long-established journals, and to scholarly journals published by university presses. In some fields, certain online venues wield cachet.)

Visit the websites of scholarly or professional organizations in your discipline, and look at their publications. You should know the major organizations in your field. (If you don't, you'll have to ask a colleague, an academic mentor, a librarian, or someone else likely to have a finger on the pulse of your field.) You know what I'm getting at: the American Anthropological Association, the Association for Asian Studies, the Association for Business Communication, the Australian Association for the Study of Religion, the British Archaeological Association, the Canadian Historical Association, the European Educational Research Association, the Modern Language Association. I could go on (and on). These organizations—and their kin—often sponsor scholarly journals that publish book reviews. On their websites, simply look for a section titled "publications" or "journals," and then read all about the possibilities.

Network, network, network. Some good advice for everyone: Don't be reserved about your interests and your goals with respect to writing for publication. If you're able to attend academic conferences, make sure to inquire about opportunities to write scholarly book reviews. You may learn of venues, you may receive helpful advice, and you may even be able to speak directly with book review editors about your interests. (At the same time, you might also hear that writing book reviews isn't worth the effort. Make sure to follow up by asking why—and evaluate what you hear very carefully.) If you don't have the means to attend academic conferences, network among your peers.

Ask a research librarian. Librarians love to be helpful. Identify a research librarian knowledgeable about your field and inquire about journals that publish scholarly book reviews. If you don't know how to identify a research librarian in your field, ask any librarian for assistance. Any librarian should be willing to show you how to use the library's online resources for tracking down recent reviews of books in your field. You can learn of potential venues by simply noting where the reviews were published.

Use a back-door approach. Say you want to do everything on the sly, and the professional organization–website approach somehow left you empty-handed. Go online and look at CVs of your advisers, mentors, or respected scholars in your field. See if they have published book reviews—and where. Score! (By learning where these scholars have presented their research, you can also find out about scholarly organizations and conferences.) Academic social networks such as ResearchGate or Academia.edu can also help you uncover networks of researchers in your field, including where they have published book reviews. Don't be shy about digging around online.

Reverse-engineer your search. Find the publisher's webpage for a book that is important to your research—one that was published between two and about five years ago. Many publishers excerpt from reviews on these pages, and they frequently indicate the sources. Reviews, after all, are badges of honor for scholarly books. Note what you find. Then, before you leave the publisher's website, follow the links to "related works" or "similar titles," noting the locations of reviews of those books, and you should uncover a trove of potential venues for scholarly book reviews in your field.

Understanding the Expectations of Review Venues

How are you feeling now? By this point, you should have a list of potential publishing outlets for scholarly book reviews in your field. You may have a mix of print-based and online-only venues. The next step is to discern which venues would be good fits for your interests and efforts. You will do so—no surprise—by visiting the websites of the journals or other outlets. In the process of investigating the requirements for book reviewers, you will uncover a lot of useful information. Some of what you should learn is described below by way of responses to frequently asked questions.

Do all scholarly journals publish book reviews? No. Only some scholarly journals publish reviews—and some journals that used to publish reviews no longer do. This point may seem obvious, but it's both easier to overlook and easier to verify in today's digitized world. As recently as two decades ago, when print still ruled, you could know at a glance whether a journal publishes book reviews: You'd simply take a look at the contents page of a recent hard-copy journal issue or would reflexively flip to the back, where reviews are commonly relegated. These days, with inconsistent online tagging or indexing of journals, spotting reviews by looking at an online issue of the journal can be hit or miss. The good news is that journals that publish book reviews will have guidelines for book reviewers. (Look for a section or link akin to "author guidelines" or "submissions.") You will need those guidelines. Also look for editorials that explain what a venue publishes.[48] You may even find some outlets that exist for the sole purpose of publishing book reviews in your field.

How do I know if I am eligible to serve as a reviewer for a particular publication? Earlier I wrote that all individuals with relevant expertise should be able to review scholarly books in their respective fields. I do not, however, set all the rules. Some journals decide which scholarly books they will review and then solicit reviews of them from established scholars. These journals, engaging in proactive commissioning, do not accept unsolicited submissions. (*American Historical Review* is one such example.) Some journals expect their scholarly book reviewers to have written scholarly monographs themselves, in an "it takes one to know one" fashion. (*Monumenta Nipponica* is one such example.) Some journals allow graduate students to coauthor book reviews only with faculty mentors as first authors. (*The Review of Higher Education* is one such example.) Journals that publish book reviews will be clear about how—or if—potential reviewers should approach them.

Journals might not actively state that, for example, they welcome book reviews or offers to review from graduate students. (For an encouraging example, though, see *Metascience*: "We do welcome reviews from graduate students.")[49] But you should take the omission of other exclusionary text as an opportunity. Here, too, you can again use the internet to your advantage. In whichever journal you are investigating, check out the author bylines of recently published book reviews, and look up these individuals. Note their statuses. Whatever role you currently inhabit—graduate student, postdoctoral researcher, visiting lecturer, adjunct instructor, assistant professor, academic professional, independent scholar—you will somewhere find like individuals who have contributed scholarly book reviews. The journals that have recently published those reviews should be friendly to a review of yours.

What publication formats exist for scholarly book reviews? The publication formats for scholarly book reviews are a function of the venues in which they are published. I previously mentioned the delays inherent in print journals. My first book review provides one such case: The book was published in 2002; I wrote and submitted the review in 2003; and the review was finally published in 2004. If you wish for speedier publication, you may opt for an online journal. Consider, for example, H-Net (Humanities and Social Sciences Online), which has been around since 1993 and annually publishes 1,500 reviews of scholarly books. If bibliometrics and altmetrics matter to you (and they should, at least eventually—they are ways for you and other researchers to keep quantitative and qualitative tabs on your scholarly output), reviews posted online will likely garner speedier attention. And, for better or for worse, you will forever be attached to the review whenever anyone searches your name online. (Before opting to publish in an online-only journal, just be sure to assess the stature of the journal within your field. Consulting with a trusted mentor or adviser can be the easiest way to do so.) As an alternative to online-only journals, most journals that still issue print copies are also available online in some fashion. And, as noted earlier, some journals will make accepted materials available online prior to formal publication, if speed is of special importance to you.

How are scholarly book reviews disseminated? Dissemination is also a function of the venue. A review that lives behind a paywall will reach a limited audience. How important is access to you? Is it enough for others to know that you reviewed a book in question, or would you like them to be able to read your review with ease?[50] Weigh, as part of your calculus, the prestige of the outlet, the visibility of your work, and the control you may have over subsequent use of your review (at heart, an issue of copyright).

Where do I find the book review guidelines for a publication? This information, available on the website of the venue in question, is key. At minimum, outlets that publish reviews will provide expectations regarding length and formatting. Some outlets will offer guidance regarding content, organization, tone, and permission (or, rarely, expectation) for using external citations. Always consult the guidelines. Believe me, you're much better off knowing before you write a review that you have a maximum of 1,000 words and that you shouldn't cite external sources. You'll save time, effort, and frustration by writing a review to exact instead of arbitrary specifications. I know because I once—only once (I learned my lesson!)—had to rewrite a review for a different venue with different length expectations and an unfamiliar citation style. (In the end, it was as if I had written two different reviews of the same book, but I got credit for only one of them.)

Regarding allowable lengths of reviews, consider this comment from historian and bibliographer David Henige: "Generally, the stipulated length of the review is not commensurate with the length or importance of the book, but conforms merely to the standards of the journal in which it is to appear."[51] Some venues allow more flexibility than others, but asking is always safer than presuming.

Who manages book reviews for a publication, and what should I expect in the process? More key information that should be provided on the website of the venue for scholarly book reviews: Who is the point person who will receive and review your submission? How will you submit your review? What will happen to it? What can you expect? Later I will encourage you to reach out to the book review editor. But, for now, just make note of these particulars.

Do some journals recommend or offer particular titles for review? Yes. Publishers are proud of their books and want their books to be reviewed. (Reviews generate interest, after all, and interest generates potential sales.) As a result, publishers routinely send notices about just-published books to key journals in relevant fields, provided that these journals publish book reviews.[52] Many of these journals keep running lists of "books received," possibly removing titles from the list once reviewers have claimed them. If you'd like an example, see the "Books for Review" page at the website of the Canadian Society for the History of Medicine, which sponsors the *Canadian Journal of Health History*.[53] Or check out the "New Books in Food Studies" resource link at the website of the Association for the Study of Food and Society, which sponsors the journal *Food, Culture & Society*.[54] Both lists offer impressive bibliographies of recent additions to their respective fields.

May I review the same book for more than one venue? Theoretically, yes, if the venues are distinct, and if you are willing to write different reviews. But wouldn't your assessment effectively be the same? One review in one venue is enough. Let others review the same book for other venues, adding their voices to the mix. (Also, you should never seek to publish the same review in more than one outlet without full cooperation of the original outlet. Online reviews are occasionally cross-posted, but the idea for doing so usually comes from the second venue, not from the reviewer, and the original source should always be acknowledged.)

How can I be asked to review a book for a scholarly journal? Here is a strategy if you like the idea of book reviewing but, for now, want to leave it at that: You may ask to have your name added to a "stable" of potential book reviewers. You do so by reaching out to the book review editor of a specific journal with a brief introduction. Include your academic credentials, your broader scholarly interests, your specific research focus, and (if relevant) your methodological expertise. Offer to be available for reviewing related books received by the journal. The risk? You should be willing to follow through if ultimately invited to review a book, provided there are no conflicts of interest.[55] (And you can't predict the timing of an invitation.) I will offer more thoughts on conflicts of interest toward the end of this chapter.

Identifying Scholarly Books for Review

Now you should have a possible venue or two in mind for your review. We are getting closer. The next tasks are identifying a suitable book for review and ensuring that one of your potential venues is willing to consider your review. If you have a book in mind, you may skip ahead. If you'd like some strategies for identifying potential books for review, stay right here with me.

I've reviewed a rather embarrassing number of books for scholarly and professional journals over the years—over one hundred fifty, in fact—so I have a few ideas about how to identify new and forthcoming books in my areas of interest. My top tips are below.

Check out the "recent acquisitions" shelf at your local library. I'm referring to a college or university library here, since such libraries are more likely to acquire a more diverse array of scholarly books than are public or community libraries. And I'm referring either to a physical shelf, if your library has one, or to a filter in the online catalog that lets you identify recently added titles. Library catalogs allow you to filter items by date of entry and by date of publication, but you may have to ask a friendly librarian to show you how to do so. (Some library websites offer more intuitive or more obviously customizable filters than others.) In libraries where new books are sent directly to the open stacks, you would be welcome to peruse the shelf or shelves on which scholarship in your subfield is likely to be located.[56]

One joy of a physical shelf of books is that you can easily browse—that is, pick up, flip through, consult the contents and references, and otherwise get a sense of whether a book is a good fit for your interests. (Remember how I discovered the first book I reviewed over twenty years ago? It was on the "new acquisitions" shelf of the local university library.) I find value in actually seeing a book before I commit to reviewing it, because it's often easy to judge relatively quickly whether a book will be a "keeper." Websites with "search inside the book" previews can approximate such browsing of contents.

Check out WorldCat.org. From WorldCat.org, a robust library network of over thirty thousand libraries in over one hundred countries, you can use the "Advanced Search" to perform keyword or subject searches in over a dozen languages and can simultaneously filter for titles published recently, say, this current year. (In addition, WorldCat lets you see which libraries own copies of the book, which may prove helpful when you'd like to get your hands on a copy. I'll say more about actually acquiring review copies in the next section.) Note, however, that WorldCat does not include forthcoming titles, and new books need to be cataloged somewhere before they will show up as results of a search.

Query new and forthcoming titles at Amazon.com. You can love Amazon.com, or you can hate Amazon.com. But one thing the company has is reach. Publisher Anne Trubek writes that "Amazon is now, for better or worse, the card catalog."[57] Here is a way to use the Amazon.com catalog for apprising yourself of new and forthcoming releases. First, use the menus to navigate to the "Books at Amazon" page, which offers multiple filters. The two most fruitful for finding new or forthcoming books are the "New Releases" filter and the "Department" filter. Activate the "Department" filter first. You can choose "History," say, and then you can further choose "Asian History" and, finally, "Japanese History." Once you've found your disciplinary home (or as close to it as Amazon's classification system allows), you can activate the "New Releases" filter. There, you may select "Last 30 days," "Last 90 days," or "Coming soon." Within the results list you can additionally sort by publication date. Voilà! Not all of the items returned will be germane, but what you may find should nonetheless be remarkable.

If you play around on the website, you'll uncover more methods to finding needles in Amazon's haystack. You may also start by typing your field or subfield in the "Books" search bar and then selecting the appropriate "New Releases" filter. The filtering system works differently on the Amazon.com app, so I usually perform my searches from a computer. And I don't expect the Amazon website to remain static. These instructions were still relevant as of late 2024, but your experience may vary.

And regarding that Amazonian reach: Check out the Amazon pages in any of the other twenty-two (as of late 2024) countries or regions, particularly if you're based in the United States and are looking for non-English-language books or books unavailable in the USA.

Visit relevant university press websites. If you're not familiar with the university presses that actively publish in your field, you should become familiar with them. (Simply note the publishers of the books you use most frequently in your work, and look for repeats.) Scholarly publishers have "lists"—that is, areas of specialization around subjects or topics. Many press websites will let you search these lists, ordering the books by publication date. Scholarly publishers also regularly publish named series that are similarly searchable. In the absence of navigational tools on press websites, university presses typically digitize their seasonal catalogs (spring and fall), with books commonly grouped by subject or series. You can easily learn what's new and forthcoming in your field by periodically visiting the websites of your favorite presses.[58] I've bookmarked a number of series pages myself for quick reference.

Search Edelweiss+ for new and forthcoming releases. If you don't like the idea of visiting press websites one by one, you'll find past and current catalogs for several hundred publishers—both scholarly and trade—at https://www.edelweiss.plus. You can search recent and forthcoming releases by keyword, access important details (including list prices), and preview media kits and book galleys (where available). Edelweiss+ is intended for use by individuals associated with the trade publishing industry, and you may be surprised by the coverage.

Consult the "books received" lists at scholarly journals or scholarly organizations. Don't forget these helpful resources that I described in the prior section. They're not always where you might think they'd be, however. For both examples I offered earlier, the lists of "books received" are housed on the websites of the sponsoring organizations, not of the journals themselves.

Indulge in social media. Here, you can let the publishers do some of the work for you. Subscribe to marketing and other messages in your fields of interest from your top presses. Follow their social-messaging feeds, scan their posts, tap into whatever methods you have for connecting with the world and keeping your finger on the pulse of matters that matter to you.

Keep your professional social network alive. When you come across new titles that complement the research interests of your academic friends and colleagues, share your insights. If any of your friends and colleagues believes in karma, someone might reciprocate with you someday, delighting you with a tip about a new title that you might otherwise have overlooked. My suggestion earlier about not being quiet about your own interests thus transfers to not being quiet about others' contributions. Ideas can change the world only when shared with others. So: Read and contribute to blogs. Listen and contribute to podcasts. Remain active, attentive, engaged.

Preparing to Reach Out to a Book Review Editor

Now, in addition to having identified a viable venue for a review, you have also identified a new or forthcoming scholarly book that you would like to review. Before reaching out to the book review editor, let me offer a few more important items of housekeeping, including some pertaining to the ethics of book reviewing.[59]

How do I know if I have a conflict of interest? You can't—or shouldn't—review a book if you are a relative or close acquaintance of the author. Even if you disclose the relationship, your views will be presumed to be biased. (Of course, you may promote the work of relatives and close acquaintances otherwise. One of the most effective ways is by citing it in your own work.) If you are named in a book's acknowledgments, you should presume that readers may suspect your objectivity in a review. At the other extreme, you should recuse yourself from reviewing books of any personal or intellectual nemeses. If you have any sort of axe to grind with the author, you should tend to your grievances in a less public manner. You should also not review a book if your primary motivation for doing so is to draw attention to your own work. Although not a conflict of interest, per se, such a situation can introduce a conflict of priorities. And such reviews also make you look bad.

A note to book authors: This story might be apocryphal, but I have heard that one scholarly publisher, at least, used to encourage its authors to name their *enemies* in the acknowledgments.

Why? The reason was so that no reputable scholarly journal would be willing to run a book review written by any of the named individuals—who might be inclined, for unprincipled reasons, to write a negative review.

Consider one special case that may apply to readers at more advanced stages of their professional careers. If you happen to have served as a peer reviewer of a book manuscript—that is, you were asked by a publisher to evaluate the suitability of a manuscript for publication—you are not automatically precluded from subsequently writing a review of the published book.[60] Peer reviewers often remain anonymous to the authors whose manuscripts they review. If you reviewed a book manuscript and the author did not out you in the acknowledgments (because the author did not know your identity), you are generally free to review the published book, provided you inform the book review editor of your prior role. Just make sure that you review the book *as published*. Refrain from commenting on any behind-the-scenes matters to which you are privy by virtue of your previous involvement with an earlier iteration of the text. Such a review will be most meaningful to everyone involved when the reviewer is a respected or well-known academic and the book author is a newcomer to the field.

Do I agree to review a book on spec? That is, should you commit to reviewing a book before you've seen a copy of it? If you know the work is bound to make a contribution to your field, go ahead. Perhaps you've read earlier works by the same author and found them to be excellent. Perhaps the book addresses a new or understudied topic and is therefore bound to have the merit of novelty, if nothing else. But is it ever possible to know, before reading a book, how valuable the book is or may be? While you are attentively reading and taking notes about a book you are reviewing, as I describe in chapter 2, you will be forming an opinion of the work. Your goal as a reviewer is to be honest; and you might very well want to avoid having to pan a book. I recommend trying to get a feel for a book before agreeing to review it, simply because agreeing to review a book marks a commitment. You can avoid discomfort down the line if you have a sense that the experience of reviewing the book will be at least somewhat enjoyable due to your appreciation of positive elements of the book.

Do I need to keep anything in mind about books in translation? Yes—I'm glad you asked. If you are proposing to review an English-language book that was originally published in another language, you will ideally be able to read the book in its original language. Translations occasionally miss the mark, and the only way to know if that may be the case is to read the original as well. If you are unable to compare the present text with the original, you will want to note this limitation both to the book review editor (upon proposing the review) as well as within your review.

How do I acquire a copy of a scholarly book I plan to review? During my graduate studies and throughout much of my professional career, I have been fortunate to be affiliated with institutions with large library collections and impressive acquisitions rates for new titles. For the majority of my earliest reviews, I began with local library copies or with copies acquired via interlibrary loan. In many cases I used these copies for the reviews, never acquiring copies of my own. If you wish to have your own copy that you can mark up as necessary, you will have to ask for it.[61] Here you have two primary options, which I explain in greater detail toward the end of this chapter: You may ask the book publisher directly for a copy yourself, or you may ask someone else to contact the publishers on your behalf and arrange for a copy to be sent to you. Either route requires first ensuring that the venue you have in mind for your review would in fact be interested in your review.

I was unaware of this protocol when I wrote my first review in 2003, using a library copy of the book. Having access to a library copy enabled me to write the review without having received any assurance that a journal would be interested in publishing the review. I could have ended up wasting time and effort, but I was lucky. So, with your target venue selected and a potential book in mind for review, let's now—finally—reach out to the book review editor.

Reaching Out to a Book Review Editor

Your target venue will identify the book review editor and will provide either an email address or a link to an online "contact" form. Remember the importance of first impressions. Ensure that you are addressing the book review editor properly by exhausting the internet to locate a correct title. Should you begin your message with "Dear Mr. Webster" or "Dear Dr. Webster" or "Dear Professor Webster"? Try to avoid the (soulless, insipid) twenty-first-century default "Dear Noah Webster." If you wish to avoid relying on a gendered honorific—a sensible reason for the twenty-first-century forename–surname default in the first place, despite the genericness—"Dear Editor Webster" would offer a better start.

Now that you have the attention of the book review editor, here are the tasks at hand:

- *Ask if the venue would be interested in a review of the book you have identified.* If the book is listed on the journal's "books received" list, ask if it is still available for review. If the journal has no such list—or if the book you have identified is not included—provide the name of the author (or editor), the title of the book, the publisher, and the publication year. Also provide either an ISBN (International Standard Book Number) or a hyperlink to the publisher's book-description page.

- *Share just enough about your background to indicate that you would make a qualified reviewer.* For example, you may cite your degrees, your areas of expertise, the title of your dissertation (even if it's in progress, provided the connection with the book you are seeking to review is clear), your current academic position, titles of relevant publications, or the names of other books you may have previously reviewed (and their venues). If an academic mentor or adviser has encouraged you to review this book, feel free to add that point, especially if this mentor has offered to guide you through the review process.
- *Note how you will acquire a review copy.* Perhaps you will arrange for the review copy yourself (see below for advice). If you would like the book review editor to arrange for a copy to be sent to you, be clear with your request. You should also indicate your preference for format (electronic or hard copy) and, for a hard copy, include your mailing address and phone number.[62]
- *Note if you are willing to review a different title, if necessary.* For example, the title you propose may have already been claimed by another reviewer or might not be of interest to your target venue. The one time I had to rewrite a book review for an alternative venue was when I had not cleared the title with the book review editor of the journal for which I had originally written the review. As I quickly learned after submitting my review, someone else had already submitted a review of the same book (but the review had not yet been published, so I was unaware of the duplication).[63] The lesson: Query first, then write.

And here's an additional tip: You might increase your odds of the book review editor accepting your offer to review a book if the topic of the book you have in mind aligns with a forthcoming themed issue of the venue—and if you can promise to have the completed review delivered in time to meet the production timeline for that issue.

What can you expect by way of response? In short, you'll either be given a thumbs up or a thumbs down for the book you recommended. If the book is approved, you will likely be directed to the book review guidelines for the venue. The book review editor may offer a suggested timeline (for example, you may be told the earliest date by which your review could be published if you are able to submit it by a certain date).

Make sure to acknowledge the book review editor's response. Confirm if you will be proceeding with the review, and consider suggesting a date by which you will aim to have the review complete. (If nothing else, doing so gives you a deadline. Just remember that tasks—especially complex ones you are undertaking for the first time—can easily take twice as long as you imagine they may. Be sure to factor in sufficient time for the arrival of a review copy if you don't yet have one, and give yourself adequate time to do the job well.)[64] If you have asked the book review editor to arrange for a copy of the book to be sent to you, be sure to let the editor know once the copy has reached you. When a venue expresses interest in a book review you have proposed, you have created the expectation that you will follow through on your offer. If you encounter an unexpected delay, just let the book review editor know of your revised timeline.

You may be thinking that this guidance involving correspondence is common sense. When I served as a journal editor between 2007 and 2009, I was surprised by the number of authors who lacked the sort of common sense I am describing here. With editors, transparency is key. When you have questions, ask. Editors want to help you prepare and present your best work. If you think editors will forget your original excitement about submitting something to them, think again. (But because memory is fallible, in my work for the *Journal of Scholarly Publishing*, I maintain a database of all contact with reviewers and potential reviewers.) The type of relationship you want is one where you are proactive, always being the first to reach out in case of actual or anticipated problems, challenges, or delays.

A copy of a *Peanuts* cartoon by Charles M. Schulz, originally published on April 11, 1966, hangs above my desk. In it, know-it-all Lucy watches as Linus, her younger brother, bends over a piece of paper, writing a letter. "Dear Editor of 'Letters to the Editor,'" Linus offers by way of salutation. Then: "How have you been?" In the next frame, Lucy queries her brother's opening question, asking, "What sort of letter is that to write to an editor?" As Linus attempts to explain in the third frame, Lucy turns and walks away, unimpressed by Linus's proffered rationale. In the final frame, Linus shouts his thesis—the punchline—in Lucy's direction: "Editors are sort of human, too, you know!"

Requesting a Review Copy from a Publisher

If you have offered to procure your own review copy of a scholarly book, here is what you should know. Some publishers identify a marketing contact for each book on the book's webpage. Others, including smaller academic presses, typically provide email addresses for "media," "marketing," or "publicity" contacts on their websites. In the absence of a clear website organization by department or function, consult the staff directory. Larger or for-profit scholarly presses may have online forms for media requests. Note that review copies intended for book reviews are distinct from review copies of scholarly books for potential course adoption by faculty members (otherwise known as "desk copies" or "instructor copies"). Make sure you are initiating the correct kind of request. If you cannot figure out the ideal contact for requesting a review copy, you may write to a generic, top-level "info@" email address, but do so only after you have searched the website thoroughly for a better fit for your request.

Requesting review copies of scholarly books may feel easier once you have a PhD in hand. If you are still a graduate student, make sure to write from (or, on a form, to provide) your institutional email address. When you request a book, you should offer the ISBN (or may be required to provide it via online form) in addition to the author and title of the book. You should note your preference for hard copy or electronic version. (I always prefer hard copies, although electronic versions have their benefits. Some publishers have policies of providing only electronic versions for review. And if you are familiar with reviewing in the world of trade publishing, you may have encountered the advance reader's copy, a bound, uncorrected proof of a book circulated to reviewers in advance of publication so that reviews can be timed for publication with the release date of the book in order to maximize buzz—and sales. Such publicity proofs are uncommon in the world of scholarly publishing, at least in the United States.) To receive a hard copy, you should provide your mailing address and phone number. You should always note the name of the journal for which you are intending to write the review. Some publishers ask for an anticipated publication date for your review. And you should assure that you will share a copy of the published review in return.

When I wrote my first book review in 2003, I had no idea that reviewers wielded such power. I would never have dared to ask a publisher to send a gratis copy of a book to me, at the time *just* a graduate student. But, by writing a review, I was effectively providing free publicity. I would be saying to the world, "Look, I read this book, and I learned something from it. If you read this book, you might learn something, too." Some years and a number of book reviews later, I learned that marketing staff appreciate requests for review copies, since the reviewers are helping the marketers do their jobs.

And *now* you can proceed with your review.

Lessons

- Scholarly book reviews serve valuable purposes within the academic ecosystem.
- You, too, can review scholarly books in your areas of topical, disciplinary, and methodological expertise.
- Never write a scholarly book review on speculation. Find a home for your review first. Then write the review to the specifications of the target venue.
- Complimentary review copies are typically available to reviewers in return for a promise to send a copy of the published review to the publisher of the book.

INTERLUDE 1

THINKING LIKE A REVIEWER

Now that you have a scholarly book to review in hand and have found a venue eager to receive your review, you are ready to begin the intellectual work of reviewing. Before you read any new book, you can never be sure what you will encounter. In the case of a book you're planning to review, you've likely read the description on the jacket or on the publisher's website, and perhaps you've read the promotional blurbs, making note of the status or affiliations of those who've provided them. But these elements are marketing tools. How well they capture the tenor and contribution of the book being described is a function of the skill—or luck—of the publisher's marketing team. The packaging is never a definitive indicator of the riches that may (or may not) lie between the covers.

Reviewing involves the thrill of discovery coupled with the challenge of forming and communicating your impressions selectively and concisely. Because other people will be invested in your impressions—not least the book review editor who has expressed interest in your thoughts about the book in question—you will want to ensure that you approach the book with a generous, open mind. Through your published review, your impressions may be the first encounter that other scholars and students have with this book, with this author, or possibly even with this particular press. A reviewer therefore shoulders great responsibility for objectivity, fairness, accuracy, and precision.

Before you embark on your own review of a book, should you read previously published reviews of the book, if you happen to come across any? Generally, no—or at least not until after you've fully drafted your review. You want to engage with the text without biases or preconceptions. Others' opinions about a work can all too easily influence your own. You should trust your own impressions, opinions, and assessments. But exceptions exist, of course. Imagine a scenario where a glowing review of a new book results in your reading that book, yet your experience with the text varies markedly from what you expected. You may wish to write your own review to serve as fair warning to others. Or imagine a case where you read a new release in your specialty and find the book to be transformative, triumphant. And then you encounter an unfairly negative review. You could seek an opportunity to review that book as a corrective, of sorts. In such a case, your primary motivation would not be "What's in it for me?" Instead, you'd be motivated to write a review by the importance of the ideas in the book, asking, "What's in it for my colleagues?" and "What's in it for my field?" Reviewers routinely think about the value-added nature of their evaluations, particularly when they sense the importance of the work at hand.

You do, however, want to read reviews of other books recently published in your target venue, especially if you are preparing to review your first scholarly book. You'll likely find presentational diversity, but you should also find consistency. Consistency results from expectations of the discipline and of the venue: the requirements regarding length, content, and tone that you learned from the venue website or directly from the book review editor. Diversity arises from the books and the reviewers themselves. A reviewer's reviews leave intellectual fingerprints: ways of determining the perspectives, positions, values, views, and other dimensions that inform the content, direction, and valence of a review.

Here's what to do: Identify and read at least three or four recent reviews published in your target venue. (More would be better, if you will be writing your first scholarly book review.) As you read them, make note of how each reviewer

- contextualizes the book within the field;
- contextualizes the book within the author's oeuvre (if the book is not a scholar's initial offering);
- uses examples from the book; and
- uses quotations from the book.

These elements serve as general framing strategies for scholarly reviews. The key question is: *Where does this book fit?* Contextualization requires knowledge and awareness of a field and its literature. Effective use of examples and quotations from the text requires attentive, inquisitive reading (the subject of the next chapter).

With respect to contextualization, note whether and how your sample reviews invoke and cite external sources. Some venues (and fields) expect such substantiation. You may even be permitted to include discursive notes, although they will count toward your word limit. Other venues will have no mechanisms for notes or references. Know what you will be allowed in your own review from the outset.

Then, consider what characteristics of the text each reviewer uses to evaluate the contributions of each book. Some of these characteristics will depend on the field and the book in question, but common attributes for assessment include the

- intended goals of the book;
- author's critical perspective;
- sources (evidence) used by the author;
- methods and robustness of analysis;
- clarity of argument and presentation; and
- stated and unstated limitations.

Next, ask yourself the following questions about each review:

- How and where in the review does the reviewer identify strengths and shortcomings of the book?
- Can you tell who might benefit from reading this book, and why?
- Is the reviewer's ultimate assessment clear?
- How is the reviewer positioned within the review, if at all?
- Did you learn something from reading the review?

Finally, ask these questions of your set of sample reviews as a whole:

- Which reviews are especially effective? Why?
- Which reviews are less engaging? Why?

You can learn a lot about academic genres by engaging with examples. Pay special attention to the reviews that strike you as most effective. In your own review, you will aim to capture the attention of your readers similarly while fully and fairly presenting the essence of the book you are reviewing. And you will aim to do so using context, knowledge, and language appropriate to readers of your target venue. Use the sample reviews as guides to a suitable tone. Keep copies of these three or four reviews, because you will return to them in interlude 2 and in chapter 3, once you're ready to write your own review.

One role of a reviewer is to be a critic, and one role of a critic is to critique. Critiquing requires that you're starting from somewhere. In your case, as a scholarly book reviewer, your somewhere is within the target readership of the book. Your preparation also includes being attuned to the goals and expectations of, first, scholarship within your field and, second, scholarly book reviews in your field and your target venue. Reviewers have their antennae out: They're collecting evidence and examples every time they engage with a book, with an author's other works, with a series, with a press. So you won't be reading just for content. Far from it. You'll be paying attention to much, much more. Thinking like a reviewer will, in fact, make you both a better scholar and a better writer.

Remember the goals of scholarly book reviews. You will aim to present a

- contextualized summary,
- clear analysis, and
- cogent assessment

of the book at hand. From these goals, you can divine the goals of scholarly reviewers: the identity you will appropriate yourself as you actively engage with a book and subsequently compose your review.

You are now beginning to think like a reviewer. Next, let's get reading.

2

Reading for Reviewing

SCHOLARS WHO READ BOOKS as part of their ongoing engagement with their fields often treat books like mines or quarries: *What's in this text that might be useful to me? How do the ideas in this book relate to my work or advance my intellectual agenda?* To such scholars, robust indexes in academic books are vital; searchable digital texts, godsends. Tired, overworked scholars can cut to the chase, extracting knowledge and connections efficiently before moving on to the next work, the next quarry. Library administrator Rick Anderson differentiates "researchers" from "readers" when it comes to scholarly books as follows: "The researcher wants to find discrete pieces of information within the body of the text and therefore treats the book more as a database of content than as a linear and immersive reading experience."[1] Even when reading the work of others, then, researchers privilege their own interests, agendas, goals.

Scholars who review books must approach them, fundamentally, as readers. You will of course have your own interests in the material; these interests may be what piqued your curiosity or are fueling your commitment to reviewing the book in the first place. But you will need to see beyond those personally instrumental needs and to engage with the contributions of the book as a whole, on the terms set forth by the author. By summarizing, analyzing, and assessing the book as a complete entity—that is, by engaging with the text through a "linear and immersive reading experience" à la Anderson—your review should prove useful to the same tired, overworked scholars who are tempted to extract, to cherry-pick, to skim. Perhaps this rationale for book reviews helps explain Nicholson Baker's comment, from the previous chapter, about book reviews serving as key influencers in the ways scholars understand the development of their fields. Effective book reviews answer this question: *How do the contributions of this book further our collective understanding of this subject or develop new discursive arenas for consideration?*

This chapter encourages you to step back and immerse yourself in the pleasure of careful, attentive reading. As a reviewer, you will be reading both for understanding—that is, for understanding the author's goals and intentions with the book—and for associating. While you read, carefully and critically, you will compare and connect what you encounter with what you know of the field, and you will use these associations to fuel your ongoing assessment of the work. In this way, you are taking what the author gives you (the book at hand) and interpreting the value of that material through the lens of what you bring to the occasion of engaging with the author's ideas (your familiarity with the field). Reviewers thus enter into dialogues with the books they review. These dialogues begin when the reviewers start considering and working their way through the texts and continue throughout the preparation of the reviews. Dialogues with books that shift paradigms within disciplines have the longest afterlives.

Here, then, I invite you to approach with an open mind the book you have identified for review. You will learn a comprehensive approach for taking in a scholarly book both descriptively and reflectively. You will receive advice on what to pay attention to, what to look out for, what to register. And you will find suggestions on what to question during the ongoing dialogic process of reading, taking notes, and preparing to review and reflect on your notes. Ultimately, the serious work of reading and attentive note-taking lays the foundation for crafting an effective scholarly review.

Understanding the Importance of Note-taking

How should I read a scholarly book that I have agreed to review? What sorts of notes should I take? How should I organize them?

Acknowledging a Bias and an Ingrained Habit

Let me confess: When it comes to reading for reviewing, I am biased toward print. Maybe I'm old-fashioned, but when I take in and commune with a book, I want a physical object—a print copy of the book itself—in my hands. I don't want to be tethered to a device. Should the power fail or the battery die, I want to be able to continue to make progress, even if I must light a candle or two. (*Candles*? Old-fashioned, for sure.) Yes, digital books have their merits: searchable text, ease of annotation, straightforward exportation of citations and textual excerpts, ability to include material (complex datasets; transcripts; translations; full-color, high-resolution images; even audio and video elements) that would overwhelm a typical print book, either in scale or production costs. When a publisher sends me a digital book for review—typically due to a policy of no longer shipping print books to reviewers—I also check out a library copy (via interlibrary loan, if necessary). The most fluid and customizable electronic-reading platforms lack precise pagination, thwarting my attempts at precise documentation. I am therefore reassured by print. As a result, the strategy I put forth in this section presumes that you have access to a print copy of the book you are reviewing. If you are working solely with an electronic book, as you may well prefer, you will need to modify my suggestions accordingly.

And now a habit, one that might seem counterintuitive for a productive book reviewer: I have a *very* hard time writing in books. I will occasionally find myself penciling the tiniest of checkmarks, in the lightest of hands, in the margins of a book. I attribute this disinclination to write in books not to any characteristic of my upbringing but rather to the fact that I wrote most of my earliest book reviews using library copies. I therefore kept all of my reading notes outside the books themselves. If you read chapter 1, though, you know better: As a reviewer, you have every right to request a review copy for your own use. So, by all means, feel free to mark up your text: Underline, highlight, adorn with exclamation points and question marks and marginalia to your heart's delight, if doing so helps you engage more actively and attentively with the text.[2] But trust me on one point (one that will become clear later): When it comes time to write your review, you'll want to move out of and away from the book itself. So make sure to transcribe any important commentaries, responses, and impressions into your reading notes, as I describe in this section.

In the material that follows, you will see that I refer to the "author" of the book you have identified for review. You may very well be working with a coauthored book or perhaps even an edited volume (though for edited volumes, you'll definitely want to check out chapter 4). Please pluralize or adapt my text as necessary to your situation.

Beginning Your Notes

With acknowledgments to environmental historian Stephen Pyne, a book review begins as a verb.[3] First, even though you have not begun reading the book, you will begin your notes.

I start such a document the moment I am committed to reviewing a book. You may keep these notes in longhand, shorthand (a lost art), or in a computer file. But (double-standard alert!) what did I just mention about my dislike of being tethered to a device? The device that I don't mind having close at hand when I am reviewing a book is my computer: I can type much faster than I can write. I read at my desk, book directly in front of me, laptop just an arm's reach away. If I find myself away from my desk for a spell (or negotiating a power outage), I can always continue working my way through the book, pen and notepad at hand. I later add these notes to the electronic file so I ultimately have, in one place, complete documentation of my impressions of the book.

At the start of the document, first enter the descriptive metadata about the book as required by the review venue. What are metadata? In the case of a book review, the primary metadata are what appear at the head of your review. At minimum, you will be asked to provide basic bibliographic information: the name of the author, the book title (and subtitle, if any), the series name (if any), the place of publication, the publisher, and the date of publication.[4] In addition, you may be asked to include the number of pages, details about special features (including maps or color plates), and the ISBNs (the thirteen-digit International Standard Book Numbers) and list prices of various publication formats (cloth or hardcover, paperback, electronic). Your target venue will have a preferred format; follow it here. If you do things right from the outset, you can use this block of metadata at the head of your review. Much of this detail, save the pagination, list prices, and special features, can be found on the book's copyright page. Ensure precision in transcribing this fundamental information.

Sometimes I struggle to identify the list prices of books I am reviewing. (Not all venues require this information. If you need it, read on.) You have options. Generally, the publisher's website includes the list price (sometimes even adjusting for major world currencies based on the country from where you are accessing the website). Publisher's websites will occasionally include links to stand-alone promotional materials for the book—and these promotional materials tend to include formats, ISBNs, and list prices across publication formats. Certain online booksellers may list the manufacturer's suggested retail prices for their wares (in addition to their potentially discounted prices). You can check to see whether the publisher of your book shares metadata with Edelweiss+ (at https://www.edelweiss.plus; see chapter 1). If you're stumped, you may always email the publishers. If you secured your own review copy from the publisher and have the name and email address of a marketing representative, start with that individual. If your review copy came from the review venue, you'll need to reach out to the publisher yourself. When a marketing contact is not listed on the book's webpage, look for the "media," "marketing," or "publicity" contacts on the publisher's website. Your question is routine and, if you explain why you are asking, should result in a speedy, informative reply.

Conducting a Preliminary Walkthrough

Now that you have recorded the metadata, return to the book itself. Admire it. You are witnessing the fruit of hours and hours of effort, intellectual and otherwise, from the author, the peer reviewers, the editors, the production team, the marketers and distributors, and others. Books published by scholarly or academic presses are team projects. Respect the results. You have been entrusted to weigh in on the product, and the responsibility is great. Five relatively straightforward goals await. The questions underscoring these goals are repeated in the appendix, in slightly different arrangement, in the sections on "context" and "content."

Goal #1: Understand the origins of the book. Here, I don't mean the origins of the ideas in the book—or the reasons the book came to be written. (You will get to those points later.) I mean simply whom to acknowledge for the book's existence. You will investigate the following:

- *The author.* Read the biographical information presented about the author within the book itself (often on the dust jacket or back cover; sometimes on one of the last pages of the back matter or on an opening page preceding the formal front matter). Then look up the author online. Record in your notes the author's full title, affiliation, major honors, and any prior publications of note. How does this book fit into the author's oeuvre?[5] You may want to mention some of this contextualizing material in your review, so it's wise to collect it now (although you will verify its currency later).

    If the work you are reviewing is an author's first book, it may be a revision of the doctoral dissertation.[6] Make note of this possibility, and feel free to corroborate the idea by cross-referencing with information you can find about the author online (look, for example, for a posted copy of the author's CV). If you have access through a research library, you may even wish to consult the ProQuest Dissertations & Theses Global database for a downloadable copy of the dissertation. The book itself, typically in the front matter or back matter, may shed light on the origin story. At this point, you just want to know if what you will be reading had an earlier life as a dissertation.

    If you are reviewing a single book by a prolific author, you need not read all of the author's earlier works. You do want to familiarize yourself with the author's prior output,

especially if the book you are reviewing builds directly on prior work, but you need not read everything. (Reading book reviews of an author's earlier works is a wonderful way to build familiarity.) If the book you are reading is a second or subsequent edition, however, you will want to make note of what is new, what is different, or what has been revised in the current edition. For comparative reference, then, you will need to have copies of earlier editions (at least the next-most-recent edition) on hand. Just remember that, in such cases, you cannot presume that readers of your review will be familiar with any earlier editions.
- *The publisher.* What do you know about the publisher? Does the publisher have a strong reputation in this field? If not, what are the publisher's disciplinary strengths? What audiences does the publisher typically serve? What titles similar to the one you are reviewing has this publisher issued? Here, you are looking for the company the book keeps by way of associative contextualization.
- *The series (if applicable).* If the book you are reviewing is part of a series, make note. Who is the series editor? What are some of the previous and forthcoming works in the series? Do you recognize any of the other authors or books?

Goal #2: Understand how the book is organized. Here, I'm referring to the structure, the architecture of the work. More formally, what you will technically be noting and recording are structural and statistical metadata. Study the contents page. List the elements of the book in your notes, including part, section, and chapter titles. Then go through and count—yes, physically count—and record the numbers of pages dedicated to the various components, from contents page and other front matter through appendixes, references, and index. Doing so will give you an immediate sense of how well "balanced" the book happens to be. I once reviewed a nine-chapter, 220-page book. I could have noted, in the review, that the chapters average twenty-three pages. (They do.) But the book is quite imbalanced: Chapters range from five pages to sixty-three pages. Knowing what to expect from the start about organization and balance helped prepare me for the reading experience to follow.

Goal #3: Understand how the book is substantiated. Now note the extent of the back matter. Pay special attention to how extensive the notes and the references happen to be. (If you are reviewing a book that uses footnotes or places endnotes or reference lists at the conclusion of each chapter, judging the collective extent of such notes is more difficult.) Next, scan the bibliography or references list, looking for authors, works, and sources you recognize. Perusing the sources is akin to looking at the author's bookshelf or sifting through piles of photocopied archival or other documentary materials on the author's desk: These are some of the works that inspired, informed, influenced the text at hand. Suitable reviewers should be familiar with at least a portion of the works cited by the author.

Next, note how the book makes use of any tables and figures. At a glance, can you understand the messages they impart? Similarly, make note of maps, chronologies, timelines, flowcharts, genealogical or pedigree charts, musical examples, glossaries, color plates, datasets, and other special elements. (If such material is not included and could be realistic for the type of book you are reviewing, while you read you will register what would have been helpful to include.)

Goal #4: Begin to consider the design and layout of the book. Former editor William Germano refers to editing and design as "the invisible virtues": "Good design, inside and out, draws the reader to the book, stages the author's brilliant ideas, and makes the act of reading a pleasure."[7] Note the typeface, the type size, the density of text per page. Note the placement of the text block on the page. Note the width of the gutter (the inner margin of the bound leaves of the book) and the outer margins. Consider the placement and content of running headers or footers. Can you tell what section or chapter of the book you are looking at when you open to a random two-page spread? Are the page numbers clear? Are any tables or figures you noted earlier rendered clearly and legibly? Does reading the notes, references, or index require use of a magnifying glass? Do any design elements distract? What about the paper refractivity and quality? The binding? Given these production characteristics, does the list price seem reasonable?[8]

Unless you are reviewing a book on design or one for which the argument hinges on the legibility of figures, these elements may seem trivial. But they will affect how you engage with the book. Make note of anything atypical, unexpected, distracting, or especially impressive. For example, book historian Leah Price, in *What We Talk About When We Talk About Books: The History and Future of Reading*, offers an eight-page "interleaf" titled "Please Lay Flat."[9] Instead of reading down the verso (left-hand page) and then over to and down the recto (right-hand page), as usual in an English-language book, each line requires you to read all the way across the page spread, your eyes jumping across the gutter up to twenty-nine times per page spread. In my reading notes for a review of Price's book, I recorded a number of observations about this section. One was that "I don't believe I've ever seen anything like this in a contemporary book." Another was that "reading this way is surprisingly difficult!" Given the topic of the book, such an unexpected design element warranted inclusion in my review, where I note that Price pushes "the boundaries of the ordinary in ways that enchant both the page and the reader."[10]

Goal #5: Begin to formulate an idea for why the book exists, based on the apparatus and the organization. At this point, you won't know how the various components of the book fit together; you'll just know that they exist and how they are ordered. Effective organizations reveal logic. Logic helps buttress arguments. Your critical wheels are already turning, even though you've just taken in the organization and substantiation of the book at hand. Revisit the chapter titles: In conjunction with the title of the book, can you sense the author's thesis?[11] ("Introduction" and "Conclusion" represent missed opportunities: Of course the material at the outset is the introduction and the material at the end, the conclusion.) You will check and recheck this nascent idea as you begin reading.

Now, having conducted a walkthrough of the text—a process referred to by qualitative researcher Ronald Chenail as "taking a grand tour of the book"—what do you expect of the book you are about to read?[12] You are welcome to record your impressions in your notes. You will be continuously recalibrating these impressions while you read.

Understanding Approaches to Careful Note-taking

In graduate school, you likely learned strategies for "efficiently" taking in scholarly works. These tricks often involve reading the conclusions and introductions first before deciding which of the substantiating inner material to consider thoroughly (versus which to skim).[13] I say "no, thanks" to this nonlinear approach when reading a book I am reviewing. Instead, I read the book from beginning to end. A conscientious reviewer needs to do more than to harvest the thesis, the contribution, the "so what?" factor of the work. Sure, those elements are important, but they will become clear during the process of engaging attentively with the book. Reading linearly allows me to assess the pacing, the scaffolding of ideas, the staying power of examples and explanations.

Reading linearly enables me to catch the type of disorganization or repetition that I might miss if I knew from the outset how everything resolves and how the author gets there. And reading linearly forces me to approach the book as a narrative instead of as a repository. Remember Rick Anderson's books-as-databases analogy from the opening of this chapter? My approach for reviewing runs counter to that instrumentalization of the text, and I encourage you to read linearly, as well. In fact, you owe such a careful reading to the author.[14]

If you were taught how to take reading notes as an undergraduate or graduate student, you likely learned the importance of differentiating between your own synopses and the author's own words. (If you weren't taught how to take reading notes, you likely learned the hard way when it came time to check quotations or sources. Or you might have found yourself, heaven forbid, unintentionally plagiarizing.) This distinction—between what you are observing about a text and what the text itself imparts—is key. Careful note-taking allows you to avoid inadvertent plagiarizing once you start using your notes for your own writing. Careful note-taking also saves you time. For long, complex books, especially, looking back through your notes is more efficient than rereading entire chapters or sections when you're keen to understand how and where in the text your own understanding of the author's ideas began to evolve.

When I read a book for review, I record three distinct kinds of notes:

- direct quotations from the text (*always* with page numbers);
- direct, factual descriptive matter *in my own words*: these entries include summaries and synopses of the author's presentation; and
- commentary: observations, asides, associations, questions, inconsistencies, errors.[15]

Because I read linearly, I differentiate between two types of comments: those that are pertinent to the section of the text at hand and those that pertain to my evolving understanding of the book as a whole. I interlace specific comments with my summaries and the direct quotations I am harvesting, linearly, prefacing the notes with an italicized QUESTION or COMMENT marker. In their own section at the bottom of my notes, I place more general comments: those pertaining to the author's bigger picture or to the broader thesis, to overall associations or considerations or implications that arise while I am reading. The comments at the bottom of my notes often form the heart of my critique, with more specific, chapter-relevant comments offering the evidence I use to support my assessment of the text.

Let me share a few strategies for bulletproofing your notes:

- Consider using different colors for the three different types of notes: direct quotations, descriptive notes, and editorial comments. You will be passing through your notes multiple times once you have finished reading the book, and you might want to use the highlighting tool within your word processor (or an actual highlighter on a printed copy of your notes), so be sure to use colors amenable to such treatment. In case the formatting is lost, preface your own comments and editorializing with obvious markers. Consider placing curly brackets around your synopses and square brackets around your editorial comments.[16]
- Even if you've decided to use different colors for different note types, *always* use quotation marks around direct quotations. And *always* include page numbers for these quotations. When a quotation crosses a page break, note

the precise location of the break within the quotation. You may insert a bracketed "END OF PAGE X" comment, or you may use a spaced slash or another obvious marker of your own devising. Such annotation is important in case you happen to end up using just part of a page-spanning quotation in your review.

- Be *very* careful with your transcription. I will mention later how you must always compare with the original text any direct quotations that end up in your reviews—one reason you will want the page numbers in your notes. But I will mention now how easy it is to make transcription errors when taking notes. (Most often, I am guilty of attempting to "improve" a text when noting direct quotations. Occasionally, I simply get a word wrong. I recently caught an error in a quotation in one of my reviews at the page-proof stage, the last chance to fix it. I had simply transcribed *critical* as *crucial*, and the error had eluded all of my prior cross-checks.) Pay special attention to textual emphases (italics in the original, for example): Aspire to accurate reproduction of what you include in your notes. (Accurate reproduction is crucial—I mean critical!) If a passage you are recording includes an error, highlight the faulty text in a different color or identify the error with a "[*sic*]" ("thus") in your notes.

Although the book you are reviewing will likely base its arguments on primary sources, for a scholarly book review, the book itself becomes a primary source. You should therefore treat the text with the same reverence and precision you would afford to any primary source used in your own scholarly work.

Discerning Noteworthy Material

To what should I pay attention while reading a book I will review? How do I know what's important enough to warrant entry into my notes?

Seeing the Bigger Picture

As with any scholarly activity, reviewing is a skill that you improve with practice. You may be tempted, upon preparing for your first book review, to record in your notes everything that feels remotely "important." Try to resist the urge. Reviewing is about filtering, highlighting, being selective and intentional. For extreme examples of selectivity (and, as a reviewer, self-restraint), take a look at entries in the "Briefly Noted" column in the *New Yorker*. The books selected for inclusion there—typically a mix of fiction and nonfiction—are encapsulated in under 130 words.

Still, I tend to end up with five to seven times the volume of notes, in terms of numbers of words, as will end up in the finished review. That is, for a 1,500-word review, I may end up with notes totaling 7,500–10,500 words. (Why the range? Books themselves vary in length. Remember that the typical monograph ranges from 70,000 to 110,000 words. My notes therefore equate to around 10 percent of a work in terms of volume. The review itself ultimately amounts to just 1 or 2 percent of the length of the book being reviewed.) If sitting at a keyboard encourages you to record too much, consider handwriting your notes instead.

What you will need to resist most strongly is the urge to transcribe long portions of text into your notes. Yes, in your review you will likely want to include some of the author's own words. But quotations, which can help demonstrate the texture of a work, should typically be used as sparingly as possible in a finished review. Quotations should support or reinforce *your*—the reviewer's—claims about the book, not make the claims for you. In your notes, then, aim to record statements or turns of phrase that expressively capture the author's voice, the author's style, or the author's claims or thesis in a way that reflects your evolving understanding of the ethos or intellectual orientation of the work. When you come across sentences that encapsulate the raison d'être of the book, add them to your notes. You might also wish to record spurious, faulty, contradictory, or otherwise problematic statements by way of building evidence for your eventual assessment of the book. You're capturing a continuum in your quotations from the text, and ideally you will have more quotations toward the "positive" end than toward the "negative" end. If your notes start filling up with negative material, you'll have a tough time writing even a neutral review. But as in any research act, you should not avoid or ignore evidence that would fail to support your claims. Stephen Pyne identifies two "nonnegotiable" rules specific to nonfiction writing: "You can't make anything up, and you can't leave out something that really matters—meaning something that, if included, would alter our fundamental understanding."[17] Observe these rules when reviewing.

I try to follow a rule of thirds in my notes: No more than one-third of my notes should be direct quotations, allowing two-thirds to be composed of descriptive matter (in my own words) and commentary about the text. The more direct quotations you capture in your notes, the more tempted you will be to include too many quotations in your review. Your own descriptions and comments should form the heart of your critique.

Have you noticed yet? Here's something really neat, in a reflexive, refractive way, about reviewing: You will build an argument about the book you are reviewing in a manner similar to the way the author of the book likely used sources. Scholarly authors use quotations to reinforce or drive home points they—the authors—are making, not to make the points in the first place.[18] Quotations thus buttress the surrounding text, wherein the argument is presented. A scholarly book review is no different. You are the author of the scholarly review, and the book you are reviewing is your primary source. You will use quotations strategically and sparingly for maximum effect.

Now, if you happen to be feeling bored by all these preliminaries—by matters that appear to be secondary to the scholarship at hand—you can get ready for the good stuff. By way of a series of interrelated questions, we'll next consider the core features that animate works of scholarship. You will consider these questions as you read, and your reactions to them will form the crux of your assessment of the contributions of the book you are reviewing. Like the questions in the prior section, the questions in the following section appear under "context" and "content" in the appendix.

Considering Content: Thesis, Argument, Substantiation

We engage with scholarship to learn about the world, to form or reform our opinions and understandings, to provide a knowledge base upon which to position our own scholarship and contributions. When reviewers engage with scholarly books, they ultimately seek to assess the extent to which these books advance understanding within a field. As a reviewer yourself, when you read a work of scholarship in the humanities or social sciences, you will be on the lookout for answers to the following questions. In your notes you will record what you find—or what you conclude based on textual evidence you encounter within the book. Initial questions are straightforward, objective: The book should contain the answers. Later questions will introduce greater layers of subjectivity.

What are the author's stated goals? You will most likely find these in the introduction or otherwise near the outset of the work. The goals might also reappear toward the end of the book, as a reminder that they have been accomplished (assuming they have). Another way of stating this question is: *What does the author believe to be the value of the book?* Look for bold, confident statements involving what the author argues, asserts, attests, avows, avers, holds, claims, questions, controverts, contends, maintains, suggests, proposes, offers, advances, surveys, assesses, reassesses, evaluates, reevaluates, destabilizes, positions, repositions, centers, decenters, recenters, focuses, refocuses, synthesizes, articulates, differentiates, delineates, determines, settles, solves, resolves, reasons, decodes, proves, concludes. Remember these forty verbs—and others like them—when you are writing your review.[19] Authors do not *talk about* topics in their books, nor do they *say* things (unless you happen to be reviewing an audiobook narrated by the author).

Who is the intended audience? As explained in chapter 1, you should belong to the intended audience: Your disciplinary background and training should have prepared you to understand and engage fully with the book.[20] Authors of scholarly works, when self-evidently writing for their peers, tend not to state their intended audiences. When they do, such information is often revealed in a preface or introduction—or possibly in the acknowledgments or an afterword. Marketers may fill in such lacunae themselves, noting in publicity materials that the book is "intended for" certain types of readers. Such a strategy is used especially with books that the publishers would like to see adopted for classroom use.

What sources does the author use? How does the author use them? Record the empirical evidence used, the methods used to gather the evidence, and the methods used to analyze the evidence. As with the author's stated goals, the primary answers to these questions are descriptive. The subjective approach to this material, which comes later, lets you address the suitability and efficacy of the sources and analytical methods and, ultimately, the conclusions the author reaches. Disciplinary knowledge is fundamental for such analysis and appraisal.

What theoretical perspectives underpin the presentation? Discern what you can about the author's epistemology, either through direct acknowledgment or through the literature in which the work is grounded. The research methodology the author employs should suit the theoretical framework.

How well does the work flow? Are the chapters logically ordered and organized? Scholarly works should have intentional structures. You already noted the architecture of the book you are reviewing in your preliminary walkthrough. Within the text, if the author does not articulate and justify the organization, the structure should be obvious to the reviewer. The material within chapters, too, should progress logically. Developmental editor Pamela Haag offers the following on subheadings: "My rule is that if a manuscript is well structured, then subheads aren't needed. And if the manuscript isn't well structured, then subheads aren't helpful."[21] (You can be the judge about whether the subheadings in *this* book are helpful.)

The objective side to these questions about flow and organization addresses whether the author acknowledges intentionality behind the organization. Note the difference between an author simply *describing* how the work is organized and more robustly *explaining* why the work is organized the way it is. Organizational descriptions commonly conclude the introductory chapters yet typically add no value to the readers' experiences. Chapter-by-chapter overviews near the outsets of scholarly books are generally as boring as chapter-by-chapter overviews in scholarly book reviews. (Yes, I've been known to record, in my reading notes, my frustration when such an overview in the introduction reads like content that could be right at home in a book proposal. At least once I mentioned such annoyance in a published review.)[22] The subjective side is the reviewer's call: *Does the organization in fact serve the author's goals?* William Germano describes the architecture of a text as the author's "secret weapon": A savvy author uses structure both to shape the text itself and to guide the reader's response to it.[23]

Getting Granular

And now our questions move into greater subjectivity. You won't necessarily know why the author made certain presentational choices, but you will be able to describe and ultimately assess the effects of these choices. In all instances, you will want to record specific examples in your reading notes. For this material, which focuses more on presentation, knowing whether the book derived from a doctoral dissertation can be helpful in your assessment.

How does the author's use of language reflect the intended audience? Here, you are not directly assessing the author's writing style (though you will do that later). Instead, you are noting the presence (or absence) of context and the use of jargon and other specialized concepts that are common currency in your field. Another way of framing this question is: *What does the author take for granted that the readers already know?* Since you are a member of the target audience, your knowledge base is second nature to you. Here, then, you are noting alignment (or misalignment) with that shared disciplinary knowledge base.[24]

Are key concepts, terms, and variables appropriately defined and used precisely, consistently? Some fields may agree on definitions of key terms; many fields do not. Here you are looking for clarity, precision, accuracy, and consistency. Success of arguments can hinge on these details.

Does the author rely heavily on acronyms? If a large number of acronyms is necessary, does the author provide a list in the front matter? Some fields adore acronyms. Even in fields with fewer shared acronyms, acronyms can streamline the presentation of certain research topics. If anything seems out of line with disciplinary expectations and norms, make note.

Does the text read easily, or is it complex and dense, with overly long paragraphs, sections, or chapters? Again, disciplines have norms. Your knowledge of similar books will provide you with a helpful comparative lens. Complexity can be a function of the subject. But regardless of the level of complexity, clarity is always possible—and ideal.

How does the pacing influence the presentation? This question relates to proportion, organization, and flow. Are important ideas given adequate space? Are digressions and asides kept to a minimum? Does the narrative keep moving forward?

Are tables and figures used effectively? Are legends, headers, and axis labels complete? Are all the tables and figures mentioned in proximal text? As you read, you will note how tables and figures are used to support efficient presentation of the author's ideas and claims. The implications of tables and figures, when keyed and captioned effectively, should be clear without needing to refer to the surrounding text. You will also note where tables and figures were not included but could have been helpful.

Engaging with the Text

What questions should I ask a text in order to assess its overall strengths and effectiveness? How can I ensure that my notes capture compelling connections, associations, and potential avenues to explore in my review?

Dialoguing with the Text

As you take notes, you are answering descriptive questions about the text regarding its contours and content. You are also responding to your own reflective, assessment-oriented questions about robustness, relevance, quality, and convincingness of the argument, the methods, the evidence, and the claims and conclusions. Make sure to externalize this dialogue, recording your evolving impressions as comments in your reading notes.

We have finally arrived at fully subjective territory. Part of your inquisitiveness involves questioning how and why you are responding to the book the way you are. Some of the questions involved in dialoguing with the text appear in the appendix, in the section on "consequences." (The questions below are those to ask and answer while you are reading. They are not necessarily questions to address in your finished review.) Answers to these questions will most directly speak to your assessment of the overall strengths and effectiveness of the book in your review.

What questions are arising as you read? How confident do you feel that the author may address these questions later in the book? How disappointed would you be if these questions are left unanswered? When I read a book for review, I keep tabs on material that feels unresolved, incomplete, tentative, or unconvincing. When wavelengths align, authors feel like mind readers: They present, typically in the next paragraph or section, material or evidence that resolves, completes, affirms, or convinces. When wavelengths do not align, I am left unsatisfied from section to section. I then must figure out why my expectations are off.

Where are you, the reviewer, heading as a consumer of the argument? How are your expectations of the book evolving as you read? You won't use this material wholesale in your review, but it will help you shape how you write about the effect of the book on your thinking.

Where in the text do you find yourself getting bored? Why? Now is the time to start assessing the author's presentational style. You may also address in your notes the level of detail provided and the relevance of such detail.

Where in the text do you feel lost or confused? Why? Authors can hide muddled thought behind muddled writing. As a reader, distinguishing between the two can be difficult: Are unclear ideas being straightforwardly presented, or are ideas that could otherwise be clear getting garbled in the presentation? The worst-case scenario is a combination of unclear ideas and unclear writing, but peer review should provide quality control for the most egregious instances of such obfuscation.

Are the theories underpinning the presentation appropriate? Are they adequately foregrounded? Here, your disciplinary knowledge will permit you to assess how the author builds on the theoretical approaches that befit your field. Be careful if you are fundamentally or ideologically at odds with the author's theoretical positioning, though. Remaining fair in a review becomes difficult when you are predisposed to reject everything the author claims.

How effectively does the author address the stated goals of the book? The answer to this question often determines the valence of the review—the strength of your positivity or negativity toward the book itself. As you near the end of the book, you should sense how well the author has fulfilled the promise offered near the outset. When the goals are met, the book succeeds. Your job in your review will be to judge how well the book succeeds. And that judgment involves your subjective sense of the value of the contribution. If an author sets out to prove something you believe to be trivial, and does so, the book is successful in reaching its goals but is unsuccessful in advancing or transforming the field. Not all books must transform their fields in order to be useful.

What significant knowledge does the book contribute or advance? Does the book extend or challenge paradigms? All books should add value to their fields in some way. Your job as a reviewer is to identify what a book does manage to accomplish, regardless of the scale of the contribution. Remember that, before the book manuscript was accepted for publication, the peer reviewers found merit in the work. If you struggle to see value at first, keep looking.

Do you ultimately trust the author? The answer to this big question will affect how you approach your review. Ideally, the author projects a command of the material and presents a clear and well-substantiated argument.

Where is the author bold, brave, daring, risky—in presentation or approach? Literary scholar Eric Hayot believes that "many audiences *want* to be startled, engaged, disturbed, and otherwise shocked out of their familiar habits."[25] Did the author of the book you are reviewing do any of these things to you? Was anything experimental about the text, given the typical expectations for scholarly books in your field? A predictable approach can certainly be effective, and it is almost certainly safe. But the pushing of boundaries opens space for the creation of knowledge. I always appreciate encountering works that take me farther than I anticipate. For me, these are the works that linger in my memory long after I've finished reading them. They offer me a glimpse of the author's reach of mind, challenging and transforming my own.

Wrapping Up Your Notes

Toward the outset of this chapter, you began your reading notes even before you began reading the book you are reviewing. You should not be surprised to learn that, even after you have finished reading the book, you will continue adding to your notes. The reason is because the digestive reflection begins once you've finished reading. What you notice—and what you note—at this stage will help you formulate your approach to the review. So don't be skimpy when you engage in these six final reflective activities, which touch on questions that appear across all three sections of the appendix.

Activity #1: Reconsider the title of the book. Is it appropriate? Does it adequately capture the scale and scope of the work? Does it say too much—or too little? If you were to come up with an alternative title for the book, what would it be? Or is the title ideal as is?

Activity #2: Reread the introduction. Does it overstate the aims or the reach of the book? Does the book cover ground that was unanticipated, given what is set up in the introduction? One of the reasons for rereading the introduction is because, theoretically, the author should have rewritten—or at least heavily revised—the introduction after the remainder of the text was completed. Scholarly books, like good essays, should come full circle. The foreshadowing in the introduction should be obvious in retrospect. Everything in the introduction should fit. The opening presentation should be pointing and projecting toward the conclusion.

Activity #3: Consider the back matter. Assess the notes, bibliographic entries, and index(es). Your job is not to be a nitpicking copyeditor—for this book, at least, it's too late for that—but you are welcome to note the relative strength of these sections. References afford abundant opportunities for errors, yet their precision serves as a strong litmus test of the attentiveness of the author, the editor, and members of the production team. (I often worry, perhaps unfairly, that if the straightforward stuff isn't handled with care, the more challenging material can't have been handled any better.) Review the index(es), and note their robustness and potential usefulness to the type of researcher introduced at the beginning of this chapter.[26]

Activity #4: Consider the length of the book. Here, you may channel your inner Goldilocks. In the ideal world, the length of the book would be "just right." You noted internal balance earlier. If parts of the book feel bloated, can you imagine them being shorter without sacrificing nuance? Not all authors heed these wise words of William Germano: "If you say everything you know about something, you've said too much."[27]

Activity #5: Consider what has changed about your own understanding or appreciation of the topic or problem addressed in the book. What do you know now that you didn't know before reading this book? What will you plan to do with this knowledge? What questions have been raised by this book that you wish would be addressed in future scholarship? Who else do you imagine could benefit from this knowledge? Would readers from other disciplines benefit from this work? If so, which disciplines? You may certainly focus on the content of the book, but I encourage you also to reflect on the presentation, the approach, and the broader implications of the work. Ideas must be expressed in order to be transmitted, after all, and how they are expressed often affects how they are received.

Activity #6: Write down how you feel, now that you have finished reading the book. Was the time you invested in reading this book well spent? What aftertaste did the book leave with you? Are you illuminated, inspired, transformed, eager to learn more, exhausted, relieved? Then elaborate on why you feel that way. Literary scholar and creative writer Jennifer Harris asks this question: "Is there something in the book that brought you joy?"[28] If you could have dinner with the author, what questions would you want to ask about the book? Often this final reflective response helps me formulate my "way in" to reviewing the book, since it connects my intellectual reaction to the book with something in or about the book that captivated, stimulated, piqued, or perplexed me.

And now you have, in your full reading notes, the valuable resource you will plumb while you are formulating and writing your review. Congratulations! Ready to write? That's the process we'll tackle next.

Lessons

- How you read a scholarly book for review will affect the quality of your finished review. You must be attentive and deliberate as you engage—critically, actively, and linearly—with the author's ideas and presentation.
- The primary source of a scholarly book review is the book being reviewed. Treat the text with the same reverence and precision you would afford to any primary source used in your own scholarly work.
- In your reading notes, record direct quotations, key ideas in your own words, and comments and questions that arise while you read. Make sure to keep these three types of notes distinct.
- While you read, you will address descriptive (objective) and reflective (subjective) questions about the text in your notes. These notes will inform your summary and contextualization of the argument of the book and your ultimate assessment of how well the book achieves its stated claims.
- When you begin formulating your review, you'll want to move out of and away from the book itself. Your reading notes will provide the raw material you use to generate the review.

INTERLUDE 2

FINDING YOUR WAY IN

Most of the time, when you're reading, you're being responsive. No, you're not being passive—or, at least, I hope you're not. But the text is being presented to you, and you're consuming it. You're following subtle (or obvious) clues and nudges within the text regarding what the author wants you to be thinking, or at least thinking about, as you read.

Once you've finished reading and taking notes on a scholarly book you are planning to review, the fun, creative part begins. Now, as you begin digesting the work as a whole, you shift from consumer to producer, from reader to writer. Your focus remains on the book itself. But you must now imagine, as a primary audience, individuals in your field who have not yet read the book. You have specific, newly gained knowledge and perspectives that they do not yet have. Just as the author of the book directed your thinking about the topic while you read the book, you are now responsible for encapsulating the work and presenting a thoughtful synopsis, analysis, and assessment to the readers of your review. How will you do so? An important early task is to figure out how to find your angle, your approach, your "way in" to the review that you have offered or agreed to write.

Journalists, essayists, and other authors often write about "hooks": opening statements that capture the attention of readers, pulling them into the text that follows. Book reviewers—well, at least thoughtful book reviewers—should care about their readers and should want them to engage with their reviews. So even if book reviews appear to belong to a staid, predictable genre, hooks matter with them, too. Return to the three or four sample reviews you read earlier to get a feel for book reviews published in your target venue. Reread just the opening paragraphs. How did those reviewers introduce the texts at hand?

I'm not omniscient, but I'm confident that the authors of those reviews opened in one of two ways: They either jumped right in, starting with a claim from or about the book itself, or they started with something else, most likely an idea germane to the work under review or to the reviewer's intentions with the review. For scholarly book reviews, both approaches can be effective.

The *jump-right-in approach* clearly acknowledges the genre of the book review in the opening sentence. Such a sentence often summarizes the contribution of the book or provides the reviewer's overall assessment. Short, sweet, to the point. Individuals in the US government refer to this approach as BLUF: Bottom Line Up Front. This approach hedges against readers with the shortest attention spans, those who are easily distracted, those who are impatient. If you could tell readers of your review only one thing about the book in question, what would it be? Feel free to give away that idea at the outset. Reviewers following this approach occasionally use the remainder of the opening paragraph to position the work in relation to other scholarship on the topic, perhaps pointing out what's novel or distinct about the work under review.

The *something-else approach* affords more room for the reviewer to put a personal stamp on the review. Readers still know they're reading a book review, but this approach can signal that the reviewer is treating the review genre more like an essay. The reviewer shares an idea, and this idea connects with the book that will soon be under discussion. (How soon is "soon"? It depends on the length of the review.) Here are a few ways to begin such a review:

- Contextualize the book by bridging a connection with contemporary events, debates, anniversaries, or trends.

- Teach the reader something germane.
- Surprise the reader with something unexpected or counterintuitive: a statistic, a finding, or a fact from or related to material in the book. (This method belongs to the something-else approach instead of the jump-right-in approach because the readers aren't made immediately aware of the source or relevance of the statistic, finding, or fact. Again, though, because the readers know they're reading a book review, they will expect a connection. The tidbit serves as the hook to interest them in reading more about the book.)
- Offer a comment about the author, perhaps acknowledging prior contributions. This approach can be especially effective when the author should be known to most readers of the review.

Stylistically, any of the above methods suit declarative opening statements or rhetorical questions. However you open your review, you want to spark your readers' curiosity and inquisitiveness, offering a tacit promise that you will resolve their desires for understanding by the end of your review.

So how do you decide which approach to use? You need not decide this instant. After I finish reading and have completed the copious notes on a book I am reviewing, as described in chapter 2, I like to let the book sit with me for at least a day before I begin drafting the review. During that time, even though I move on to other tasks, I keep thinking about what the book left with me: *What questions did it answer? What questions did it raise? Where am I noticing resonances with or connections to these ideas in my other work?* A way in to the review often occurs to me when I am tending another task, so I quickly jot down the opening sentence or sentences that have come to mind. Depending on where you are and what you're doing when inspiration strikes, you could also capture your thoughts with the voice recorder on your cell phone.

At the outset of the next chapter, I detail how to use your reading notes to start formulating a general structure for the scholarly book review you are preparing. Often, when I am undertaking those iterative steps, my opinion shifts regarding the best way in to the review. Sometimes, though, the way in comes to me earlier, occasionally when I am still midway through the book. Inspiration tends to strike once I've realized what the book *means* to me, either by association or by transformation.

I've used all the approaches listed above as openers to reviews I've written over the years. I don't have a favorite. I do work hard to ensure, though, that each opening signals that the review to follow will be worth reading. Revisit the first paragraphs of your sample reviews once more. Which ones draw you in? Why? Study the strategy and aspire to find as effective a way in for the book you are reviewing. I know you can do it. And I'll be sure to help you out along the way.

Feeling ready to write?

3

Writing a Scholarly Book Review

NOW THAT YOU'VE finished reading and have taken extensive notes on the book you are reviewing, you're ready to begin composing the review. You have been recording thoughts and ideas all along: noting significant passages from the text; summarizing the author's ideas; and recording your own observations, associations, questions, and asides. You have also begun to consider your "way in" to the review. By this point, as well, you have a sense of your overall reaction to the book: positive, neutral, or otherwise. As long as you were reading attentively and recording your impressions throughout, you should have more than enough material from which to construct your review.

Did you note how, in the first sentence of the prior paragraph, I used the term *composing* instead of the term *writing*? The reason is simple, even if the distinction is nuanced: You still have a lot to process before you begin writing the text of the review itself. This chapter walks you through distilling your notes, framing your assessment, and ultimately presenting your ideas about the book in a convincing and compelling manner. One goal in your review is to allow yourself to serve as a conduit for the author's ideas and intentions. But, since you are also offering your opinions and assessment, you will want to let your personality shape your review. After all, a single-authored review offers one reader's experiences with a book. Own your review. Put your own stamp on it, to whatever extent your review venue will allow.

I charge you to approach the process of writing your review with confidence. You've read the book, so you now have an opinion about it.[1] Your task, as reviewer, is to present that opinion and justify it with examples from the work at hand and from your field at large. Reviews without opinions—without arguments—are simply summaries. Yes, an argument requires you to insert yourself into the review, at least as the sentient being who is producing the review.[2] What is a book without a reader? Just a bunch of words. When read, the text acts as a bridge between the author and the reader. Remember this point: A book review is not *about* you, but it is not *without* you. Just as the author created the book itself, you will create the review. Your review will necessarily be influenced by your background, perspectives, orientations, prejudices, preferences. Embrace them. The more reviews you write, the more comfortable you will feel in acknowledging these sources of your impressions.

Distilling Your Reading Notes

How do I begin to make sense of my reading notes? How do I reasonably reduce the large number of wide-ranging ideas in my reading notes into a small number of focused ideas worth invoking in my review?

Winnowing and Focusing

As I mentioned in interlude 2, after I finish reading a book for review, I aim to set the book and my notes aside for at least one day. This time provides a bit of distance from the active work of reading and allows me to begin intellectually processing the book as a whole. Yes, I have been processing all along. But processing the overall contribution of a book is different from processing its individual components while encountering them for the first time. Distance allows my feelings about the book to strengthen (if my impression is a positive one) or to soften (if I am less impressed by a book). This mellowing is important. All scholarly books have merits, and, in the case of less impressive books, identifying positive elements is often easier with some distance from the text.

In the previous chapter I recommended that you linearly read the book you are reviewing. This approach allows you to encounter the ideas in the book as the author intended you to experience them. Successful scholarly arguments hinge on evidence, on logic, on interpretation, on beginning with the shared—the known—and advancing into new territory. Reading linearly allows you to experience the intended progression of ideas, thus enabling you to evaluate more comprehensively both the conclusions reached and the methods, empirical and rhetorical, employed to reach them. Your reading notes should therefore reflect two progressions and evolutions of understanding: the author's and your own. When you turn to your notes to begin debriefing the book (for your contextualized summary of the book's argument) and its effects on you (for your clear analysis and cogent assessment), you will pay close attention to these two developmental strands. At their juncture lies the space where shared meaning is created.

Earlier I encouraged you to reread the introduction of the book you are reviewing after finishing the book. I did not tell you to reread the entire book, no matter how nervous you may feel about having missed something or getting something "wrong" in your review. Note this accusatory comment to authors and public speakers from journalist and policy writer Charles Wheelan: "If your intended audience does not understand what you are trying to tell them, it's your fault, not theirs."[3] From the perspective of the reader, then, if you missed something, or misinterpreted something, you are not entirely to blame.

But you will read and reread your reading notes. These you will pass through multiple times, each time winnowing the material into a smaller and more manageable number of ideas for inclusion in your review. Remember the proportions. Your notes should be many times longer than the space you are allocated for your review. You must be selective, discriminatory. I imagine the hours and hours of footage a filmmaker or documentarian collects while preparing, say, a ninety-minute film. The majority of material in your notes will end up on the analogous cutting-room floor. Do not despair, for you will need all the material to bring attention to what is most important. In your review, you will not be able to mention everything worthy of inclusion.

You may consider the point of compression to be both a strength and a weakness of scholarly book reviews. As a strength, selectivity forces you to emphasize only what you determine to be the most important material, respecting the limitations on time (that of the readers of your review) and space (in the review venue, assuming it is a print journal). The weakness? You have much, much more you could say about the book than space permits. If you feel disappointed by how selective you must be, given the richness of your notes, I have a bold suggestion: You are welcome to offer to share your full reading notes with the author once your review has been published. I have done so myself. In one case, my notes became a starting point for preparation of the second edition of the book. Which gift was greater, that of my notes to the author or that of the author imparting to me the value of my notes?[4]

Just as I favor print books for review, I prefer to print out my reading notes before proceeding to review them. You need not do the same, of course. But regardless of whether you review your notes on paper or on screen, I encourage you to turn on line numbering before proceeding. (In Microsoft Word, for example, you can enable line numbering in the Page Setup section under Layout.) I appreciate the respite from electronic devices, since my compositional habits involve returning to my computer. With a printout of my line-numbered notes, I sit somewhere comfortable and well lighted, pencil, pen, or highlighters close at hand. The book itself might or might not be within reach. At this point, I am focusing wholly on my notes, which should contain everything I need to create a comprehensive outline for my review.

(Relax. Don't let the word *outline* quicken your pulse by conjuring up flashbacks of secondary-school English class, where points were deducted for improper formatting. I'm using the term loosely to refer to an ordered presentation of ideas. You'll not find me using Roman numerals.) Outlining can help writers stay focused on what matters, which is especially important when space is limited—such as with scholarly book reviews.

If you've conducted qualitative research involving transcripts or other documents—or any sort of research involving repeated passes through a dataset—you'll see resonances in my approach with reading notes. But, despite all of the suggestions and instructions I have been proffering, I am not proposing a science of scholarly book reviewing. Formal content analysis is not what this task is about. Instead, you must rely on your expertise and your scholarly sixth sense—your intuition, your gut, your inclinations—when evaluating what is most important to include in your review. You will not find "right" approaches. Unless you happen to be coauthoring your review (see chapter 4), no one else will be triangulating anything with you. You are charged with presenting *your* impressions of a work, and you are the original source of the material you will be mining for those impressions.

I keep invoking this point for a reason. The more deeply you believe that the review is a function of *your* responses to the book at hand, the easier it is to conceptualize scholarly reviewing as a creative, intellectual act. The easier it is, as well, to think of yourself as an expert on the book at hand. If the two of us were to review the same scholarly book, our reviews would be distinct. And they *should* be distinct. If your discipline supports a journal that publishes omnibus reviews, you may have seen different scholars' views of the same book published together.[5] Occasionally, authors are invited to respond to the responses to their books: living proof of the fact that scholarly book reviews contribute to scholarly conversations.

So get comfortable with a printout or your electronic file of your line-numbered reading notes. I will guide you through four passes of your notes. You do not need to complete all of these passes in one sitting. (In fact, taking a break of a day or more before the final pass through your notes can be helpful.) You should, though, aim to complete each full pass through your notes without substantial interruption, since you will be holding your response to the entire book in your head each time you finish reading through your notes. Be prepared for the first pass to take the longest. The first full reading through your notes is when you reacquaint yourself with the entire book in one sitting.

Pass #1: Begin to identify what you want *to say about the book.* This material is different from what you *need* to say about the book. (I start with the *want*-to-say business, because focusing on the *need*-to-say business can easily overwhelm your allocated space with description and summary. And you're writing a scholarly book review, not a scholarly book report.) Pay special attention to the comments and questions you registered about the text. *Which comments and questions do you now find to be the most insightful? Which would likely be most interesting to others in your field? Which bring up connections and associations that extend the value of the book into other contexts?* Flag these points in some way: by circling or starring the line number, by drawing a line or making a checkmark in the opposite margin, by underlining or highlighting, or (if you are working on a word processor) by calling out the text in any manner that does not affect the line numbering. On your first pass, you will likely identify too many points of insight and interest. But you will continue to refine and reduce the list, prioritizing your ideas so that those most worthy of mention end up in your review.

If you have a lot of notes, this first pass can take some time. You are reminding yourself of the purpose of the book and your reactions to its presentation. You are beginning to calibrate how positive you will be able to be in your review. You are beginning to identify themes and resonances across your notes. You should feel moments of déjà vu, but you should also come across reminders of startling thoughts, comments, and questions that the act of reading this book invoked. Relish those reminders. They offer evidence of your intellectual engagement with the text. And they illuminate instances of communion with the power of the author's ideas and implications.

Break #1: Reflect on what you just identified in the first pass through your reading notes. One of the reasons I take a break between reading a book and reviewing my notes is because the distance allows me to see my thoughts afresh. Long, complex scholarly books, especially, may take me several days or even weeks to read, on top of my other responsibilities. Reviewing my notes sequentially thus compresses that time and reminds me of the architecture and contributions of the work as a whole. Reviewing all my notes from the book is akin to speed-reading the entire work. My notes offer a refresher, a crash course in everything the book impressed upon me. After my preliminary pass through the notes, I need another brief break. In this space, I begin to consider themes, connections, associations. I look for claims I can make about the book that can be substantiated by examples from across the book. I litter the margins of my notes with instances of "cf."—Latin for *confer*, or "compare"—and I cross-reference line numbers within my reading notes. When clusters of themes and associations emerge, the likelihood increases that I will make space for those core ideas in my review. They become major reflection points, not stand-alone details of interest that I would plan to include if space were unlimited.

Pass #2: Identify what you need to say about the book. I embark on this easier step next so I can distance myself a bit from the ideas I flagged in the first pass through the notes. The need-to-say material is more descriptive and, therefore, more objective. Much of it you recorded in your preliminary walkthrough of the text. *Who is the author? What is the purpose of the book? How is the text structured?* Remind yourself of this material, flagging it in a different manner (with squares around the line numbers, different marginal markings, dashed or squiggly underscores, whatever works for you).

Break #2: Reflect on what you have identified in your first two passes through the text. Are ideas coming into focus? If you had previously envisioned a way in to the review, does that approach still seem reasonable? Or has another issue or set of issues risen to the fore, suggesting a new theme or throughline for your review?

Pass #3: Reread your notes, paying special attention to the direct quotations you recorded. You are now looking for sentences or phrases that eloquently or memorably speak to the themes and insights you began to identify in the first pass. You are also looking for purely descriptive materials that address the purpose and goals of the book in the author's words—material that will serve your contextualized summary of the argument of the book. Underline or otherwise highlight these notable quotations.

Break #3: Congratulate yourself for having engaged with your notes as carefully and deliberately as you engaged with the book under review itself. If other obligations are calling, you may now step away from your notes for a day or more. In the next pass through your notes, which may or may not be the last before you begin outlining your review, you will focus on the subset of notes that you called out in your first three passes through the text.

Pass #4: Review your notes, this time reading only the points that you identified in your prior passes. In the earlier passes through your reading notes, you may have ended up identifying too many points to cover in your review. So you must now become even more selective. *Which of the points that you previously flagged are the most substantive? Which have the most intellectual merit? Which will be of greatest interest to others? Which are likely to be the most particular to your reading of this book?* Distinguish these points from the others by adding an additional checkmark or asterisk or layer of underlining, perhaps in a distinct color. These points will be the ones around which you'll plan to structure your review.

Break #4: Finally, if you've not done so recently, take a moment to remind yourself of the readership of the target venue for your review. (In theory, at least, you should be a reader of the publication yourself—or you should be among those likely to engage with the contents of the publication.) If you are new to the venue, you should survey recent contributors, topics, and scholarly and methodological approaches. Look for a recently published editorial that highlights the goals of the publication—or remind yourself of the venue's aims and goals by revisiting the publication's website. This information is invaluable when you are deciding on how to focus or frame your review. What is likely of interest to the readers of your target venue should be at the forefront of your mind as you begin to structure your review.

Sorting and Organizing

Now that you have passed through and marked up your reading notes, you are well on your way to identifying the material that you will address in your review. You may need to keep going through your annotations, winnowing further. A group of core ideas will eventually emerge, and your next task is to extract these ideas from your notes. Once you have done so, your concentrated ideas will be together, and you will be able to begin sorting and organizing your most significant thoughts about the book.

I know that templates can be effective for plotting out many genres of academic writing, from cover letters to CVs to scholarly journal manuscripts (in certain disciplines) to grant proposals to book proposals—and many more. But here I do not present a template, per se, for scholarly book reviews, in part because templates smack of mental shortcuts and intellectual standardization. In a book on reviewing published nearly a century ago, journalism professor Wayne Gard notes the tedium that would result from template-driven book reviews: "The particular form of a review—the arrangement of its various elements—is less important than the fact that it should have a form of some kind; the fitting of all reviews to a single outline would soon result in monotony."[6] Later, Gard writes that "the most acceptable reviewer is not one who has mastered a handy formula, but one who brings to new books an adequate knowledge and a philosophic understanding of life and of literature."[7] Sage advice, yes. Reviewers must know something about the topics of the books they review, and they must be able to place these books in a broader, representative context. To be maximally engaging, the resulting reviews should not be formulaic.

Another justification for avoiding templatizing is simply because every scholarly book is different.[8] Reviewers should take what they are given, reflect on what the authors have offered, and produce reviews that sufficiently honor the intellectual objects being reviewed. As long as they present a summary of the argument, an analysis, and an assessment, scholarly book reviews can and should be as distinctive as the books upon which they are focused.

Also, when you consider the length of typical scholarly book reviews—just 1,000 to 1,500 words, sometimes more, sometimes less—that means you have between just six and ten paragraphs (sometimes more, sometimes less) to present, analyze, and assess the work at hand. You will need all the flexibility you can muster within such limited space, and templates would stifle your creativity.[9] In my mind, a process differs from a formula. So instead of a template, I present guidelines, suggestions, goals. If you know what you're aiming for, you can produce a review that respects the book under review while satisfying your readers' needs.

To proceed, return to your reading notes. If you had stepped away from a computer, return to the digital version of your notes and pull out the clusters of ideas—the comments, the summaries, and the quotations—that you identified as most important in your final pass through your notes. Copy these ideas to the bottom of your reading notes or into a new document. (You should no longer need the original line numbers. Just ensure that complementary ideas are grouped together.) These notes become your *working notes* for the review. Remind yourself that you'll have between about six and ten paragraphs for your review, so you should have no more than six to ten substantive ideas for your review, preferably fewer. Your working notes will likely have several examples of supporting evidence per main idea. As you write your review, you will consolidate some of these substantive ideas, and you will likely be forced to cut some others.

I imagine you'll intuit how to proceed. I date myself by pointing out that this intellectual combining-and-ordering exercise is one that I was first taught to carry out with index cards, with one card per idea or piece of supporting evidence. (I haven't used index cards in ages.) These days, for scholarly book reviews, I study the clusters of ideas on my computer screen, mentally arranging and rearranging them until a tentative order logically presents itself. If you enjoy the tactility of such a process (or think you might), go ahead and print out your working notes, leaving space between the thematic clusters. Then cut the clusters apart so you can arrange and rearrange them on a table or other workspace. To return to the documentarian analogy, these snippets form the material that you will be organizing for your finished product, but even some of this material will not make the final cut.

When I am working on a preliminary arrangement of main ideas for a review, I am simultaneously considering my way in to the review. I typically write scholarly book reviews linearly, so knowing how I'm planning to start helps me identify a suitable organization for my ideas. At this point in the process, though, I may still be sorting out my opening move, so I let the ideas themselves suggest an order to me. And now I can no longer ignore the valence of my ideas. In a book review, only the purely descriptive details are neutral. Everything else involves a level of evaluation. This evaluation—your assessment as a reviewer—is what makes a book review a review and not a report. The readers of your review expect assessment. So how does what you think about a book affect how you organize your review?

Assessing the Text

How do I weigh the merits and demerits of my comments? How do I measure their valence (positivity or negativity)? How do I ensure that I am being fair and impartial in my assessment? What approaches or material should I avoid in scholarly book reviews?

Identifying Weaknesses

You will note that, until the end of the prior section, I had so far avoided commenting on the orientation of your ideas and insights—whether positive or negative, supportive of or critical of the text. Let me offer some thoughts on the matter, now that you are figuring out what to emphasize in your review. In chapter 1, when I introduced scholarly book reviewing as a form of peer review, I qualified book reviewing as "post-publication" peer review. The manuscript of the book you are reviewing should have been scrutinized by informed peers before the text was finalized. Those informed peers should have afforded due diligence to the manuscript, pointing out its major flaws and weaknesses. The most substantive weaknesses should have been addressed in revisions to the manuscript prior to publication. In your review, you shouldn't set out to ignore any remaining flaws or weaknesses, for "there is always room for highlighting crucial errors of fact."[10] Nevertheless, you should aim to emphasize the positive aspects of the book as published. What's done is done. No book is perfect. Deficiencies in copyediting, for example, should be brought to light in a review only when errors are pervasive, are unexpected (based on your experience with prior works by the same publisher), or conspire against understanding the author's intentions.[11] Professor of English and prolific author Leonard Ashley observes that "any one of us who has published extensively knows that once a book is in print it is almost magical how one can open it at random and find a typographical error. Some reviewers delight in making huge fun of this sad fate."[12] Your goal is not to be that type of reviewer.

Instead, your goal is to be fair and measured, assessing the book on balance of its merits. Yes, if you discover substantive weaknesses that may have been overlooked in earlier rounds of peer review (or that may have arisen as a result of revisions encouraged by peer review), you should mention these weaknesses when success of the author's argument hinges on them. But nitpicking is unnecessary and, generally, unwelcome.[13] Use your allocated space to focus on more important matters. Still, the types of flaws that are worth mentioning in a review include the following:

- overlooked or ignored data that would redirect the author's conclusions;
- overstatements or inflated conclusions supported by neither the data nor the logic of the argument;
- factual errors that lead to spurious conclusions;
- faulty logic;
- smaller errors or inconsistencies that would not prove problematic for knowledgeable readers but that could mislead or confuse newcomers to the field; and
- production-related issues that conspire against effective presentation of the author's ideas.

If you simply dislike an author's conclusions, that's one thing.[14] But if the conclusions are flawed, that's another. Ensure when you point out such weaknesses that you are criticizing the book, or the processes underscoring the preparation of the book, not the author. The author may still take such criticisms personally, of course. (Historian Paul Fussell referred to negative reviews as "the truly crushing calamity for authors," after all.)[15] But you can nonetheless soften the blow by focusing your comments on the book itself.

Why is it that weaknesses are generally easier to identify than strengths? Is it because of how we are trained in graduate school: to be suspicious, to be critical, to question everything we are offered? Or is it because ideas (and therefore books) are always works in progress and thus can always be refined, finessed, improved? If you as a reviewer recognize that a book reflects (or should reflect) an author's (and publisher's) best efforts at that time, then you may be inclined to be more gracious in your assessments. In fact, in chapter 2 I encouraged you to consult the author's biography and online profile at the outset of taking notes on a book because empathy comes more easily if you conceptualize the author as a person.

Just as scholarly books themselves may have "fatal flaws," so too can book reviews. One of your jobs as a reviewer will be to avoid committing any of the following, all of which concern scholarly and writerly ethics:

Critiquing an imaginary book that you wish the author had written instead. Historian James Cortada describes this inclination as the "most common sin" perpetuated by book reviewers. This sin involves offering "the wishful description of how you would have written the book if you had the time, energy, and knowledge to do it" yourself.[16] *New York Times* columnist Ligaya Mishan concurs, identifying the same gravest problem at the end of one of her own reviews: "This is the worst thing a reviewer can do, to judge a book against the one not written."[17] Review the book at hand, not what you wish the author had written instead.

Using the book as a platform on which to grandstand or foreground your own ideas. Your review should be about the book and about the ideas the author is presenting, not about you or about what you wish to discuss instead.[18] Plenty of other venues exist for scholars to express their ideas about their pet projects, perceptions, and prejudices. Use book reviews for reviewing books.

Making personal attacks on the author or the publisher. As soon as any comments you include incline toward the libelous or defamatory, beware: Your target venue reserves the right to reject your review for publication. If you are unsure how any such comments may be construed, share a draft of your review and solicit the opinion of one or more trusted colleagues before submitting your review. Then, upon submission, flag any sentences or sections of note, asking the book review editor to weigh in on the matter. If your review venue overlooks such comments and publishes your review anyway, you—not the publisher—will likely be responsible for any subsequent legal damages. If you cannot, in good conscience, review a book without condemning the author or publisher, do not write the review.

Venturing into plagiarism territory. As long as your review stems from your reading notes, your text in the review should be your own, save any properly cited quotations from the book itself. Be careful, always, of accusing an author of plagiarizing, since such comments in a review can venture into the territory of libel and defamation, and venues may avoid publishing such a review.[19] (After all, *plagiarism* is "the worst word in the scholar's vocabulary.")[20] The proper approach to handling suspected plagiarism in published work is to alert the publisher privately about your concerns. At the time, provide documentary evidence to support your claim. The publishers will handle the matter from there.

Addressing Weaknesses

Reconsider the clusters of ideas that emerged from your working notes. As you review the list, shifting and sorting and arranging, you should see ways to organize these ideas. Take note of which ideas are positive, which are neutral, and which are neither. You might wish to lead with the positive, filling as much of the review with such material as you can. (What's not to love about an optimist, or someone who is generous?)[21] The negative points you may plan to address in a single paragraph or section near the end. Depending on their severity, these points may be ones that you ultimately do not mention in the review. And always remember that assertions about a text—especially about flaws or weaknesses—must be supported by evidence. Trust the words of literary scholar Roy Wolper: "The cramped space of a review may seem to offer little room for both judgements and proof. It is tempting to document some assertions, slide over others. Such skating is wretched, since neither reader nor writer has ground for belief."[22]

Linda Simon, former director of the Writing Center at Harvard University, agrees with my general approach. She encourages appropriating "a spirit of patience and generosity" and using the compressed space in a scholarly book review to emphasize the positive.[23] Alternatively, you can weave your criticisms throughout the review, inserting them where logically appropriate to the discussion.

How do you decide which approach to take? Use your overall impression of the book as a guide. If the strengths outweigh the weaknesses, as will ideally be the case, you should focus on the strengths throughout, addressing toward the end any weaknesses that you deem too large to overlook. If the strengths are counterbalanced by weaknesses, consider a back-and-forth approach, just being aware that some readers will try to keep score if you present your impressions in such a way. Especially when using an alternating approach, you will need to clarify your overall assessment of the work in an obvious location. The most common locations are either the outset—using the jump-right-in approach described in interlude 2—or the conclusion. After surveying numerous published reviews before embarking on his first scholarly book review, literary scholar P. J. Klemp "noticed that the introduction [of a scholarly book review often] set the tone for the review by indicating whether the reviewer felt charitable or hostile" toward the book.[24]

If the strengths are too few to warrant anything other than a generally negative review, consider recalibrating your standards in light of the context. Please do not misconstrue this suggestion: I am not asking you to *lower* your standards. Never do so. You are, after all, beholden at minimum to the standards and expectations of your discipline. Instead, consider your power and authority relative to that of the author of the book you are reviewing. Sociologist Phillipa Chong, in an insightful analysis of literary reviewing, presents the "informal rule that critics should go easy on first-time writers."[25] That is, you shouldn't seek to "demolish, destroy, and bury" a newcomer to your field.[26] Demonstrate some patience, some generosity. Show some grace. Remember that authors are only human (although AI is catching up). Temper your criticisms as much as you are willing, provided your disciplinary obligations remain intact.

But what if the power dynamic is reversed, and you—the reviewer—are facing the prospect of criticizing a senior scholar in your field? First-time reviewers are often in this situation. Here, then, you are wise to tread carefully. Lynette Felber, former editor of *Clio: A Journal of Literature, History, and the Philosophy of History*, notes that doctoral students and other "fledgling scholars [are] painfully aware that they could one day encounter a book's author on a search committee or on an external promotion evaluation."[27] I share Felber's quotation not to stoke paranoia or to cause you to self-censor. (Felber notes, as well, that even tenured professors generally take no delight in publicly offending their colleagues.) Instead, your goal is to be as confident as you can in your assessment. Genuine, substantiated criticisms are always warranted in scholarly reviews. But if the prospect of grudges unsettles you, do your best to seek books about which you can be authentically positive in your reviews.

Singing Praises

Enjoy yourself when you are writing a positive review. Such reviews are generally the most fun to write. Positive reviews, after all, make many people proud: the authors (and their employers), the acquisitions editors, the peer reviewers, the copyeditors, the marketers, the publishers. They indicate to everyone involved that the efforts of researching, writing, vetting, editing, producing, marketing, and distributing the book were worthwhile. Positive reviews describe scholarly success stories, so you should enjoy the hand you are playing in sharing such an accomplishment with the world.

When you are writing a positive review, you are welcome to express your positivity from the start. Critic S. Stephenson Smith emphasizes the importance of sharing the "dominant impression" a book leaves with a reviewer.[28] Allow this impression to serve as the backdrop to your presentation. Let it flavor your review from the outset. Delight when you can praise a strong addition to the literature in your field.

Presenting Your Assessment

How do I ensure that my review will be deemed acceptable by my target review venue? How do I structure my review to emphasize what matters most? How should I use quotations from the text? How do I end my review?

Crafting Your Review

If you are eager to begin writing, you have found the right section of this book. And if you are eager to begin writing, you can thank your reading notes. Remember this excitement: It means that you have something you want to say, something others may be interested to learn. Because the generative nature of reviewing is reactive, all you are required to offer in a scholarly book review is a measured response to a book. What you are inventing and creating by way of a review is a way to present your response.

If you ever feel blocked in the process, simply review your working notes or your reading notes. Remind yourself that, while you were reading, you had lots of reactions and responses to ideas in the book. Let your organized working notes directly feed into the first draft of your review. Yes, reviewing can be that straightforward. You have no reason to feel stuck or at a loss for words. And don't be deterred by a blank page or screen, either. Nothing you initially write is written in stone. Columnist Anna Quindlen extols "composition first, cleanup later."[29]

Before you begin writing your review, remind yourself of the readership and the book review guidelines of the venue for which you are writing. Know your word limit from the start, and keep tabs on the running number of words while you write. Venues may be somewhat flexible regarding the lengths of reviews they will accept, but you can't count on it. You should aim for your review to be under the prescribed upper limit.

I noted in chapter 1 that the standards for book reviews are distinct from the standards for peer-reviewed journal articles. In short, whether proactively or reactively commissioned, book reviews submitted for publication to scholarly journals are generally not subjected to formal peer review. Instead, the book review editor tends to decide whether the review will be published. (In challenging cases—for example, with overtly negative reviews or with those including comments that could be read as ad hominem attacks on an author or publisher—the book review editor may consult with the journal editor before deciding how to proceed.) As a reviewer, your goal should be to deliver a well-written, insightful review that meets the expectations of the publication venue in terms of length and general approach. Book review editors tend not to argue with their reviewers' opinions. They have no motivations, really, for rejecting quality material that addresses a mission of the publication. Remember: You read the book, and, as long as the book aligns with your field of expertise, you are qualified to offer your opinions.

As you begin fleshing out your outline, keep in mind this principle for scholarly books, from Pamela Haag, that applies equally to scholarly book reviews: "Proportionately, big things should take up a big space; small things, a small space."[30] (For *things* read *ideas*.) You will quickly find that reviews require remarkable compaction, remarkable concision. You will learn to craft tight, value-filled sentences, because your ability to address a reasonable portion of your substantive ideas—and to offer an adequate summary of the contents of the book—will depend on your parsimony with words and your ability to resist getting bogged down in minutiae. Always keep this comment by philosopher David Shatz in mind as well: "When word limits force a book reviewer to choose between expressing judgments about style and expressing judgments about substance, comments on substance should be given priority."[31]

Once I'm ready to commence writing a review, I prefer to begin at the beginning. I first craft my way in, so I know the theme around which I am building the review. (Consult interlude 2 for some ideas about beginnings.) My way in also helps me set the tone for the review. In the ideal world, my finished review will mirror the ideal essay, coming full circle, returning to the central theme or idea presented at the outset. But I don't necessarily imagine the ending when I am writing the beginning. Instead, I write myself there, following the thread that connects the clusters of ideas identified in my working notes. Even if my way in does not follow the Bottom Line Up Front principle described in interlude 2, I generally like to frontload my most compelling ideas. Reviews of scholarly books don't require maintaining much suspense.

Especially near the outset of a scholarly book review, declarative sentences of need-to-say material can slow down the presentation, bore the readers, or both. (*Who is the author? How is the book organized? How many chapters does it include?* And so on.) I instead let my ideas about the book—the want-to-say material—guide the sentences, slipping the objective, descriptive material into sentences that already offer value-added content. Toward the start of your review, for example, you will need to introduce both the book and its author, providing the full title and the author's full name upon first mention. When you incorporate such material into sentences that serve other purposes, you are allowing your voice and your ideas to propel your review forward. And you want the review to keep moving forward as you summarize the book's argument, analyze it, and assess it.

You will describe the contents of the book—and its goals, its argument, and its conclusions and contributions—in the present tense, even in the case of a posthumously published book. The research behind the work occurred in the past and should be such attributed, but the resultant book is very much a living artifact of the present. Its words are there for you to relish today. Its ideas are alive. Note that the American Psychological Association, for one example, calls for using the past tense (e.g., *suggested*) or present perfect tense (e.g., *have suggested*) in literature reviews, even when citing just-published work.[32] If you are accustomed to such conventions, you will need to be intentional in maintaining an active present tense in describing an author's views and conclusions in a scholarly book review. The shift may feel strange at first.

I've already discounted templates as lacking the necessary flexibility for structuring compelling scholarly book reviews. At any point in the process of composition, though, you are of course most welcome to refer to the three or four sample scholarly book reviews you consulted earlier. Samples, when done well, become exemplars; and exemplars offer aspirational models. Samples differ from templates because they present *a* way to structure your ideas, not *the* way. Across your set of sample reviews, you should see a variety of approaches. If one approach appears particularly effective to you, feel free to appropriate it, if it suits both the book you are reviewing and your response to it.

How, then, should you present the ideas from your working notes once you've found—or while you are still finding—your way in to your review? You may do so however you like, however makes sense, however feels natural to you. You may wish to start with the ideas that you find the most compelling, the most telling of the book and its contributions. For example, consider answering any of the following questions near the outset of your review:

- What does the author set out to do, and what does the author accomplish? (Recall the list of forty verbs indicating authorial intent presented in chapter 2.)
- What prior knowledge is disrupted, unsettled, repositioned by this book?
- How do you see your field—and the world—differently now that you've read this book?
- What is something that surprised you—something you were not expecting to encounter in this book—that you continue to think about?

These questions involve your perceptions about the contribution of the book to your field and its impact on you as a reader. They address why the book matters to your field and why the book matters to you. Readers of a review appreciate learning this material because it helps them understand what they might learn if they were to read the book themselves. Answering these questions in a review emphasizes the *so what* as much as it does the *what*.

Across your set of sample book reviews, remind yourself how the reviewers found their ways in and introduced the books at hand. Then try it yourself. Write your way in to your review. Introduce the book using whatever approach seems most fitting to you. Lead with something you found compelling about the book. Then let your working notes suggest your next move, and the next. Don't worry too much about transitions between sentences or paragraphs. (In compact texts, such as book reviews, transitions are less necessary than you might think. In all academic writing, you can generally excise *furthermore* and *moreover* and their kin without loss. Don't believe me? Try it sometime.) And don't waste precious space with signposting: setting up, structurally, what you will be presenting in the review. If you need to write such material for yourself to keep your outline in mind, fine. But make sure to remove such text later. As long as you stay on course, a review is short enough that your readers will not get lost. They need no road maps. I love this reminder from economist Deirdre Nansen McCloskey: "You're a writer trying to keep your reader, not the American Automobile Association."[33] Keep maintaining your readers' interest front of mind while you write. Or, as William Germano compellingly puts it, "don't just write *about*, write *for*."[34]

Congratulations: Your review is beginning to take form.

Quoting from the Text

In the prelude, I differentiated "scholarly" book reviews from "literary" book reviews, arguing that scholarly reviews can aspire toward the literary in how well they can be written and how pleasurable they can be to read. If you take a look across literary book reviews—again, consider reviews published in the *Los Angeles Review of Books*, the *New Yorker*, the *Times Literary Supplement*, or your favorite such periodical—you may note that these reviews don't over-rely on quotations from the books under review. In fact, you'll find reviews with hardly a quotation from the texts at all. In writing your scholarly book review, you will likely want to quote from the text you are reviewing. But, for maximum effect, you will want to do so selectively, calculatedly. Literary book reviewers can thus teach scholarly reviewers the importance of standing ground in a review and not allowing the author of the book under review to monopolize the presentation textually.

In chapter 2, I encouraged you not to overdo copying quotations from the book into your reading notes. Earlier in this chapter, you did not focus on those selected quotations until the third pass through your reading notes. From experience, I have learned how tempting—and easy—it can be to craft a review as a string of quotations from the author. I admit to having written reviews where the balance is off: reviews where I have not remained disciplined and have included too many quotations from the text. When an author is especially eloquent, the inclination to over-quote can be quite strong. You may feel that you can demonstrate your attentiveness as a reader by curating and offering the most gracefully presented and revelatory thoughts like islands in an archipelago, with your accompanying text merely bridging these examples of the author's profundity and wit. But you must not do so. Readers of your review are seeking your opinions about the book, and you should present them in your own words, not the author's.

What you must do, then, is form the skeleton of your review with your own ideas. When the time is right to allow the author's own words to receive the spotlight, you may quote selectively. Try to avoid quoting whole sentences (especially if they are long and complex): You often can't afford to surrender so much space.

A single 50-word quotation in a 1,000-word review has already consumed 5 percent of your review. But do try, in your quotations, to allow the author's voice to emerge, especially when it is distinctive. (I realize that these two suggestions might seem contradictory, though authorial voices can appear in short statements and turns of phrase.)

I also noted earlier how I try to keep quotations from the text from comprising no more than one-third of my reading notes. Quotations from the text should comprise a *much* smaller portion of your review. The extent of the saturation of your review with direct quotations will be, in part, a function of your field. In fields where *how* the ideas are presented matters as much as the ideas themselves, reviews may contain more direct quotations. But how many are too many? You must be the judge. While you are composing the review, I recommend zooming out from the page (assuming you are using word-processing software) and performing periodic "squint tests": squint at the page, looking for quotation marks. How overwhelming are they? (The squint test also works to assess paragraph length and to identify distinctive punctuation, such as the dash, that some writers tend to overuse—I used to myself and possibly still do. Of course, you can use your word processor's Search feature, as well, to identify all the cases of quotation marks in your text.) If you find yourself using what feels like too many quotations, identify ideas that you can present in your own words, then revise accordingly.

To gauge reasonableness with respect to numbers of quotations, you are also welcome to refer to other reviews recently published in your target venue. Some authors are just more quotable than others, though, so let what you see in published reviews be a rough guide, not a strict constraint.

As your review unfolds, ensure that you are not presenting quotations sequentially. Such is a sign of reporting instead of analyzing or synthesizing. If you have clustered ideas effectively in your working notes, you should not be presenting chapter-by-chapter overviews of the book in your review, nor should you be necessarily covering topics in the order presented by the author.[35] A thematic presentation makes citing text from across the volume, nonconsecutively, much easier.

When you have finished your review, always double-check all quotations with the original text. You will be surprised how easily transcription errors can creep in, even when you have tried your best to be careful.

Filling Out Your Review

No scholarly book reviews write themselves. But your working notes, duly organized, provide you with a list of the ideas you identified as most important to present. Let your notes guide you as you write, being at least periodically mindful of your word limit. You will inevitably need to sacrifice an idea or two (or more) for want of space. Trust me: You're better off providing a few solid, well-supported ideas about the book than trying to cram everything you think into the allotted space. After all, you need to balance your analysis and assessment with your summary of the book's argument. A review that is predominantly analysis will be understandable only by others who have read the book. And that's not the point of a scholarly book review.

Here I offer some suggestions and principles to keep in mind while you flesh out your review.

Mind your verbs. Remember to describe the work in the present tense: The author *examines*. The author *suggests*. The author *argues*. The author *concludes*. What does the author *not* do? The author does not *say* or *talk about* anything in a book, so don't let those conversational verbs—which, sure, we might use colloquially when discussing a text with a colleague—slip into your written reviews.

Mind your adjectives. Whenever you are tempted to use what I consider to be "empty" adjectives—for example, *engaging, enlightening, fascinating, captivating, stimulating, intriguing, interesting* (the worst offender)—remember always to justify your assessment. Better would be to avoid such adjectives in the first place and simply to explain how the book delivers, letting the readers of your review determine whether they might consider such an approach to be engaging or enlightening or the like.[36]

Mind your adverbs. Adverbs diminish the force of your prose, weakening your authority. Minimize them. Novelist Stephen King agrees: "I believe the road to hell is paved with adverbs."[37] In academic writing, Helen Sword notes, adverbs and adjectives alike can "supply more clutter than color, more padding than precision."[38] Ensure that your modifiers are necessary.

Keep the review focused on the book—and the ideas it contains. At the same time, do not be afraid to bring in outside knowledge (your own or others') to support your assessment. (Just remain cognizant of the stance of your venue regarding external citations within reviews.)[39] Invoking such knowledge will help bolster your credibility as a reviewer and will help elevate the scholarly nature of your review.

Differentiate clearly between your ideas and the author's ideas. As a book review editor, I encounter attributional confusion surprisingly often in drafts and submissions. Agentless, passive voice is a common cause.

Be precise. Be accurate. Precision and accuracy bolster your trustworthiness as a reviewer. As Roy Wolper notes, "Whether one likes it or not, a review's authority is due to its own body. A weak rationale, muddy organization, slipshod proof—all such stifle belief."[40]

Be careful when noting that an author doesn't mention something in a book. Being factually wrong in my description of a book in a review might be my biggest fear. Electronic books—that is, those with searchable text—ameliorate this fear. But because I prefer reading hard-copy books, I know that my credibility as a reviewer hinges on my ability to be confident about and accurate in my claims. (What if I missed the single mention that negates my assertion? This fear drives my attentiveness while I am reading. Of course, readers of your review likely won't know that you are wrong if you make a faulty claim about a book. But the author of the book certainly will.) Remember, too, that you are reviewing the author's book, not a book on the same topic that you would have written. If something was omitted from the discussion, perhaps the omission was intentional.

If you need to be critical of the work, make sure you criticize the book, not the author. I have made this point earlier in this chapter, but it bears repeating here. If you read much about writing for scholarly publication, you have likely seen a similar message when it comes to handling reviews of your work that you have submitted for peer review. A manuscript of a journal article that is rejected, for example, is just that: a *manuscript* that is rejected. *You*—the author—are not being rejected when such a decision is tendered. But the ways in which authors identify with manuscripts of journal articles differ from the ways in which they identify with their published books. Negative reactions to books carry greater sting. Authors are occasionally wont to respond to such criticisms as if the reviewers had brazenly criticized the intelligence or the looks of one of their children. As the reviewer, avoiding ad hominem comments helps to reduce (but not entirely remove) the sting. Providing examples from the text to justify your criticism also helps.

When you can be positive, rejoice. Scholarly books represent labors of love. Reciprocated love surpasses all. When the finished product exceeds your expectations, don't be afraid to sing praises.

Make sure to mention how the book transformed you. Robert Milardo explains that effective book reviews "indicate how the reviewer's views changed as a result of reading the book."[41] Elsewhere I've seen this goal described as pointing out "the thinking the book provoked in your mind."[42] If you'd overlooked this point previously, you can generate an answer by asking—and then answering—"so what?" in response to the book.

Make sure to include an excerptible sentence or two. Publishers appreciate pithy sentences that they can lift from published reviews, quote on their websites, and use in marketing materials. Try to include a strong sentence, capable of standing on its own, that summarizes your assessment of the value and the contributions of the work. Publishers might latch on to different text—reviews tend to be "ransacked for quotes"—but at least your review is being noticed and appreciated.[43] When scholarly books that were originally issued in hardback are subsequently issued in paperback, stimulating quotations from reviews (especially reviews in prominent publications) are often included on the back cover or occasionally on "praise pages," pages inserted prior to the front matter, supplementing the solicited blurbs from well-known individuals in the discipline. And, resulting in a frisson of delight when the fact was brought to my attention, a quotation from one of my reviews was even used on the *front* cover of a second edition of a book.[44]

Now, if you feel that your review is sound but just not that compelling, skip ahead to the second section of chapter 5 for some additional writing-related suggestions. Many of the suggestions in chapter 5 are of the "gilding the lily" variety, but they may help you infuse some pluck into a review that you believe could use a bit more life. As Gail Pool notes, "a dull review fails to do its book justice."[45] Make sure any reviews you write aren't dull.

Concluding Your Review

So far in this chapter, I have not invoked the list of questions in the appendix. The reason is simple: You addressed most of the questions presented there in your reading notes. By using your reading notes as the starting point for crafting your review, your review already addresses the questions you felt are most germane to the book. Nonetheless, you may wish to peruse the appendix to remind yourself of any key material that you might not yet have mentioned in your review. Do not let yourself be overwhelmed by the list of questions. Just scan for points you may have overlooked. (Ralph Alan McCanse also includes a robust list of "critical considerations" in his *The Art of the Book Review*, and he prefaces his list with the caveat that "no single review need make use of all of them or even many of them.")[46] When I write reviews based on my working notes, I occasionally overlook two important points germane to assessment. Make sure to bring out these two matters as you conclude your review, or insert comments to these effects earlier in your review:

Have you offered your overall assessment? Will a reader of your review know how you feel about the book? When I love a book, I want to make sure my impressions are clear. When I am indifferent about a book, my assessment is measured. When I am not too impressed by a book, I may be a bit coy when it comes to my overall assessment, perhaps because I never like to say, "Don't waste your time with this book." Still, a direct approach is usually best in a scholarly book review. Even if you summarize and analyze quite thoroughly but fail to assess, your readers will inevitably wonder how you feel about the book. Don't leave your readers hanging. Do avoid an unimaginative "This book is a welcome addition to the literature" statement, though. Your review should describe and assess the contributions of the book without resorting to prepackaged opinions. Readers of your review can decide how welcome such material happens to be.

Have you noted who could benefit from reading this book—and why? Including this sort of comment helps readers of your review envision the usefulness of the book to themselves, either directly (for their own scholarly interests) or indirectly (if, for example, they might consider assigning the book for a class or recommending it to advisees or colleagues). Do avoid an uninspired "This book is required reading" or "Everyone should read this book" refrain, unless you qualify the statement sufficiently.

And now you must consider your conclusion. Do you wish to come full circle, invoking the opening of the review? Everyone loves when an essay does so. A scholarly book review, though, need not be an essay. (You can read about review essays in the next chapter.) If you can naturally nod toward your opening in your final sentences, go ahead. But don't attempt rhetorical contortions. Your readers' attention should remain focused on the book you are reviewing and on your assessment of it, not on your prose pyrotechnics.

Some venues allow (or expect) their book reviewers to title their reviews, with the title of the book under review given in the subtitle of the review. (The predictable formula is "[Your Brilliant Review Title]: A Review of [*Title of Book Being Reviewed*]." Occasionally the subtitle is omitted, with the context clarifying the subject of the review.) If you are writing for such a venue, take a cue from titles of other recently published reviews. Keep things short and sweet. Invoke a "theme, concept, or interpretive perspective" that you develop in your review, offering readers a sense of your sense of the value or a key contribution of the book.[47] Like finding your way in to the review, coming up with a suitable title requires thought and reflection. Take the task seriously, and ensure that the title of your review respects the book at hand.

Reveling in Near Completion

How do you feel now? Have you given your review your best efforts? Let yourself be inspired by these words of prolific writer (and reviewer) John Updike: "Each of my efforts is the best I can do at that time, on that project."[48] You are not finished yet. Let your review rest for a day or more before rereading it. How does the review strike you after this short break? Approaching your review with fresh eyes allows at least two potential weaknesses to surface and thus to be edited out or otherwise addressed: mean-spiritedness and dullness. Revise as much as necessary, but don't muffle your opinions. After all, "nothing is duller than a review which has been revised into utter blandness."[49] Do make sure to remove all traces of snark, however. (Snarkiness may feel fun in the moment, but its juvenility embarrasses in hindsight.) Share your revised review with a colleague, asking whether your description and assessment are clear. In short, treat the review the way you should treat any piece of scholarship prior to submission: with distanced objectivity, with attention to matters macro and micro, and with a sense of your future readers in mind. Your name will be on the byline, so you should want the review to be the best it can be.

Lessons

- On successive passes through your reading notes, you will generate working notes that organize your most compelling comments on, reflections about, and assessments of the book you are reviewing.

- Your working notes will provide the outline from which you write your book review.
- The book review is not *about* you, but it is not *without* you: You are needed to give substance and form to your opinions and ideas about the book you are reviewing.
- An effective scholarly book review offers a contextualized summary, clear analysis, and cogent assessment of the text under review.

INTERLUDE 3
CELEBRATING COMPLETION

Congratulations! Did you imagine you would get to this point—having a complete and nearly finalized version of a scholarly book review that follows the guidelines of your target venue and effectively summarizes, analyzes, and assesses a scholarly book? (I knew you could do it, of course.)

I feel the most excitement when I'm *almost* finished with a scholarly book review—that is, once I've fully drafted a review and have addressed all the core points I wish to make about the book that space will reasonably permit. Seth Perry refers to "cracking" a project: In terms of structure and organization, everything in the text more or less works, and the end is in sight. At this point I am done referring to my reading notes and my working notes. My attention shifts wholly to the text of the review itself. I continue revising, improving the language and the flow, otherwise polishing the presentation. Once I am satisfied with my efforts, I will often share the review with a trusted colleague for comments. (I never skip this step in the case of a negative review, when I ask my colleague to confirm that I am clearly criticizing the book, not the author.)

After this "cooling off" period, while awaiting my colleague's impressions, I then return to and scrutinize the review again, this time with fresh eyes. If given suggestions for improvement, I revise accordingly. Before submission, I once more check all quotations with the text (not with my notes), verify the metadata (with both the book itself and the publisher's website), and confirm that the author has not recently changed jobs or received an especially prestigious award (for example, a Guggenheim or MacArthur fellowship) that warrants mention in the review. I read the final version aloud, ensuring felicity and fluidity of prose. Once I feel that additional slight improvements to the text meet diminishing returns, the time to submit has arrived.

If the submission portal for your venue asks or allows for a cover letter, you will remind the editor or book review editor of your prior correspondence. Your submission is of the "as promised" variety, so you need not reintroduce yourself or your qualifications. Instead, you should

- provide brief bibliographic information about the book you have reviewed,
- indicate the number of words in your review, and
- note that you have expressly prepared the review for this venue and are thus not submitting the review elsewhere.

If you would welcome comments or suggestions from the editor, you may say so at this time. You may conclude with an anticipatory, goodwill-expressing sentence akin to "I appreciate your willingness to consider this review for an upcoming issue of [publication name]."

In case the venue has no submission portal and you are simply emailing your review to an editor, you should include, in the body of your accompanying email message, the information that would otherwise populate a cover letter. Brevity in such correspondence is welcome, since the message is effectively a letter of transmittal.

And in case your target venue has a submission portal that bypasses the cover-letter step for book review submissions, then you need not worry about the extra layer of goodwill toward the editors. Reviewing is itself an act of goodwill, and editors are happy to have material to publish.

What comes next? After you celebrate your submission—yes, make sure not to skip that essential step in whatever way is meaningful to you—you can expect confirmation of receipt from the editor or book review editor of your venue. (Or you may simply receive an automated acknowledgment from the manuscript-submission system.) Depending on the venue, you may subsequently receive comments or suggestions for improving your review. I remember receiving comments on my first review, the unsolicited one I submitted to *Business Communication Quarterly* in summer 2003. The book review editor asked if I would bolster my summary of the book under review and, in the process, tone down my criticism. At the time, I likely did not appreciate the suggestions as much as I do in retrospect. Today I am grateful to have been asked to take a softer approach in my critique of the first scholarly book I reviewed. I complied with the requests, revised and resubmitted the review, and was able to celebrate again when the review was published the following year.

Even in cases where you may have been approached by a journal or book review editor to review a scholarly book, venues reserve the right to decline to accept what you submit. If such a thing happens to you, ask for justification for the decision, if a reason is not offered at the time your submission is declined. Perhaps the publishers discerned a conflict of interest. Perhaps your review crossed a line and included what the publishers could classify as defamatory, tortious, or otherwise unlawful matter. Or perhaps your review just wasn't up to snuff, and the editors didn't want to commit to the time-intensive work of developmental editing. If you've been following the advice in this book, though, you should have avoided all of those potential problems in your review, submitting a product that your venue should be pleased to accept and publish.

Assuming all is well with your review, you may next proceed through copyright protocols (depending on your venue). Pay close attention at this stage, saving copies of relevant documentation for your records. You may be asked (or required) to assign the copyright of your review to the publisher, in which case your review becomes the publisher's property and may be repurposed later without your knowledge or compensation. You may still be able to use your review for other purposes, perhaps after a fixed embargo period has elapsed, possibly provided you request permission from the publisher in advance.

Different venues have different stances on the copyediting of book reviews. Editorial hands vary from light to heavy, and my reviews have been subjected to both extremes prior to publication. Many have been published verbatim to how I submitted them. (Those reviews make me nervous, since I know I'm not perfect.) Some were effectively rewritten by overzealous editors—an odd situation when made clear, from the revised text, that the editor had not read the book under review. Regardless of the editorial approach taken, you will likely receive a final version of your review for approval prior to publication. Be prepared if you are new to scholarly publishing: The turnaround time for reviewing final page proofs can be remarkably brief—often no longer than one week. Be mindful of these timelines if you are ever off the grid for weeks on end. Language like the following commonly accompanies page proofs: *If we do not hear from you by [the stated due date], we will assume that you are satisfied with the proofs, and your review will appear in the journal as it currently stands.* At this point in the process, as well, substantive changes in the text usually cannot be accommodated.

Do reread your review once it has been published. Doing so will allow you to see your review in the context and company of other material: other scholarship, perhaps, or at least other reviews. If you spot errors, weak arguments, infelicitous phrases—for distance allows us to spot them more easily—take note, but do not despair. Simply strive not to repeat such errors or weaknesses in future work. *Kaizen*, the Japanese concept of continuous improvement, offers an approach that students and scholars should wisely appropriate.

Also make sure to let others know about your review. Add the review to your CV with its final pagination or URL. If your published review exists behind a paywall, be sure that you upload only the pre-copyedited version—that is, the final version you submitted—to institutional repositories, personal websites, or academic social-networking sites (such as ResearchGate or Academia.edu). (The copyright materials often outline how you may rightfully disseminate your work.) You might also want to take it upon yourself to share a copy of the published review with the publisher of the book you reviewed. In theory, the review venues should take this step—I did when I edited a scholarly journal between 2007 and 2009, and I do now as book review editor for the *Journal of Scholarly Publishing*—but the courtesy seems to have become less common than it should be, given the ease of disseminating digitized materials electronically. (In the good old days, scholarly book publishers were physically mailed paper copies of published reviews of their books. These copies were variously known as "tear sheets," "reprints," or "offprints." Nowadays, PDFs rule the day, though I delight in using the outmoded language when emailing PDFs to book publishers.)

If you feel that letting others know about your book review smacks of indulgent self-promotion or careerism, then at least make sure that others learn about the book itself, especially if you found it to be valuable. Cite the work in your own scholarship. Personally recommend the work to colleagues or students. Reviewing a scholarly book gives you a memorable intimacy with the content, facilitating future connections with the work and its ideas. You might not be surprised to learn that quite a number of the books I've cited in *How to Review Scholarly Books* are books that I have reviewed.

And should you alert the book's author to your review yourself? If you loved the book and wrote a positive review, why not? Everybody loves fan mail, and word will get around eventually. I once emailed the author of a particularly scintillating book of his I'd reviewed, attaching a copy of the review. He replied soon thereafter, with appreciation, adding that he'd forwarded my review to his mother!

I have heard that reviewers may sometimes share drafts of their completed reviews with the authors of the books under review before finalizing the reviews. In such cases, the books are typically technical volumes, and the reason for sharing is to save the reviewers from accidentally misrepresenting the text. If such may be the norm in your field, go right ahead. In most cases, though, you would want to wait to communicate with authors until after your reviews are published.

Now that you have successfully reviewed a scholarly monograph, perhaps you are ready to review an edited volume or write a review essay of multiple, related titles. Or perhaps you would like to explore coauthoring a review alongside a colleague with complementary expertise. Scholarly book reviewing offers many possibilities, so I've written the next chapter with you in mind.

4

Considering Special Cases

EVERY SCHOLARLY BOOK is different. Every scholarly book reviewer should thus feel free to address each book on its own terms, offering a contextualized summary, clear analysis, and cogent assessment of the text in whatever way seems most appropriate to the text at hand. In the preceding chapters, I offered approaches for reading scholarly books (chapter 2) and writing scholarly book reviews (chapter 3) that apply, primarily, to single-authored or coauthored monographs. In the humanities and book-oriented social sciences, such books are the types upon which scholars typically stake their careers. They are thus key works in both the advancement of scholarly ideas and the advancement of individual intellectual agendas. In the previous chapters, I also assumed that you, the reviewer, are addressing a single book and are completing the review by yourself.

But the landscape of scholarly publishing—and the potential for scholarly book reviewing—is much greater than I have so far portrayed. Scholars frequently write, edit, compile, or contribute to academic books of many stripes: edited collections, textbooks, handbooks, and other reference works (including almanacs, atlases, bibliographies, catalogs, concordances, dictionaries, directories, encyclopedias, festschriften, gazetteers, glossaries, and indexes). Given the distinct purposes of such books, all require special considerations when being reviewed. Of these diverse types of scholarly works, edited collections are most likely to be reviewed by other scholars in scholarly journals, so I offer specific advice for reviewers of such volumes in this chapter.[1] But because I want you to welcome the challenge of reviewing a diverse range of scholarly books, I also offer general thoughts on reviewing anthologies, scholarly editions, and reference works.

Perhaps you are aware of two or more recently published books on similar or complementary topics, and you would like to review them together. Review essays—also known as comparative reviews—allow reviewers to offer their own arguments about a topic while considering the contents of (and analyzing, and assessing) two or more books. Such reviews, too, require additional considerations.

Or, perhaps, knowing that scholarly writing need not be a solo activity, you are drawn to the communal aspects of writing and would like to coauthor a scholarly book review. If any of the above possibilities applies to you, you have found the right chapter.

With any type of "special" review, be sure to inquire with the book review editor of your target venue as to viability and any exceptions to the allowable length before you begin writing.[2] Reviews of single monographs are the default in most published reviewer guidelines. For review essays, especially, you may be given some latitude. Just do not expect a doubling or trebling of the maximum length for a review of two or three related works. More realistic is adding another 50 percent to the maximum allowable length for a review covering multiple titles. Some review editors may be more (or less) generous, so always make sure to ask.

Reviewing Edited Volumes

What should I keep in mind when reviewing an edited volume? What challenges do edited volumes present to their reviewers?

Contextualizing Edited Volumes

Edited volumes include collections of new (or mostly new) material by different contributors and anthologies of previously published works either by a single author or by different authors. To be maximally useful as contributions to the scholarly literature, both types of edited volume require intellectual framing. I consider edited collections at the outset of this section. At the end, you'll find some ideas for reviewing anthologies and scholarly editions, plus some tips for reviewing other types of reference works.

When it comes to edited collections—in this case, volumes including newly sourced contents, primarily if not exclusively—perhaps you've heard that such volumes are "where good publications go to die."[3] Chapters in such collections can also be regarded as "vita stuffers," because the peer-review process is often handled directly by those involved in the curation of the volume.[4] Yes, even in the book disciplines, well-placed journal articles tend to have more visibility—and tend to be much more persuasive to hiring, promotion, and tenure committees—than chapters published in edited collections. Regardless of contributors' and editors' motivations, I am seeing an increase in the number of edited collections being published, especially by for-profit academic presses. I have my hypotheses as to why.[5] No matter why and how these volumes come to exist, they form part of the scholarly literature. And, because edited volumes can indeed offer meaningful contributions, you may find yourself wishing to review such a volume.[6]

Edited collections pose particular challenges to reviewers. As collections of chapters written by different contributors, these works are commonly uneven or imbalanced. William Germano is right: "It seems almost impossible to publish a collection of essays all of which are genuinely uniform in quality."[7] The scholars who shepherd such volumes through the publication process can do only so much to ensure that the contributors remain on target, that they approach their tasks with similar levels of thoroughness and attentiveness, and that they ultimately deliver materials that cohere illuminatingly around the central charge or theme. When done well, though, edited collections bring together diverse perspectives and viewpoints, providing readers with cross-sectional approaches to a problem or a question or an idea.

One delight of reading and reviewing edited collections is coming across new and emerging voices. After reviewing an edited collection, I sometimes reach out to specific contributors whose chapters most impressed me, letting them know that I will be on the lookout for their next publications. I also suggest venues, typically scholarly journals, that could be interested in these scholars' perspectives and future work.

Taking Notes on Edited Collections

The very hallmark of edited collections—their ability to present a diversity of perspectives and approaches germane to a central theme—complicates readers' linear engagement with the texts. Just when you, the reader, have come to understand one contributor's worldview, you are forced to move on to someone else's. As a reviewer, then, one job is to keep the perspectives, ideas, and contributions straight. This task begins with your preliminary walkthrough of the text, as described in chapter 2. When you proceed through the volume and record the constituent parts in your notes, you will need also to record their attributions. For monographs, I encourage thoroughness with respect to investigating authorial identities, affiliations, accolades, and more. For edited volumes, you need not expend much time at the start familiarizing yourself with the editors or contributors. The reason is one of practicality. Assuming that you have only the standard space for your review, say, 1,000–1,500 words, you will need to focus on content, not the backgrounds of the contributors—unless their backgrounds are what prove to make the volume successful as a whole. (And you will know that point only after you have read the collection.) Edited collections typically include brief biographies of the contributors either in the front matter or in the back matter (or occasionally at the outsets or ends of the respective chapters). In your preliminary walk-through, these biographies should prove adequate for your needs. Contributors' titles (or positions) and affiliations (or locations) are all you need to note from the start. Be aware, at the very least, of the geographical or cultural diversity of the contributors. This diversity may end up being germane to which material you cover in your review.

Here are a number of additional points to keep in mind when you read and take notes on an edited collection:

Pay special attention to the justification(s) presented in the introduction. Whether an edited collection makes sense as a whole is often a function of the intellectual and organizational framework. The editorial introduction should offer the key to why and how the collection came into existence. All scholarly books should have clear raisons d'être. What unifying question or questions do the collected chapters address? What charge was issued to the contributors? And how were the contributors identified? (Was the edited collection stimulated by a conference? Did it result from a call for contributions? Or did it result from a well-networked scholar who proposed the idea to a number of colleagues? Answers to the origin questions, unfortunately, are not always offered in editorial introductions, but they may emerge elsewhere in the volume.) Seek to understand the origins of the collection so you will know how to engage with the chapters that follow.

Read and evaluate each chapter on its own terms. When reading edited collections, you have no choice but to reset your expectations at the outset of each chapter. This constant readjustment can detract from a sense of cohesiveness yet nonetheless has its advantages. For one, your optimism for the volume can be reinstated with each successive chapter. Unimpressive chapters can be followed by brilliant ones. Compared with monographs, edited collections can also more easily be read in fits and starts, as long as your unit of occasional consumption begins at the level of the chapter. Edited collections do not necessarily benefit from the luxury of extended engagement and can be effectively read piecemeal. Compared to cohesive, single-voice monographs that proceed like highly orchestrated multicourse meals, edited collections can feel like the all-you-can-eat buffets of the scholarly book world.

Keep track of how your overall impression of the volume evolves. Some chapters will be hits. Others may be misses. If the collection is especially lengthy, you need not let yourself get bogged down in the chapters that are misses. Yes, you still need to read them and should summarize them briefly in your notes, but you can otherwise let your dearth of notes signal the deficiency of any such chapters. Pay special attention, in your notes, to the hits, for these are the chapters you will want to emphasize in your review.

Emphasize themes, approaches, and ideas in your notes. The most effective reviews of edited collections tend to take a cross-sectional approach, highlighting ideas that cut across multiple chapters. Make sure your chapter-level notes record perspectives, methods, and conclusions that address the themes identified by the volume editors. But also be on the lookout for other overlaps, including complementary and contradictory views about issues not emphasized by the volume editors.

Note the extent to which the chapters appear to be in conversation with one another. I am favorably biased toward edited collections where the contributors demonstrate awareness of ideas in other contributors' chapters. A level of internal cross-referencing, whether direct or indirect, often elevates an edited collection from an assortment of related thoughts to something approaching a more developed, more unified whole. The volume editors are typically responsible for such reverberations within an edited collection. Sometimes the origin story contributes, as well. If the collection arose from a scholarly conference, for example, the contributors were likely exposed to the ideas of their fellow contributors. And the contributors may know each other on personal as well as intellectual bases, adding to a sense of intellectual familiarity or compatibility.

Flag any outliers. If a chapter seems not to fit with the collection, register the nature of the discord in your notes. Unless the editors explain, you won't know why it was ultimately included. You might find, amid a cloudy firmament of mediocre chapters, one that shines brightly. Or you might find the opposite: an edited collection with just one or two nominal chapters within an otherwise stellar field. For example, I have reviewed edited collections wherein the author of one chapter simply missed the mark with respect to the intended audience of the volume. (I could have hypothesized any number of reasons for why the volume editors included such a chapter, anyway, but such hypotheses are typically irrelevant to the review.)

Reflect on the organization and coherence of the volume. In your reading, how well do the chapters fit together? The editors should have explained the organization in the introduction. They may have thoughtfully clustered the chapters into thematic sections. Do the sections cohere? Did you notice any obvious gaps in coverage? Be reasonable with this last question, of course. Focus on the editors' intentions with the volume, not the direction you might have taken with it yourself. Know, too, that plans for edited volumes do not always come to fruition. Occasionally a promised chapter—one that would have filled an obvious gap or served to balance the work—is never delivered (or is delivered yet deemed unacceptable due to quality or length or other reasons), and the volume editors must proceed without it.

Note inconsistencies of presentational matters. You will likely not comment upon such particulars in your review, but I often presume editorial indolence when chapters in an edited collection follow different citation styles, punctuation conventions, or spelling preferences. Unless one intention of the volume is to respect variations in World Englishes, either the volume editors should ask the contributors to follow a particular style sheet or the publishers should require the volume editors to ensure that all chapters conform to the same style sheet.[8] In the absence of either scenario, the publishers should take it upon themselves, at the copyediting stage, to rectify any remaining infelicities in the manuscript. But, for better or for worse, the types of publishers that appear to be most willing to publish edited collections these days are also the types that seem less concerned about stylistic consistency. (I once joked in a review that reviewers are the most likely individuals to read edited collections straight through, anyway. Readers who cherry-pick only the chapters of greatest interest are unlikely to notice inter-chapter inconsistencies.)

Revisit the introduction. As I suggested in chapter 2, when you finish reading a single-authored or coauthored book that you are reviewing, you should always reread the introduction. The same strategy applies to edited collections, where the introductions often provide an even more important role in explaining coherence. Rereading the introduction to an edited collection once you have finished reading the volume will allow you to match your experiences with the editors' expectations of them. Did you pick up on any themes not identified by the editors? Does the ordering of the chapters make sense in retrospect? Do you agree that the chapters, together, rise to the collective effect suggested by the editors?

Edited collections frequently demonstrate another dislike of mine: published works that are structurally imbalanced. When a book opens with framing material that functions like an introduction, I expect to encounter similar material at the end that functions like a conclusion, returning to key themes and emphasizing primary takeaways. Edited collections tend not to include such concluding chapters, thus ending up like open-faced sandwiches.[9] Their introductions therefore function as the sites of synthesis, creating an odd situation: The volume editors know how everything hangs together (because they have read everything); readers of the volume do not yet have such perspective on the material. In fact, few things are less engaging than introductions to edited collections that present chapter-by-chapter synopses. Fortunately, I have seen creative solutions to this perspectival and presentational problem. In the introduction to a coedited volume (with Richard Bradford and Madelena Gonzalez), publishing expert Alison Baverstock thoughtfully interjects her own ideas, opinions, and experiences into the chapter-by-chapter preview she presents.[10] This strategy so impressed me that I mentioned it in my review of the volume.[11] Perhaps part of the reason why the strategy works is that Baverstock wrote the introduction herself instead of coauthoring it with her coeditors, as is typical of introductions to coedited collections. She wrote from her own perspective, not attempting a collective view. If "too many cooks spoil the broth" has an idiomatic opposite, Baverstock demonstrates it in her tasteful introduction.

And, for edited volumes, few things feel more anticlimactic than introductions that too thoroughly summarize the material that follows. In one volume of transcribed interviews that I reviewed, for example, the interviewer qua author (qua compiler) highlighted many of the most memorable quotations in the substantial introduction without sufficient spoiler alerts. The result? As I put it, "the déjà vu felt upon [subsequently] encountering the original quotations *in situ* reduces the joy of discovery that feeds narrative excitement."[12]

Writing Reviews of Edited Collections

Compared with monographs, edited collections may take you a bit longer to process, mentally, once you have finished reading them. With monographs, you can be formulating your approach to the review more directly as you work your way through the book. Because each chapter in an edited collection may come from a different perspective or serve a different purpose and thus may potentially alter your impression of the whole, you may need additional time to let your sense of the volume *as an edited collection* settle.

So take some time, allowing a day or two for you to think occasionally about the edited collection but not yet focus pointedly on how you will review it. You can use this time to consider your "way in" by reflecting on what the collection as a whole made you realize, made you question, made you think. Did your rereading of the introduction corroborate your impression of the contents? When you are ready, begin the iterative process of converting your reading notes to working notes, following the reductive principles presented in chapter 3. Be aware that, especially if your notes to each chapter are thorough, you can easily feel overwhelmed by your reading notes for lengthier edited collections. Avoid getting hung up on your notes to any particular chapter, particularly if the chapter is one of the weaker in the collection. In order for your review to capture the essence of the collection, you will need to be selective in what you address.

The need for selectivity in reviewing becomes one of the true pleasures of reviewing edited collections: You can focus on the strongest chapters and simply not mention the weak ones. Because you will—or should—not be offering chapter-by-chapter synopses, and because you'll find little reason to refer to the chapters by their chapter numbers (since each chapter likely stands alone), readers of the review should not easily notice which chapters have been omitted from your review. (The collection editors may notice, and the unacknowledged contributors will notice. But you have done no harm by sparing these contributors whatever negative or neutral comments you could have offered on their chapters.) You may, if you wish, mention the unevenness as a justification for your focus. But because edited collections have high points and low points, I have a tendency not to state the obvious. Instead, I simply emphasize the most impressive chapters, describing them as "standout" or "strong" or "especially valuable" chapters.

As you are passing through your reading notes, then, make sure to identify the standout chapters. These are the ones you will want to mention in your review. Do yourself a favor now, though, and ensure that you are not diminishing the diversity of the work by identifying only chapters by like individuals. In other words, assuming diversity of contributors within the original collection, make sure you have not highlighted only chapters by contributors from or residing in a certain country, or who share the same first language (if discernable), or who are of the same gender identity. The brief biographies included in the volume should assist with this task. While you're at it, if the original collection lacks contributor diversity, ask yourself whether the volume might have made a greater contribution if a more diverse cohort of contributors had been involved. A note about contributor diversity (or lack thereof) might be worth mentioning in your review. Such sentiments would be far from unprecedented.[13]

If, for some reason, the book review editor asks for chapter-by-chapter synopses, please feel free to explain that you are preparing a synthesis, not a summary. That is, you are writing a book review, not a book report. Still, you may find a way, in your review, to mention all of the contributors by name, even if you do not dwell on the contents of each chapter. I occasionally attempt this goal when I am reviewing an edited collection of reasonable length that includes especially diverse perspectives. What's "reasonable length" for this approach? It depends, of course, on the length of your review. I managed the feat in a review of an edited volume with sixteen contributors writing from ten different countries, but I was granted a generous 2,100 words for that review.[14]

Protocol suggests, upon reviewing an edited collection, that you should identify the editor or editors before naming any of the contributors. The reason is simple: Because the volume editors are responsible for the existence of the collection, they should receive top billing. You will also likely want to introduce the theme of the collection before introducing any of the constituent parts. But don't feel that you must be bound by protocol. If one chapter rises far above the rest, and you wish to focus your review on that chapter, you may very well identify the author of that chapter before introducing the volume editors. I have a lot of edited collections on my shelves, and often what keeps them there, consuming precious space, is the strength of a single chapter.

In your review, you will play the role of emcee as you pass the metaphorical microphone from contributor to contributor you have chosen to highlight. You will need to take special care to ensure clear attribution of ideas. In proceeding from your working notes to an outline for your review, then, you will want to note when you will introduce various contributors. You will work to arrange a thematic presentation of ideas that prioritizes mentioning the standout chapters. Creating the outlines for reviews of edited collections is a process I find quite intellectually enjoyable. I liken the creative process to adjusting Tetris pieces to fit solidly into a block. I organize the review by key themes or questions, making certain to present the stated goals and to offer my assessment of how effectively the collection addresses those goals.

Remember these pointers when writing a review of an edited collection:

- *Address how the constituent parts cohere and complement one another.* Comment on the breadth, the range, the diversity of viewpoints, examples, contributors.
- *Focus on the standout chapters.* Feel free to be selective in the material you cover. You need not mention the misses.
- *Assess the success of the volume by measuring how well the chapters ultimately reflect the editorial framing.* Edited collections can be successful in ways neither intended nor expected by the editors. You may identify such a value in an edited collection as you read. If so, make sure to mention it in your review.

Reviewing Anthologies and Scholarly Editions

When reviewing anthologies of previously published works, your job is to contextualize the value of the collection, addressing the sensibility of the collection as a whole. In short, is the collection needed? If the works are by a single author, you should be familiar with that author's oeuvre. The volume should serve a purpose: Forewords or introductions are helpful illuminators of intent. Your review will focus more on the *why* than it does on the *what*, since the works in an anthology have already had their moments in the sun, and their individual contents are thus already known.[15] You will, though, consider what was selected for inclusion—and, unless the work is comprehensive, what was excluded. How are the pieces organized? (If not explained, the organization of elements in an anthology should be obvious.) Has the collector or editor provided any valuable contextualizing commentary? You will also address the *who*: Who will find the collection useful? Consider also the accessibility of the contents prior to their being brought together in the present volume. Does the work serve to supplant or to supplement? Is the bottom line with the anthology one of convenience?

Scholarly editions are annotated works of canonical literature, collected correspondence, musical scores, or other historically or culturally significant materials transmitted by hand, often with multiple extant versions and thus opportunity for multiple interpretations. Reviewing a scholarly edition requires familiarity with the contents and any earlier editions (as well as with the surrounding scholarship). Nonspecialists should stay away from such reviews. Assuming you are a relevant specialist, your job as reviewer is to assess the strengths and weaknesses of the edition with respect to soundness of scholarship and accessibility to students and scholars. Does the interpretation or presentation have merit and propel scholarship forward? The editorial apparatus is central to the review. To digital humanist Elena Pierazzo, "an edition can only be called scholarly if it presents the supporting argument for the establishment or interpretation of the text."[16]

Reviewing Reference Works

Almanacs, concordances, dictionaries, encyclopedias, handbooks, and other reference works present reviewers with special cases that require special considerations. Such works are written to be consulted (indeed, referenced) once the works' structures and purposes are understood. Reviewers thus need not read such works straight through. The selectivity required in reviewing reference works makes such reviews, by nature, tentative. In most cases, the reviewers have just perused the texts, not actively used them, as intended, for projects other than the review at hand. Musicologist Carl Dahlhaus concludes the following: "Dictionaries and encyclopedias are, strictly speaking, scarcely reviewable. The merits that distinguish them and the deficiencies that mar them reveal themselves only during the course of years—or even decades—of use."[17] Yet reviews of such works, done well, can help others assess the potential inherent in the promise of usefulness. Here is how to proceed.

To review a reference work, you should carefully read the prefatory matter—the "how to use this book" material. You should also read any editorial essays or other expository materials related to the contents of the volume as a whole. Then you should closely read a representative selection of content across the work, being mindful of the two primary evaluative criteria for reference works: accuracy and utility.

Accuracy. Because errors render reference works useless (or, depending on the field, even dangerous), reviewers should pay special attention to material they know well. Scrutinize the text.[18] Even in less familiar material, internal inconsistencies will raise red flags. In one handbook I reviewed, for example, inconsistencies and illogical constructions (that is, obvious typographical errors) allowed me to identify mistakes in Czech, Dutch, Italian,

Georgian, German, Korean, Pennsylvania Dutch, and Spanish text. (And, although I am an editor, I am no polyglot. I wasn't actively seeking such errors; I just couldn't ignore them.) Into my review, then, went this sentence: "No single copyeditor could possibly be expected to be able to proofread all of the languages represented in this text."[19] The message? Be careful if you are tempted to use this handbook as an authoritative resource.

Utility. Yes, *users*, not serial *readers*, are the intended audiences of most reference works. Users have specific questions, and reference works offer answers. When reviewing reference works, you should emphasize utility. Describe the content. Explain the organization. Identify the findability of material, whether through logical ordering, robust indexes, or helpful cross-references. Note running heads and other locational markers within the material. Presentational matters of layout and text attributes (typefaces, readability) are worth commenting on when they affect the ease of usability of the volume. The same handbook with the foreign-language challenges includes, helpfully, a four-color political map spread across the endpapers. Unhelpfully, though, the binding obscures substantial portions of Western Europe and West Africa.

When reviewing a reference work, consider how users would otherwise acquire the information contained therein. In other words, what needs are served by the work? Think in terms of access, convenience, clarification, distinction, explanation. What other resources does this reference work supplement or, ideally, supersede? I am focusing on print resources in this book, but reference works can often benefit enormously from digital or online treatment, allowing searchable and sortable text, cross-referencing at the click of a hyperlink, real-time updates, and more. Consider the nature of the material within the context of your field when addressing the matters of practicality and ease of use.

If you are reviewing a revised version or a subsequent edition of a reference work, comment on what's new and different. What has been improved from prior editions? (So, yes, you will need to compare the new work with at least the next-most-current edition.) Why should someone who owns an earlier edition of the resource spring for an upgrade? Take, as an example, musicologist Dennis Shrock's *Choral Repertoire*, published in 2009 by Oxford University Press. The nearly 800-page resource "present[s] and discuss[es] the choral music of the most significant composers from the Western Hemisphere throughout recorded history."[20] For the second edition, published in 2023, Shrock notes the following: Since 2009 "the landscape of choral music has changed considerably. There is much more information available to us today about composers and their repertoire, including, and significantly, information about previously overlooked women composers and composers of color."[21] As a result, the volume has expanded to over 900 pages, and users will find much new material in the second edition. The revised work reflects a redefinition of the canon of the Western choral tradition, demonstrating how reference works can form, inform, and reform their fields.

One reference work that I read from cover to cover for a review is the ninth edition of style guru Kate Turabian's *Manual for Writers of Research Papers, Theses, and Dissertations*, published in 2018.[22] The first third of the volume, textbook-quality material on research and writing, was straightforward to read. But the effect of reading the final two-thirds of the text—the material on source citation and style—felt alternatively meditative and punitive. (Green tea became my crutch for maintaining focus on the text.) I use the opening of my review to survey how the work had evolved from a 60-page booklet on formatting issued in 1937 to the 477-page guide we have today. A portion of my review therefore addresses how the book came into being—and how it came to be central to the training of generations of students and scholars. Reviews of new editions of iconic reference works thus have the potential for veering toward essay territory, with the reviewer offering thoughts on the staying power and continued relevance of the works. (If you're now curious to learn more about retrospective review essays, you'll find additional thoughts at the end of the next section.)

Writing Review Essays

What should I keep in mind when writing review essays? What challenges do review essays present to their reviewers? How do they create special opportunities for offering intellectual contributions?

Contextualizing Review Essays

Review essays present two or more related books in conversation with each other—and, effectively, with the reviewer. Compared with reviews of single books, review essays involve greater levels of intellectual creativity and freedom. They can thus more easily make greater intellectual contributions.[23] In a review essay, the reviewer is expected to present an original argument, one that complements (and possibly complicates) ideas presented in the books under review. The reviewer can therefore take greater liberties within the review and need not regimentally summarize, analyze, and assess each title under consideration. (The emphasis is on *regimentally*. I am still referring to scholarly book reviews here, so the basic expectations must be met.) And since two or more works are being considered, the reviewer is often allocated more space to write this type of review. Review essays of 2,000–3,000 words are common. They also typically invoke external research.

The "literary" style of book review essay—the kind I described in the prelude, and usually more *essay* than *review*—tends to be solicited by venue editors. The reviewers are often high-profile writers and thinkers capable of writing engagingly for nonspecialist audiences; the venue knows that subscribers will be interested in these reviewers' ideas. Essayist Adam Gopnik of the *New Yorker* is one such master of the craft for works of scholarly nonfiction. Historian Jill Lepore, for the same publication, is another. Perhaps you aspire to be a Gopnik or a Lepore yourself. If that's your goal, find a well-regarded role model—your taste may vary—and read as much of that writer's oeuvre as you can. You will find a distinctive and recognizable voice. Dissect the approaches, the structures. You'll likely find no clear-cut patterns, since essays tend to be personal, meditative, inflective. The approach I present here is slightly more functional, given that I am describing review essays published in scholarly journals and therefore written for more specialized audiences. You can start here with the basics and then read and write your way toward Gopnikdom or Leporedom.

How do you identify books that would make good pairings or groupings in a review essay? The general strategies for identifying scholarly books, presented in chapter 1, work here just as well. You simply don't stop searching after you've identified a single book. If you're being attentive to new releases in your field, sometimes you'll just get lucky. An early review essay of mine considered the two scholarly monographs published in the United States in 2005 with the word *rearranging* in the title or subtitle.[24] (Both happened to involve Japanese religion, my former area of attention. And both happened to focus on religious sites I had previously visited. I couldn't believe my luck.) Years later, as part of a larger review essay, I reviewed a pair of books, published just weeks apart, with the same title.[25] (Talk about feeling scooped!

Thankfully, one of the two has a subtitle.) In another instance, in 2021, two leading scholarly presses published books on revising scholarly writing. I had an instant hook: "You might think that two books on the same rather niche topic, published the same year by two major university presses, would have a lot in common. In the case of this pair on revising scholarly book manuscripts in the humanities and social sciences, you would be wrong."[26]

Before you embark on composing a review essay, you must ensure that your target venue will consider publishing what you submit. Propose what you are imagining to the book review editor of your target venue, which will ideally be a journal catering to a well-defined discipline or subdiscipline.[27] Expect the editor to consider your proposal only if neither or none of the books you are suggesting for your review has already been reviewed or scheduled for review in your target venue. If the venue does not have a history of publishing review essays, briefly explain why you sense that the books belong together in a review. (Easier said than done, I know, before you've read the books. Just be imaginative.) If the instructions for reviewers do not specify word limits for review essays, make sure to ask. I've written review essays addressing two, three, four, and five related titles, and the range in number of words per title has been quite broad. (On one end, a five-title review essay totaled 2,500 words, or an average of 500 words per book. At the other end, a two-title review essay totaled 3,000 words, or 1,500 words per book.) You will want to know the number of words you have at your disposal before you begin your review essay.

Since 2005, I've written over two dozen review essays addressing a total of seventy books. I recommend that you cut your teeth on reviews of single books. (You'll have plenty of time to catch up with me later.) Review essays simultaneously reflect a scaling up and a scaling down of the skills involved in reviewing single titles. They represent a scaling up because you activate additional aptitudes to generate your argument and present a cohesive essay. They represent a scaling down because you must be even more selective in what you present in your review: "Trenchant efficiency" is required.[28] Yet I am convinced that anyone who is qualified to review a single book can review a pair or more in combination. If you're ready for the challenge, read on to learn my general approach.

Constructing Review Essays

Review essays can be joys to write. Although your point of departure will emerge from the books under review, review essays require you to offer your own ideas, interpretations, connections. They give you the space to be more of a scholar, not just a reviewer, within a familiar disciplinary context. When embarking on a review essay, you should acquaint yourself with both (or all) proposed books before you begin reading. You want to prime yourself to be on the lookout for shared themes, points of intersection, and other elements that will allow you to position the books in conversation with one another within your review. You are not *judging* any of the books yet. You are merely preparing yourself to be attentive to matters that may inform the argument you craft about the books in your review essay.

My reading notes for the first book in a proposed review essay often include comments akin to "I wonder what [other authors whose books I am reviewing together] will have to offer about this point." (These are the elements I have imagined to be points of intersection between or across the books.) Then, when I am reading the other books for the review, my notes reflect my evolving dialogue with the authors in conjunction with ideas—both expected and unexpected—presented in the other books I am reviewing together. I always aim to be thorough and careful with my reading notes for each book (following the method explained in chapter 2). But the act of reading books that will be reviewed together invites real-time comparison. We do something similar whenever we read within our field: We position what we are encountering alongside what we already think or know. In the case of books for a review essay, at least some of that comparative material is also open to analysis and assessment. The reviewer projects and triangulates within a bespoke space: the initially internal forum within which the ideas for the review itself are constantly being evaluated and reevaluated. This dialogic forum incubates the ideas that will ultimately sustain the review essay.

After you've identified possible shared themes across the books you are reviewing, here's one way to engage with the process of writing a review essay:

One at a time, attentively read and take notes on the books you plan to review together. I know of no magic way to know which reading order is ideal. Simply dive in. When others are binge-watching shows on television, you can relish something more productive: binge-reading your curated selection of books for a review essay.[29] Or, as your schedule permits, you can fit the reading and note-taking into the interstices of your days and weeks, making incremental progress on the review essay alongside other projects and obligations.

When you are reviewing your reading notes, pay special attention to the themes you had previously identified—and to any unexpected resonances. You will proceed similarly from reading notes to working notes (see chapter 3) for each title, but you will do so with the additional filter of themes and resonances between or across the books you are reviewing together. The process of determining what points to raise in a review essay can in fact be more straightforward than the similar process for reviews of single books. You will focus your efforts on making room in your review essay to explore the most resonant topics and issues. You will likely find yourself cutting material that is specific to only one of the books under review, unless that material marks a point of distinction within an established theme.

List the themes and resonances in a new set of working notes. After reading across each set of working notes, you will generate a set of combined working notes for your review essay. I call these notes, predictably, *essay notes*. In the essay notes is where you capture the themes and resonances between or across titles. Start by listing the most salient themes. When considering the books as a pair (or trio, or quartet), what are the first ideas and issues that come to mind? Continue dipping into your working notes and, as necessary, return to your reading notes while you flesh out material for your essay notes. You are identifying the material you will use to create an outline for your review essay.

Consider the most effective way to arrange the themes and resonances. Finding an effective "way in" to a review essay is paramount. (If you want your essay to come full circle, you'll want to consider the ending when you're crafting the beginning.) Equally important is determining how, when, and to what extent to present each of the books under review. I let the organization and presentation arise organically based on themes and ideas. Reflecting on your essay notes will help you discern which idea makes the strongest starting point for your review essay. You can thus lead with whichever book connects more or most robustly with your opening premise.

Follow the outline in your essay notes as you write the review. You will find that review essays naturally reject chapter-by-chapter overviews of the books under consideration. (If you read chapter 3, you shouldn't have been inclined to use such an approach in the first place, anyway.) Your themes will serve as the backbone of the essay. I find, though, that I gravitate to a style of review essay that hybridizes a thematic presentation with a book-by-book presentation. Unlike the literary approaches used by Adam Gopnik or Jill Lepore, my review essays are more *review* than *essay*.[30] I aim to review the books under consideration as fully as possible, even though I can't guarantee that each work will be allocated equal space in the review. (Be mindful of, but not obsessed by, the balance as you write.) I stitch together initial presentations of the books using a technique borrowed from Japanese linked verse: I end the initial presentation of one book with an idea that segues into introducing the next book. (Imagine essay notes that include a thematic Venn diagram. As reviewer, you can write from overlap to overlap, completing the presentational circuit in any number of orders.) After introducing and contextualizing each book, I reconsider the various themes between or across the books, using my remaining space to highlight differences and particularities—and to offer my assessments of the texts, comparatively.

Try to include stand-alone sentences or phrases that the individual publishers can quote. When you tightly knit a review essay, the books under review share the spotlight. Praise is often relative, comparative. Nevertheless, you can still try to include sentences or phrases that directly address the individual books in your review essay. The publishers will be grateful, especially in the case of positive comments.

Use the comparative dimension of review essays to draw attention toward strengths and away from weaknesses. Remember how, in a review of an edited collection, you can simply avoid mentioning any chapters that are especially weak? In review essays, you can say the least about the weakest book of the lot. (Alternatively, unless you're fulfilling an obligation, you can cut the weakest books from your reviews altogether.) Readers of your review essay will know which book or books impressed you the most. On that note, in fact, I have been known to *add* books to reviews to soften the blow of what would otherwise be a not-so-positive review of a particular book. (The situation arises most frequently when I have agreed to review books on speculation. I should know better by now.) In one case, I transformed a planned review of a single book into a review essay—but the first book I added in an attempt to salvage the review didn't live up to my expectations, either. So I ended up adding a third book to the mix. My review focused on the excellence of that final addition, deflecting at least some attention, I hope, from my less-than-glowing comments about the other two books in the review.[31]

Remember that your argument in a review essay can—should—emerge from the books you are reviewing. You do not want to use a review essay to soapbox or grandstand. That approach, as I mentioned in chapter 3, is one of James Cortada's "five mortal sins" commonly committed by book reviewers.[32] But don't let the need for an argument hold you back, either. If critics of book reviews attest that book reviews are written by people who don't have anything else to write about (ouch!), do your best to prove them wrong. As long as you have selected books that are in your wheelhouse, you will have something of interest to offer. Your argument can even be a rhetorical one that exists for the purposes of your review. For example, my review of the two 2021 books on revising opens with an argument in the form of a challenge: *Let me tell you just how different these two books on the same topic happen to be.* But I also develop an argument that stems from the premises of the two books. I present a continuum of revision from the macro (a re-imagining of the potential of a manuscript) to the micro (a re-seeing of the text at the level of the sentence or word). The two books happen to reflect the two extremes. I did not have such an argument in mind when I read the pair of books, and I had never written independently on the specific topic. But the books themselves activated my understanding, accomplishing, in short, what all good books should do: cause the readers to think, to reflect, to grow.

Try to bring your essay full circle. If reviews of single books commonly end with recommendations or assessments, review essays offer more flexibility. Consider returning to your "way in," even if by simply repeating one of the key words or concepts of your opening sentence or paragraph. Such intentional moves may operate subliminally, but they can help create in your readers an impression of mastery over the essay genre.

Considering Retrospective Review Essays

Of all the types of reviews described in this book, the retrospective review essay comes the closest in content, form, and length to a scholarly journal article. Typically focusing on a single work of import to a field, the essay describes the influences of that work on subsequent scholarship. (Sometimes such reviews, often for valedictory or memorial purposes, tackle the highlights of an influential scholar's oeuvre. Those pieces can lean toward biography or even hagiography.) A retrospective review essay shares knowledge that the author of the book under review could not foresee at the time of writing. Such a review marks the ultimate exercise in placing a book in context—and that context is provided by the reviewer, not by the book. Writing an effective retrospective review essay thus requires adequate temporal distance from the subject as well as deep perspective on the relevant field or fields. Broad awareness is also vital, since such essays are essentially exercises in connecting the (intellectual) dots.

If your graduate thesis or dissertation pivots on a key historical work of scholarship, you may already be in a position to write a retrospective review essay. If you are farther along in your career, you may wish to write about an important work that has remained central to your scholarly deportment and development. Anniversaries offer reasonable rationales for such essays, as do anniversary editions of texts themselves. For example, Jan Bardsley, a scholar of women's studies, wrote a 6,000-word retrospective review essay shortly after the publication of the twenty-fifth-anniversary edition of anthropologist Liza Dalby's *Geisha* in 2008.[33] This essay, which includes a bibliography of fifty-five sources, is clearly a work of scholarship. In the opening paragraph, Bardsley presents her core argument and offers a compelling proposal for reconsidering Dalby's book in light of developments over the past quarter century.

Bardsley's retrospective review essay thus sits in the space between scholarly review and article, skewing heavily toward article. Before you venture to write such an essay of your own, ensure that your target venue will be interested. You may be required to submit the piece as an article manuscript, not as a book review. (If so, you should feel blessed, not cowed, by the extra attention garnered through full-blown peer review.) Regardless of the classification, you will want the additional space. I can't imagine a retrospective review essay doing justice to a work in the minimal space typically allocated to a scholarly book review.

All scholarly reviews serve to illuminate. Retrospective review essays especially serve educational purposes (and can thus be excellent ways for students to understand developments within their fields), so you should not presume that all the readers of your essay will have read the work or works in question. At the same time, your essay must satisfy readers who are familiar with the history of the field. The balance is challenging. Yet writing such reviews offers the potential to demonstrate your knowledge and intellectual abilities to a greater extent than typical for reviews of recently published books.

Coauthoring Reviews

What should I keep in mind when coauthoring a scholarly book review? What challenges do coauthored reviews present to their reviewers? What rewards do they offer?

Presenting a Process for Coauthoring

Critic Anthony Lane quips that authorial independence is ideal: "Writing, like dying, is one of those things that should be done alone or not at all. In each case, loved ones may hover around and tender their support, but, in the end, it's up to you."[34]

In fact, what's up to you is that you have a choice when it comes to writing reviews of scholarly books: *Write alone, or write with a colleague?* Coauthoring a scholarly book review offers a low-stakes entry into the world of collaborative scholarship.[35] And it forces a delightful task: discussing a scholarly work with a colleague.

Here, to keep the process more manageable, I am assuming that you and one colleague will embark on a coauthored review. If you feel a third opinion would markedly strengthen your review, you'll need to adapt my suggestions accordingly. But do try coauthoring with just one partner first. With a relatively brief and straightforward project like a scholarly book review, the more, the messier. (If you have a number of colleagues who would be interested in reviewing the same book, you could consider proposing an omnibus review. If you have an even number and everyone is keen to coauthor, simply pair off and identify different venues.)

If you're new to the idea of coauthoring, or if you're new to the idea of coauthoring a scholarly book review, here's what you do:

Identify a colleague whose interests align with yours—someone whose thinking or whose writing you admire—yet who is not your intellectual doppelganger. Perspectival diversity improves the value of collaborations. If you will both be acquiring copies of the book for review (see below), you need not worry about geographical proximity. If you will be sharing a single physical copy, you will want to choose a collaborator who is nearby.

Pitch the idea of coauthoring a book review in whatever manner works best for your relationship. One of you will have to identify the book (something you would both be interested in reading—and both be qualified to review) and the venue (somewhere you would both be pleased to have your views published). (See chapter 1 for details.) Perhaps the selector and venue-finder can take the lead and be listed as the first author—something you'll want to decide before beginning the project. Or you could divide these two tasks. (You could even predict that the arrangement will work and propose a two-review collaboration, with authorship order reversed for the second coauthored review. Such a plan could help encourage a successful initial collaboration.) It's wise, as well, to make a written agreement regarding task division and the intended timeline. If you initially discuss the idea in person, a follow-up email message with these details will suffice. You simply need to agree about who will be doing what, by when.

Secure a review copy (see chapter 1). The lead reviewer should undertake this legwork. If you secure this copy from the publishers or from your intended review venue, you will want to discuss (and decide) who will keep the copy once the review is complete. Also revisit the intended timeline once a copy of the book is in hand, since review copies can occasionally take a while to materialize.

Take turns reading the review copy (see chapter 2). Alternatively, you could both secure copies of the book, perhaps one of you doing so from the library or via interlibrary loan. You will likely need to use this approach in the event that you and your coauthor are geographically separated. Publishers are typically willing to share only one print copy per intended review, not per reviewer (in the case of a coauthored review). However, publishers may grant some latitude with electronic versions. If you're sharing the same review copy (not a library copy), whoever is less likely to want to mark up the text should read the book first. Both reviewers should initially form independent opinions of the book and not be influenced by marginalia or other annotations made by the other reviewer. You should both take your own reading notes.

Schedule a meeting to discuss your thoughts on the book. How long will you need? Start with an hour, but expect that you will want more time. Before the meeting, review your reading notes and prepare a preliminary version of working notes for discussion. These notes can simply include the most striking themes, questions the book stimulated, and other issues you feel may warrant inclusion in the review. You may wish to share your reading and preliminary working notes with your coauthor in advance.

Enjoy your discussion of the book. Discuss what, in your separate readings, worked and what didn't. Revel equally in similar observations and in divergent opinions about the text. The agreements and disagreements will provide material for a compelling, nuanced review. "We gain the most from collaborating by paying attention to differences and valuing them," write three collaborators.[36]

Decide how to proceed with the drafting of the review. Here is your chance to swap leadership roles in the case of mixed impressions of the book. In other words, if one of you has a more positive impression of the book, perhaps the more enthusiastic one will offer to take the lead on the writing, potentially renegotiating authorship order. Before commencing the writing, I recommend that you discuss and settle on a tentative outline for your review. (This discussion may require a second meeting.)

Prepare a first draft of your review. You may try whichever method seems best suited to your personalities and work habits—though, of course, you might not know which approach is ideal until you try one or more:

- Have the lead author draft the full review, incorporating ideas shared by the coauthor. Psychologist Paul Silvia would take this approach: "Paradoxically, the best way to cowrite a paper is to shut out the coauthors and have one person do the writing."[37] This approach is likely the most efficient, but it might seem to defeat some of the purpose of coauthoring.
- Divide the review into sections, with each coauthor drafting a portion of the review. (This approach requires an agreed-upon outline in advance.) Both coauthors will have to pay strict attention to their allocated word limits. This approach will necessitate deeper revisions for style, tone, and voice once the drafted pieces have been combined. The lead author should be responsible for the initial revisions required to unify the review.
- Asynchronously cowrite the review. Cloud-based word processors allow you and your coauthor to access a shared working draft whenever convenient, fleshing it out in turns (or even simultaneously, if writing schedules overlap). This approach does not require that you apportion material. Instead, following the outline, each coauthor will just pick up where the other left off, adding a few sentences or

paragraphs during each writing session, until the draft is complete.
- Synchronously cowrite the review. This daring approach works surprisingly well for some writing partnerships. If you are the type of writer who benefits from accountability to remain on task, and if you and your coauthor both have schedules that can accommodate, you could try this approach. Be prepared: Sparks or fireworks may result.

Review the first draft, sharing comments with each other. Regardless of which coauthoring approach you try, both coauthors will want to review the first full draft. Take advantage of word-processing features like Comments (allowing you to flag text, ask questions of each other, and offer suggestions for rewording) and Track Changes (allowing for more invasive yet still obvious editing).[38] You could also come together and read the review aloud, allowing you to discuss changes to the text.

Revise as necessary. You might want to seek the opinions of another person before you finalize the review (similar to what you would do if you were writing a book review by yourself). You would ask this reader to evaluate your description and assessment of the book for clarity and stylishness. Be aware, though, of diminishing returns that can result from prolonged back-and-forth revising. The goal of a coauthored review is to add richness and perspective to a response to a scholarly work, not to sacrifice far more time than that extra dimension is worth.

Agree on a final version of the review. Be ready: Coauthorship requires compromise. The lead author should take care of submitting the review, handling editorial correspondence (copyright forms, page proofs), and keeping the coauthor apprised of the disposition of the review along the way.

Don't forget to celebrate. Celebrate the successful submission, and then celebrate the publication of your review. Reflect on your partnership, and, if you hit it off with your coauthor, consider collaborating on future projects.

Taking It Further

If coauthorship suits your disposition, consider challenging yourself to coauthor a review essay or a retrospective review essay. These more complex reviews will require a different approach—and more time. Years ago I enjoyed coauthoring a review essay that included an edited collection: Pulling it off required quite a bit of negotiation. We essentially used a divide-and-conquer approach, and instead of blending our voices throughout, we each "owned" half of the review, focusing on different practical dimensions of the texts under review.[39] Did it work? You can be the judge.

One of my goals with this book is to demonstrate how writing scholarly reviews is not an act independent of other academic or intellectual pursuits. In interlude 4, I explore how the skills honed by reviewing benefit other aspects of a scholarly life. Then, in the final chapter, I continue the theme of taking things further by exploring ways to cultivate a connoisseurship of the art of scholarly reviewing and, ultimately, to expand the promise and potential of scholarly book reviews.

Lessons

- Reviews of special types of scholarly books—including edited collections, anthologies, scholarly editions, and other reference works—require special considerations as reader and assessor.

- Review essays allow reviewers to position two or more related books in conversation with each other. They require reviewers to present an intellectual argument in order to tie the works together, thus elevating the scholarly merit of the form.
- The selectivity required for reviewing edited collections allows reviewers to focus on the standout chapters and not mention the misses.
- Retrospective review essays approach scholarly journal articles in length, temporal investment, depth of insights, and educational value. Of all the types of reviews, they are the most likely to "count" as serious works of scholarship.
- Coauthoring scholarly book reviews embraces the collaborative nature of scholarship, allows more than one perspective to be shared within a single review, and encourages intellectual growth and fellowship.

INTERLUDE 4

TRANSFERRING YOUR SKILLS

In chapter 1, I presented a number of benefits of scholarly book reviewing, emphasizing the contributions that book reviews make to the scholarly ecosystem. In chapter 5, I revisit those benefits, emphasizing the personal dimension. Here, I consider how the skills of scholarly book reviewing transfer to other facets of the scholarly life.

Because scholarly book reviewing requires you to be inquisitive, forces you to be attentive, and allows you to marshal your abilities to assess others' intellectual contributions objectively and succinctly in writing, you can most easily transfer these fundamental skills to pre-publication peer review of scholarly manuscripts. Skilled peer reviewers for scholarly journal manuscripts are perennially in high demand and short supply. Peer review, which is perhaps best learned under the auspices of a mentor, seems to be infrequently taught in graduate school. Once you have submitted a scholarly journal manuscript yourself and have come to understand the value—and power—of peer reviews in the vetting of scholarship, you will recognize the primary differences between pre-publication peer review and post-publication peer review. Pre-publication peer review:

- questions the robustness of empirical methods, the soundness of analyses and conclusions, the veracity of claims, the quality of presentation; and
- focuses on weaknesses in design, interpretation, and presentation, offering suggestions for improvements prior to (potential) publication.

In pre-publication peer review, the reviewer asks: *Is this material making an important and necessary contribution to knowledge? Even if the contribution is sound, how can it be improved?*

In contrast, as you've learned from this book, post-publication peer review—of which scholarly book reviewing is a primary form—shifts the focus away from calling out weaknesses to emphasizing strengths. The primary question answered by a scholarly book review is not whether the work is making an important contribution to knowledge but what that contribution is—and how it is made. Peer reviewers prior to publication have thus done the dirty work of vetting and helping to strengthen a book manuscript. Because the book was ultimately accepted for publication, someone other than the author saw merit in the presented material. A published scholarly book should incorporate the suggestions of peer reviewers, reflect the author's best efforts, and make an identifiable contribution to the literature. Otherwise, it should not have been published.

Once you've proven you can review a scholarly book, you can certainly serve as a peer reviewer for scholarly journal manuscripts in your field. If you're wondering why I am shifting from books to journal articles here, the reason is simply because pre-publication reviewers of scholarly book manuscripts do not volunteer: They are solicited by the publishers. Yes, peer reviewers for scholarly journal submissions are also solicited by journal editors, but the stable of reviewers is one you can offer to join—in the same manner as you may have volunteered to serve as a post-publication reviewer of scholarly books for a journal. (See chapter 1 for details.) You will reach out to the journal editor and will share your credentials, your research interests, your methodological expertise (if in the social sciences), and your willingness to serve as a peer reviewer in your area(s) of specialization. You are welcome to attach a copy of your CV. Then, you can eventually expect to be called upon to review manuscripts submitted to that journal.

One more difference you may find between reviewing scholarly books and reviewing scholarly journal submissions is the level of instruction given. Scholarly journals tend to have rubrics that peer reviewers of submitted journal manuscripts are expected to follow. You can expect to address pointed questions about methods, sources, conclusions, and presentational matters in your review. Guided by these evaluative questions, you will draft comments that will be shared directly with the author (or authors), and you may also offer confidential comments to the editor. Your audience, therefore, is known (and narrow); your demeanor throughout your review is that of an educator or consultant. You are operating in service of your field, in service of knowledge. Like post-publication reviewing, pre-publication peer reviewing also counts as service to your discipline. You should indicate any journals for which you have served as a peer reviewer on your CV.

Notice one additional difference: Pre-publication peer reviewers wield greater power over their fields than do post-publication peer reviewers. Pre-publication reviewers serve as gatekeepers. Post-publication reviewers serve as commentators. In chapter 1, I noted how scholarly book reviews can nevertheless elevate certain works, shifting them into the spotlight and drawing attention to their merits and contributions. When commentators alight favorably on a scholarly book, they can help to ensure that its message is received by scholars who continue to shape the discipline. As gatekeepers, pre-publication peer reviewers wield direct influence on a field by helping to decide what gets published in the first place. As commentators, post-publication scholarly reviewers wield indirect influence.

If you are new to the enterprise of peer reviewing journal manuscripts, do not hesitate to ask for assistance. Share a draft of your first review with a colleague or mentor—much in the same way I've suggested you do, in chapter 3, with a draft of a scholarly book review. A supremely helpful mentor would be willing to review both the manuscript itself and your review of it. You would also be welcome to ask the journal editor for comments on your review prior to finalizing and submitting it. Not all journal editors have the time, patience, or inclination for such developmental work. But if they know what's good for the enterprise, an early investment of their time and attention could pay dividends with respect to the collective quality of future peer review. Why? You may improve as a reviewer, and you will likely return the favor, sharing your skills and knowledge with others over time. (Editorial intervention also represents a strategic move: You should be more inclined to agree to future peer-review requests from an editor who has supported your development as a peer reviewer.)

Where else can you use your evaluative and writing skills? Depending on the nature of your work, you might be asked or invited to conduct internal program evaluation or assessment. (When you do so for an external organization, you can be compensated for your time.) Program evaluation typically involves the collection of data (an additional skill set), but it ultimately involves the assessment of those data and the delivery of a written report. You would use similar faculties to evaluate the efficacy of a curriculum, for example, as you would to evaluate how well a scholarly author delivers on a goal: *What are the intentions? How well are those intentions being met? Where are those intentions falling short? What is the evidence?*

Your evaluative skills can also prove useful as a reviewer of grant and conference proposals. Express willingness to serve on grant-review committees, whenever possible, and volunteer to serve on a conference committee for a scholarly organization to which you belong. You will work with rubrics and may find that, unlike with journal manuscripts, your assessments remain internal. That is, not all scholarly or professional organizations or foundations offer feedback on proposals: They are simply accepted or rejected. Conference presenters often aspire to share their work in progress, so reviewing conference proposals affords you advance notice regarding potential new directions in your field. Ditto for grant proposers, where an added benefit of serving on grant-review committees (from the perspective of learning about competitiveness) is the possibility of panel discussions about applications. Learning what others prioritize and how others assess work in your field can be revelatory.

And perhaps you would like to transfer your skills as a scholarly reviewer to members of the next generation of scholars and researchers. If you teach or otherwise work with undergraduate or graduate students, I've written the postlude with you in mind. There, you can read about teaching scholarly book reviewing in the classroom.

Our work is not yet over. In the final chapter, I consider ways to embrace the concept of continuous improvement and growth with respect to scholarly book reviewing. Such improvement involves both inward and outward dimensions, from refining your approach to the craft of scholarly reviewing to aspiring to additional service roles within the greater scholarly ecosystem. Who knew that the practice of reviewing harbors such promise, such potential?

5

Improving the Craft and Context of Reviewing

ROY WOLPER, cofounder and longtime coeditor of *The Scriblerian*, a review journal for eighteenth-century literary scholarship, emphasizes the challenges of writing book reviews with an apt analogy: "Because of the necessary compression, a review is like an omelette, more difficult to master than it appears."[1] I agree. But skills can be practiced. Skills can be learned. With a little time and dedication, you, too, can crack the genre of the scholarly book review. Julia Child and colleagues, in their classic *Mastering the Art of French Cooking*, offer thirteen pages of detailed instructions and illustrations on how to master the omelet.[2] The primary goal of *How to Review Scholarly Books*—which, granted, is a touch longer than thirteen pages, lacks nifty line drawings, and doesn't yield anything edible—is to present an approach for writing effective scholarly book reviews. As I am sure you've noticed, "effective" invites interpretation. And the skills supporting this approach and this academic genre do not exist in a vacuum.

Skills can also become second nature. I've written so many book reviews that I can rather quickly form a preliminary opinion of any book I pick up, provided it's in a field that I know something about. Reflexively and simultaneously while I engage with the content of a book, I can ask the questions I've presented in earlier chapters and listed in the appendix. Of course, my job becomes to question this preliminary opinion iteratively, allowing it to be reformed, reevaluated, reassessed as I progress through the book, alert to the author's intentions with the work. I know that the first several book reviews I wrote required much more direct intentionality on my part as a reader (first) and a writer (second). I had to learn both what to observe and how to discern the most notable characteristics of works of nonfiction. With years of practice, I refined my evaluative ability and cultivated what I like to think of as a sense of connoisseurship with respect to the art of reviewing.[3] I continue to grow into this identity as a connoisseur of scholarly book reviews.[4] The practice of improving as a reviewer and a writer never ends. Anyone who claims otherwise is, well, wrong.

Interlude 4 offered some ideas for applying what you now know about scholarly book reviews to other evaluative forms, including reviews of scholarly journal manuscripts, reviews of grant and conference proposals, and program reviews. Here I return to the focus of this work, offering some thoughts and strategies for continuing to strengthen your craft as a reviewer and as a writer. I do so by asking you to reflect on what you have learned about reviewing scholarly books. I then share some approaches I have used or seen in book reviews that you are free to appropriate yourself. These approaches can, with a dash of creativity, be transferred to other genres and situations. And I conclude by considering additional ways to improve as a reviewer, as a writer, and as a thoughtful and engaged contributor to your field.

Reflecting on the Value of Scholarly Book Reviewing

What skills does scholarly book reviewing allow me to practice and develop? How does reviewing inform scholarly identity? How does reviewing improve writing?

Tallying Personal Benefits of Scholarly Book Reviewing

In chapter 1, I presented a number of benefits to scholarly reviewing by way of explaining its place and importance in the scholarly ecosystem. Many of these were benefits to your scholarly field. Only some were of the "What's in it for me?" variety. Writer Margaret Renkl bridges these benefits: "I read because I need to learn, or because I am eager to support the work of other writers."[5] Replace *read* with *review* and *or* with *and*, and you'll understand my perspective on scholarly book reviewing.

Now that you've written a scholarly book review, you should agree with me about the following personal benefits:

Reviewing allows you to practice the intellectual work that underscores all scholarship. Reviewing requires you to read, understand, engage with, and reflect upon another scholar's ideas. In graduate school, you are trained within your discipline to undertake such work per the traditions, norms, and expectations of your field. Reviewing thus affords you an opportunity to demonstrate and to refine your intellectual acumen.

Reviewing keeps you connected to your field—and to its developments. The farther beyond graduate school you get, the greater effort you must make to remain attuned to developments within your field. Reviewing recently published scholarly works helps keep you aware of new directions, new perspectives, new voices within your field. And reviewing scholarly works carries greater accountability and more memorable impact than just reading them. If the best way to learn something is to teach it, the second-best way to learn something is to write a scholarly review of it.[6]

Reviewing teaches you to be attentive. If you found yourself not trusting your reading notes and frequently returning to the book you were reviewing while you were writing your review, then you can continue working on your attention and discernment skills. For the first several books I reviewed, I remember not knowing how to know what warranted recording in my notes. Eventually I realized that reviewers cannot be comprehensive: Space simply does not allow it. That revelation freed me from obsessiveness, allowing me to enjoy reading and note-taking—and to be more curious, more inquisitive, more responsive while I read. I recognized that stronger and more generous reviews result when I approach the book as a reader, primarily, and as a reviewer, secondarily. Counterintuitive, I know. (That comment is akin to saying you can make a better omelet if you approach the task as an eater rather than as a chef.) But reviewers—in the guise of critics who fixate on criticizing instead of engaging in fair, measured critique—seem predisposed to identify flaws instead of to celebrate excellence. Reviewers should not behave like restaurant inspectors seeking code violations, although reviewers, too, must be attentive to details. As a book reviewer, you should revel in what is admirable, what is exciting, what is noteworthy in a good way about the books you review. You should look for the awe in each book you review.

Reviewing allows you to refine your communication skills across more than one genre and more than one register. To review a book, you communicated with at least one editor and possibly with members of a publisher's marketing team. Such correspondence, although routine, can help build confidence by requiring self-acknowledgment of expertise. Then, to write the review, you marshaled your training and disciplinary knowledge, channeling this awareness into production of a succinct text that demonstrates your knowledge and your ability to communicate effectively with your disciplinary peers. After submitting your review, you may have engaged in additional correspondence with editors and production personnel. You may have shared a copy of the published review with the publishers of the book. And you even may have corresponded with the author. These interactions cement your identity and indicate your belonging to a community of practice.

Reviewing enables you to develop relationships within your field. Some scholarly fields or subfields are quite small. Everyone knows everyone else. Wendy Laura Belcher told me that, in some subfields—hers is African literature—scholars communally divvy up books for review so that no new releases are overlooked. Imagine: scholars supporting one another, encouraging one another, ensuring that one another's works are read and reviewed and appreciated. Even if your field is large, your work will be appreciated at the very least by the book review editor of the venue that publishes your review. To editors, well-crafted material to publish is a gift. You may impress the editors so much that they "become curious about your own research," paving the way toward future publications in your field.[7]

Reviewing, as a service to your field, lets you visibly share your talents. You can contribute to the collective goodwill of your field by continuing to volunteer your talents as a scholarly book reviewer. I don't know how often you think about the broader scholarly ecosystem, but cultural critic Kevin Dettmar explains that the academic profession "runs, albeit secretly, on an intergenerational economy of debt and indebtedness, an exchange of quiet acts of professional courtesy and generosity."[8] Reviewing is one such act. Book review editor Sean Sturm places reviews within the "vital gift ecology of the scholarly community."[9] Education scholar Ann Chinnery refers to book reviews as "act[s] of intellectual generosity."[10] And I could go on. If you want to feel good about yourself for a moment, writing scholarly book reviews allows you to contribute to this ecosystem.

Reviewing forces you to be focused, concise. I learn and relearn this point every time I write a review. I remind myself of the sensibility behind William Strunk Jr. and E. B. White's "omit needless words."[11] I remind myself, too, that concision affords a boon to the reader, because it offers the gift of time—time that you've liberated for your readers by getting to the point, sticking to the point, and avoiding superfluity.

Reviewing improves your writing. This point may be the most important. When you evaluate a text, you must justify your assessment. If something in a text is ineffective and you wish to criticize it, you must pinpoint the weaknesses. Books with identifiable weaknesses are thus gifts, in a sense: They force you to figure out the problems, and they demonstrate what to avoid in your own scholarship. If something in a text is effective, though, the book offers a master class in how to produce your own writing with similar effect. You simply need to pay attention to the structures, the methods, the approaches being used. Anna Leahy notes how writing book reviews cultivates the skill of "writerly reading."[12] Such attentiveness enables reviewers to inform their own writing craft and to "propel creativity to new and uncharted territory."[13] Journalist Ted Conover agrees: "The masters' secrets are right in front of us, if only we take the time to appreciate their craftsmanship."[14] As a writer, then, you simply must remember what has impressed (or not impressed) you in the works you have attentively read. And you must actively apply these positive strategies and approaches to your own writing.

Embracing the Work—and the Challenge— of Scholarly Book Reviewing

I know what you're thinking: Reviewing scholarly books is work—*extra* work, *uncompensated* work. Why can't you just read attentively, always, as a way to improve your writerly craft? Why do you need to take the extra steps and actually write reviews? Why not just appropriate what you notice, what you learn from master writers and incorporate that knowledge—structural, organizational, presentational, stylistic, linguistic—into your own scholarly writing projects (journal articles, books: the projects that "matter")? You know how I feel: Scholarly book reviews "matter," even if in different attributive and contributive ways. As citizens of a scholarly community, letting others write reviews (and reading and benefiting from those reviews yourself) without actively contributing to the reviewing ecosystem yourself is like regularly listening to public radio without ever making a donation of your own. Academe is not immune from the free-rider problem.

If you're not sure you'll ever be convinced that scholarly book reviews can aspire toward scholarship themselves, consider the following goal, from Ralph Alan McCanse: "A review should be as presentable as if it were going to be, itself, the subject treated by some other reviewer."[15] Lexicographer Michael Adams concurs: "A good review should be citable: for information it provides; for the questions it poses, for questions that may drive future research; and for the views it takes of the state of the profession, its needs and prospects, a view with which future research may be in dialogue."[16] What an inversion! And what a vision! Now the challenge is not just to take the job of reviewing seriously and do the job well. The challenge, instead, is to elevate your reviews so that they become the exemplars used by others.

In the next section you'll find an array of strategies to consider toward such an end.

Exercising Creativity in Your Reviews

What are some strategies or approaches I can try in my scholarly book reviews to help elevate my prose or deepen the effect of my reviews?

Enlivening Your Reviews: The Why

By this point you should know that in order for a scholarly book review to become an exemplar, it must be intelligent, measured, and reflective of the work under review. It must evaluate its subject to the highest disciplinary and ethical standards. Readers should come away with a clear sense of the scope of the book, its argument, and its contributions. And readers should know how you, the reviewer, were transformed by reading the book. Exemplary reviews accomplish all these goals with authority, commitment, and style. Now, you might assume that the greatest editorial compliment I've received about one of my book reviews is that it is "very well written." Not so. (Everything you write for publication should be well written, no?) Instead, when an editor told me that he "always learns something" when he reads my reviews, he had identified my purpose. *That's* why I write scholarly book reviews: to educate, to motivate, to inspire.

Still, don't presume that I necessarily *disapprove* of a workmanlike approach to writing scholarly book reviews. The genre requires that the tasks of summarizing, analyzing, and assessing be undertaken in a compressed space, after all, resulting in a certain mode of predictability. In the prelude and in chapter 3, though, I called out the clichés of "Everyone should read this book" and "This book is a welcome addition to the literature."

You can easily avoid those inert statements by sharing the sentiments, if appropriate, in your own more original words or through the way you choose to approach your review in the first place. In chapter 3, I also called out the use of templates as recipes for boredom. As Ralph Alan McCanse cautions, "there is not, and should never be, one strict pattern for review writing."[17] The tasks of summarizing, analyzing, and assessing need not always be undertaken in the same manner or order.

In writing, scholarly or otherwise, I always favor stylishness and wit. What reader would want the opposite? And I have good news: Cognitive psychologist Steven Pinker concludes that "there is no [academic] field in which you can't be stylish."[18] And even better news, from former editor Rachel Toor: "Attractive writing—brave, personal, narrative, zingy, imaginative, funny—will not make you appear any less smart."[19] Granted, some of the ideas I propose below would not be appropriate for certain topics or for certain books. You must always remain respectful and professional, treating your subjects with the dignity they deserve. But I nevertheless believe that if you make a scholarly book review fun for you, as the reviewer, you'll make it fun for the reader. Writer, editor, and critic William Zinsser includes an entire chapter on humor in his *On Writing Well*.[20] And the longest chapter in Stephen Pyne's *Style and Story*, another book on writing nonfiction, addresses humor. To Pyne, who is both a master of metaphor and an aficionado of alliteration, "a sprinkling of comic wit can spice the text like a dash of chili powder."[21] Don't be afraid to season your text with a touch of levity.

To elevate your writing overall, you should follow the recommendations of writing sage Helen Sword, who encourages writers to favor concrete nouns and active verbs; to keep nouns and verbs close together; and to cut unnecessary prepositions, adjectives, adverbs, and pronouns.[22] These straightforward suggestions can help activate your prose, making it both easier to understand and more engaging to read. Another way to break out of boredom and stuffiness in your academic writing would be to read writer Amitava Kumar's *Every Day I Write the Book: Notes on Style*—and then to entertain some of his creative suggestions.

Enlivening Your Reviews: The How

Here you will find a dozen additional ideas for enlivening your reviews. They range from the commonsensical—many of which you have likely seen before—to the audacious.[23] You should be able to imagine how these ideas could be applied to other genres. I give you free rein to use as many of these strategies in your writing as you wish, wherever and whenever you deem them appropriate. Just remember, always, that rhetorical decorations will not compensate for a lack of reflective, analytical substance in your scholarly reviews. Your primary goal is to approach the review as a scholar. But you can—and should—approach the review as a scholar who is also a writer. Take pride in letting both identities happily coexist.

Strategy #1: Ensure that your paragraphs are not all of similar length. Mix things up. Don't be afraid of the one-sentence paragraph, either, when you want to make a bold, stand-alone statement. Liberate your scholarly reviews from the prescriptive idea that, in academic writing, "each paragraph should consist of a topic sentence, one to three supporting sentences, and a strong closing sentence."[24]

Strategy #2: Ensure that your sentences also are not all of similar length. Academic writers have a tendency to favor longer, more complex sentences, assuming (wrongly) that such sentences reflect a higher order of thought. Short sentences refresh your readers and force you, the writer, to be direct, precise, lapidary. Use short sentences at least occasionally. Longer, more complex sentences can be fine, provided you don't pile one atop another (atop another). If you'd like to learn to streamline your writerly voice, read nonfiction writer Verlyn Klinkenborg's *Several Short Sentences about Writing*.[25] I'll admit that I had to read Klinkenborg's book twice before his principles really sank in. Years and years spent in graduate school will do that to you: rewire your very approach to language and, by extension, to the world. Knowing what tendencies to resist, or why to resist, or how to resist often comes later, once you have more experience (and its kin, confidence).

Strategy #3: Eschew hedge words and noncommittal language. This point is especially important for graduate students and academics who are just getting started as scholarly book reviewers. Do not weaken your authority—your authoritativeness—by unnecessarily qualifying your claims. Be bold, not meek. You have something to offer. In the space of a scholarly book review, your opinion of the book should not be up for negotiation. No waffling! Banish the type of tentativeness you may have allowed to taint your writing in graduate school: tentativeness that feels polite and respectful yet in fact demonstrates lack of assurance or confidence. At the same time, avoid tearing a book to shreds. Remember to emphasize the positive. Just be brave and imbue your writing with confidence and commitment.

Strategy #4: Embrace analogies, metaphors, and other figures of speech. These moves need not be left to writers in literary or artistic fields. Like examples, analogies and metaphors help concretize your abstract thoughts and theories. Concretizing aids memory and, thus, retention. (You likely remember the review-as-omelet analogy offered by Roy Wolper at the start of this chapter.) Eric Hayot notes, too, how figurative language "expands the referential sphere of your prose."[26] Use some. You—

and your readers—may be startled by the effects. Just be careful not to venture into the territory of the cliché. Clichés, to Pamela Haag, "disorient readers, pulling them out of" the world of your text "and into a cliché-inspired land of watched pots that never boil, obstinate mules, and shoes that don't fit."[27]

Strategy #5: Make sure that all of your paragraphs start with a different word. Or at least try to write a review that way. This approach helps you avoid an obvious chapter-by-chapter summary. I have seen many reviews where a number of successive paragraphs start with "In"—as in "In chapter 1, the author . . ." followed by "In chapters 2 and 3, the author. . . ." (And so on.) Book review editor Charlotte Wright refers to the worst version of such reviews as "mere lists of chapter headings put into paragraph form."[28] Yawn. Yes, you can mix up the first words yet retain a chapter-by-chapter approach, but such cosmetic alterations may remind you that the chapter-by-chapter approach is better left to the writers of book reports, not of book reviews.

Strategy #6: Dare to write a review as an acrostic. Use the first letters of the first words of each paragraph to spell the author's name (if of appropriate length) or some other central theme or key word of the book. Perhaps nobody will notice, but perhaps someone will. According to William Zinsser, "surprise is the most refreshing commodity in nonfiction writing. Snoozing readers are startled awake to find that a writer is actually trying to entertain them."[29] A scholarly book review, entertaining? Why not?

Strategy #7: Don't be afraid of puns and other wordplay, where appropriate. For inspiration, consult critic Justin Chang's or Anthony Lane's movie reviews in the *New Yorker* or articles in a recent issue of the *Economist*. In a review of a 2019 documentary on Macedonian beekeeping, Lane presents a wildly effervescent (and onomatopoetic) bovine image: "Even a baby left to itself on the dungy farmyard ground, with cows mooching around, seems

O.K."[30] In the *Economist* I've recently encountered a composer who leapt at the chance to write a ballet score, a profile of hemp-related industries that are growing like weeds, and a review of a biopic of Elvis Presley where the cinematography is "all shook up." You don't want to go overboard, of course. ("Growing like weeds" is, after all, a cliché.) But your language should actively resist the staid, the stuffy, the soporific.

Strategy #8: Embrace imaginative vocabulary. I love coming across obscure terms that were previously unknown to me: They help keep language vibrant, surprising, alive. Students and scholars—those who will be reading your review—should always be seeking to expand their vocabularies. So consider engaging with the limits of your vocabulary, trying out new, exciting words of the type described by journalist Hunter S. Thompson as "word-jewel[s]."[31] Perhaps this strategy is most suitable if the author of the book you are reviewing embraces esoteric vocabulary. Regardless, I have slipped words like *chrysopoetics* (transmutation of substances into gold), *éclaircissement* (an enlightening explanation of something previously inexplicable), and *strigine* (owlish) into reviews I've written within the past few years.[32] And I always try to provide contextual clues to allow readers at least to approximate the meanings without having to rush to a dictionary. Reading widely and voraciously is the most enjoyable way to pick up such delightful terms, such trouvailles.[33] But online resources can also prove useful. I especially enjoy browsing the resources curated by linguistic anthropologist Stephen Chrisomalis and available via his remarkable *Phrontistery* website, which includes a 17,000-word dictionary of "rare, cool, and unusual words."[34] Prepare to be impressed.

Strategy #9: Slip in a set of interrelated words that may or may not connect with the topic of the book itself. When I was an undergraduate, I attended a lecture by literary critic Helen Vendler that has stayed with me for decades. Vendler was working on the manuscript to *The Art of Shakespeare's Sonnets*, and she shared several examples of how Shakespeare had repeated related words or sounds across the quatrains and couplets of individual sonnets.[35] You can do something similar in a book review. Pick a theme, and then sprinkle related words across your review. You can aim for one thematic word per paragraph. Again, perhaps nobody will notice. But therein lies the thrill of creation: You, at least, will know the secrets contained in your texts. In one review, I tucked in the words *point, roundly, shape, squares,* and *triangulate.*[36] In another, you'll spot *beguiles, casts, conjuring, curse, enchant, enigma, initiates, magic, spell,* and *spirit.*[37] Others I'll leave for you to discover on your own. You can take this amusement one step further by basing the themed words around the author's last name. Dive into etymology if you wish. Just don't distract your readers or compromise your message with verbal contortions.

Strategy #10: Consider allowing the author's voice to transfer to your review. Here, I'm not referring to writing "parody" reviews of the type that were periodically offered by book critic Michiko Kakutani of the *New York Times*. I'm also not encouraging reviewers of turgid texts to replicate such bombast in their reviews. Instead, if the author of the book you are reviewing does something well, try the approach on for size. When I reviewed each of Stephen Pyne's pair of books on writing, I found myself appropriating alliteration more than usual.[38] When I reviewed Deirdre Nansen McCloskey's *Economical Writing*, I eschewed semicolons, which McCloskey describes as "grossly overused" in academic writing.[39] (She's right.) Here I am encouraging creativity, not competitiveness, per se. Phillipa Chong issues a forthright challenge, noting that "the best [literary] reviewers elevate their writing in a way that can actually rival or even surpass the writing they review."[40] And Eric Hayot issues a similar challenge to writers in his *Elements of Academic Style*: "This is a book that wants you to surpass and destroy it."[41] If a book you are reviewing inspires you to elevate your writing, go for it. The reviews I have written have taught me a lot about what works in my own writing, thus contributing to my writerly voice.

Strategy #11: Use a review as a corrective to a peccadillo in your writing. As I've explained before, reviews are not about you. But because they spring from you, you are welcome to use the space in a scholarly review to flex your writerly muscles. For example, if you know you have a tendency to pile up long, complex sentences, force yourself to write a review with no sentence longer than, say, thirty words.[42] (The sentence you just read has twenty-nine.) If you know you overuse semicolons, write a review without one. If you know you overuse dashes or passive voice or the word *which*—well, you get the picture. Any writerly habits that verge on battologizing—excessive and tiring repetition—are game for intervention. Again, you should not let your challenge interfere with the presentation of your summary, analysis, and assessment. You may not be able to banish all lengthy sentences or semicolons or dashes or instances of the passive voice or occurrences of *which*. But at least you can actively work at minimizing them. Helen Sword, in *Stylish Academic Writing* and *Writing with Pleasure*, encourages experimentation and suggests taking measured risks in our scholarly writing. Why not let one such risk have a positive effect on your writing? You never know if it will unless you try.

Strategy #12: Let yourself into the review, where (or if) appropriate. The nature of the topic—and the register of your review, and the conventions of your discipline and your review venue—will determine how visible you can be in your review. Reviews cannot be completely disembodied: Opinions and assessments must come from somewhere. At the same time, a review cannot be about you but instead must be about the book at hand. Decide how comfortable you are with revealing yourself and your preferences and your biases, then consider letting yourself into the review. Helen Sword notes how the most stylish scholars humanize themselves in their writing with first-person anecdotes or asides.[43] And Walter Nord, former book review editor of the *Academy of Management Review*, appreciates when reviewers indicate the implications of their own "reflexivity" on the judgments they offer about scholarly books.[44]

Do try some of these strategies. Or at least consider doing so. (Writer Erin Pushman encourages writers to "keep an I-want-to-try-that list where you note interesting approaches or risks writers have taken that you would like to try in your own way.")[45] Strive to tuck art into the margins of your reviews.[46] And if you find a different approach or inspiration that works for you, please let me know about it. I'd love to expand my list of suggestions and ideas. Write to me directly, or why not offer your ideas in a review of this book. The more pleasure you take in writing scholarly book reviews, the more enjoyable your readers will find your reviews.[47] I agree—no surprise—with historian Carolyn Eastman, who believes that writing scholarly book reviews should be one of the "most enjoyable forms of academic writing."[48] And remember, as William Germano so clearly put it, that you're writing *for*, not just *about*.[49] Imagine yourself reading your reviews, and give yourself something to savor.

Improving as a Reviewer— and Improving Reviewing

How can I become a better reviewer of scholarly books? How can I contribute to the betterment of scholarly book reviews?

Striving for Greater Impact

With practice, you will become better at the skill of scholarly book reviewing. I thus encourage you not to stop with just one review. Anyone who routinely undertakes creative projects—and, yes, scholarly book reviews are such projects—knows that learning transpires through doing. Practice the skill, yet don't allow yourself to become fixed in your ways. You can always seek to be improving your reviewing skills by actively reflecting on your processes and your products.

I introduced the Japanese concept of *kaizen*, or continuous improvement, in interlude 3. It's germane once more. Look for incremental ways to improve quality that seem worth the investments of time or energy. (Perhaps reading this book has been one such investment for you.) Here I share some additional strategies for continuing to improve as a reviewer, as a writer, and as a contributor to your field.

Seek out and read other reviews of books you've reviewed. Once you've finished writing a scholarly book review, you should enjoy coming across—and reading—other reviews of the same book. Revel in the opportunity to see how another reader responded to the same work. You will be reminded, if you have forgotten, just how subjective reviews happen to be. If you do not encounter any duplicate reviews, then you have done your part to save a book from intellectual oblivion by demonstrating, as Eric Hayot reassures, that "no one writes into a void."[50] (Authors whose books are never reviewed, however, may *feel* as if they've written into a void.)

Seek out and read reviews of books you've read. When you are in graduate school, you enjoy the luxury of time for attentive reading and the expectation that you will discuss scholarly works with others. You learn how others approached the works, how others responded to them, how others' thinking has been changed by them. Reviews share such material publicly, providing a foil for your impressions. Reading reviews is thus both a shortcut for scholars who wish to bypass reading an entire work and an opportunity for reflection, for reconsideration, for reevaluation. Embrace these attributes. For each review you read of a book you've also read, ask yourself: *If I were to have reviewed this book myself, how would my review have differed? What did this review illuminate for me that I had previously overlooked?*

Read more reviews of books you've not read. Maybe you're not seeking shortcuts, per se, but are simply curious about the world around you. Let yourself be curious. Sure, you'll need to stay in your intellectual lane when you're the reviewer. As the reader, though, you should roam widely, trusting others' expertise and insights and evaluations. I am convinced that the greatest advances in scholarship occur when scholars remove their blinders, welcoming perspectives from other purviews.[51] For interdisciplinary scholars, especially, book reviews can serve as "catalysts of association, connection, and transformation: three intellectual actions that drive the advancement of knowledge."[52] Plus, you'll build up your armamentarium of scholarly reviewing strategies that work (or don't work) in maintaining your interest in a book and its contributions to a field. According to critic George Woodcock, the "ideal reviewer must . . . make these few words [of a review] so alive in the reader's mind that they will—at secondhand—evoke an active interest in the book discussed."[53]

Read other types of reviews to find other ideas, other influences, other approaches. Across genres, reviewers share the goals of contextualizing, analyzing, and assessing. So why not engage critically with reviews of different genres: memoirs, literature, the visual and performing arts, film and television, restaurants. Examine how different types of reviewers contextualize and deliver their opinions. Scholars can learn a lot about the writer's craft by reading intelligent evaluative nonfiction, even if the topic is television, or dance, or contemporary music.[54] You've likely noticed my references to the *New Yorker* earlier in this book. Conveniently, you'll find reviews of literature, the visual and performing arts, film and television, and restaurants within the pages of that magazine. Some will be just capsule reviews. Let them teach you how to present the essence of a work (or a place, or an experience). Others will be extended reviews. Let them teach you how a review can take the form of an essay. If you reject the idea of journalism being useful to your scholarship, you should read the introduction to critic Jeffrey Williams's *How to Be an Intellectual*.[55]

Send a "gracious note" to a reviewer whose work has impressed you. I can't recall when I first learned of the term *gracious note*, but such a note, written to a stranger, simply expresses your appreciation, gratitude, or praise, asking for nothing in return. I recently received such a note from a scholar in Malaysia, and the message made my day. Sending gracious notes feels almost as good as receiving them.

Capitalize on your linguistic skills by reviewing a non-English-language work. Although English has apparently become the scholarly lingua franca, if you happen to be able to read another language, and if scholarly books in your area of expertise are published in that language, challenge yourself to review one such book for an English-language publication. (Because you should never write reviews on speculation, you will want to confirm that the identified outlet for your review will welcome your review, despite the inaccessibility of the original text to many or most readers of the publication. Since 2018, for example, the journal *Metascience* has been publishing English-language reviews of books published in other languages.[56] I encourage more journals to follow suit, because these sorts of reviews should be more prevalent across fields.) Reviews of works published outside the Anglophone sphere can expand worldviews, share otherwise inaccessible insights, and counter the natural inclination toward parochialism and cultural myopia. Author Jhumpa Lahiri, who reads, writes, and translates translinguistically, sees great benefits in "stepping away from one's linguistic point of gravity."[57] And Eric Hayot explains how reading academic work in other languages operates like traveling abroad: "The dislocation provided by unfamiliar sights and rhythms will make you more conscious of how you think and work where you are most at 'home.'"[58] The exercise of reviewing non-English-language scholarship potentially "shocks the system" and could therefore result in the greatest liberating effect on your own thinking and writing.[59] Try it, if you're able.

Involve others in your process of reviewing scholarly books. In chapter 3 and interlude 3, I explain how I always share near-final drafts of less-than-flattering reviews with a trusted colleague before submitting them for publication. But why not share all your drafts with trusted colleagues? Why not regularly ask where your argument or your presentation could be improved? Then, if you find someone whose comments help improve your reviews, invite that person to coauthor a review with you, as described in chapter 4. If you're already worried that book reviews "count" for nearly nothing and therefore feel that a coauthored book review would be worth even less, you're missing the point of this collaborative venture. (Besides, half of nothing is still nothing.) Ponder these incentives identified by Helen Sword: "When two or more people 'click' over a piece of writing, their ideas are amplified, their pleasure is increased, and the intellectual impact of their thinking becomes greater than the sum of its parts."[60]

Encourage others to review scholarly books. No, I'm not offering this idea as a way of drumming up sales of this book. Instead, I'm offering it because I believe in the value of well-written scholarly book reviews. To Walter Nord, "book reviews that emerge from deep readings by experts who are reflexive and sensitive to context can be very valuable for the scholarly community."[61] We—and our scholarly communities—should want more of these types of reviews. You can do your part by encouraging others to do their part within the scholarly ecosystem. To Michael Adams, "writing book reviews should figure in every scholar's career, from beginning to end."[62] Amen.

Mentor others in the art of scholarly review. It's one thing to encourage others to write scholarly book reviews. It's another thing to help them learn how to do so.[63] This suggestion has so much potential for college or university instructors that I devote the postlude of this book to the idea.[64] If you're not an instructor yourself, you can find opportunities to share your knowledge. For example, you can offer to volunteer with a journal that publishes reviews in your field, noting your willingness to support first-time reviewers. If you work in higher education, you can reach out to the library, to the writing center, or to academic departments or units with graduate students in your field. Consider proposing or offering workshops on scholarly book reviewing at your institution or at a professional conference.[65] I annually mentor a small number of doctoral students on the craft of writing scholarly book reviews, and I marvel at the care and commitment they bring to the process. They live up to the promise asserted by Seth Perry about graduate students being the "best readers": "Graduate students *read*: for seminars; for qualifying exams; for obsessive, self-flagellating dissertation footnotes; and, potentially, for writing reviews. Expertise and experience are important but ultimately fungible qualifications for book reviewing; time, care, and attention are rare, and indispensable."[66]

Encourage the editors of scholarly journals that have never previously published book reviews—or that may have ceased including them—to consider introducing or reintroducing them. You will need evidence that a robust body of new scholarship germane to the readership of the journal exists. Or, depending on your field, you could be bold, suggesting that the journal publish retrospective reviews. As described in chapter 4, these reviews can offer remarkable surveys of disciplinary evolution and are particularly helpful to graduate students and other newcomers. Be prepared, of course, to step up as a contributor yourself—and to rally others to contribute.

Consider volunteering to assist or serve as a book review editor. Perhaps the best way to have your finger on the pulse of a field is to involve yourself with a clearinghouse for new publications. Such commitments are not for those deprived of time, however. Faculty members have their own expectations or requirements for scholarly contribution and engagement. If you hold an academic position, understand the service as a responsibility that will reduce the time you have to tend to other obligations. Yet the benefits can be great, even if the role itself has its challenges. Consider how others have reflected on the role.[67] And be sure to consult with senior mentors before accepting such a position.

Making Room for Scholarly Reviewing

So far in this book, I have refrained from quantifying the time that reviewing scholarly books requires. Everyone operates at different levels of efficiency and engagement, and everything we do is relative to our skills, our interests, and our other obligations. To boot, as I've noted more than once before, every scholarly book is different. Writing reviews of some books (usually the most impressive and inspiring ones) can be exercises in joyfulness. For others, the experience is quite different. Each variable in the calculus of converting time into completed reviews is thus distinct. (I do wish that book metadata would routinely include numbers of words: When it comes to approximating the amount of time that reading any given work will take, knowing the number of words is more useful than knowing the number of pages, since word densities per page vary by publication.) Reviewing well takes time. Together, the identifying time (for both the book and the review venue, chapter 1), the reading and note-taking time (chapter 2), the reflecting and writing time (chapter 3), and the finalizing and submitting time (interlude 3) underscore the reviewer's dedication to the work.

We make time for what we value. I propose that everyone who is interested in contributing to the scholarly discussion in an academic field should make time for reviewing scholarly books. I presented the benefits in chapter 1 and revisited them at the outset of this chapter. If you're worried that reviewing scholarly books will cannibalize your time for undertaking research with greater impact, remember Joli Jensen's "buddy log" metaphor that I offered in chapter 1: Smaller projects can help keep the momentum for larger projects. And in his *Clockwork Muse*, sociologist Eviatar Zerubavel proposes the idea of "A-time" and "B-time." The reactive nature of scholarly book reviews makes reviews something you can undertake, at least in part, during your B-time, the time that "requires less intense, focused concentration."[68] Perhaps you could aspire to identify the book and the review venue during your B-time, read the book and draft the review during your A-time, and then revise the review during your B-time. In other words, no matter how busy you are, if you adequately protect your time for writing and other creative pursuits, you should be able to make room for writing the occasional scholarly book review. Doing so could even help you become more productive with your other projects.

Another argument for beginning to write scholarly book reviews in graduate school—in addition to Seth Perry's proposition that graduate students make the "best readers"—is that the first review will take the longest. Graduate students (especially those aspiring toward academic careers) can most afford the temporal investment in developing skills as a scholarly reviewer earlier rather than later. I can't begin to quantify the number of hours my first scholarly book review required, over two decades ago. (In part, I can't remember. But I'm also sure the number would feel embarrassingly large to report. Initial scholarly book reviews, by their novelty, are wholly A-time projects, until the skill is learned.) Completing my one hundredth review, nearly two decades later, surely required only a fraction of the time of that original review.[69] And that hundredth review was no hack job. It was simply the culmination of years of practice and of refining the strategy that I have offered in this book. Today, on top of a full-time job, I can usually craft a scholarly book review—including the time it takes to read and annotate the book—in a few hours per day (more on weekends) spread across ten days to two weeks.

Read. Write. Relish. Take any or all of these suggestions in this chapter—in this book—and put them to work for you. Apply them to your writing, to your scholarly book reviews, to your life. Be brave, be bold, be ambitious, and propel the genre of the scholarly book review forward. And make sure to let your reviews cross-fertilize your other enterprises. In the process, you will build your confidence, your credibility, and your capacity for meaningful reflection, assessment, and contribution to your scholarly community.

Lessons

- If you commit yourself to writing scholarly book reviews at least occasionally, your skill as a scholarly reviewer will improve. You will also be contributing to the scholarly ecosystem by performing valuable intellectual service to your field.
- Scholarly reviews offer an ideal space to take measured, creative risks in scholarly writing. You should strive to be bold with your scholarly book reviews. Reviews that are enjoyable to write should be enjoyable for others to read.
- Envision the many ways you can share your talents as a scholarly reviewer: as a promoter of scholarly book reviewing, as an encourager or mentor for new reviewers, as a book review assistant or editor. Then try one or more of these roles.
- Writing scholarly book reviews affords you numerous personal, professional, and intellectual benefits. At minimum, engaged, reflective reviewing can improve your own writing—and your own scholarly practice.

POSTLUDE

TEACHING SCHOLARLY REVIEWING

Why Teach Scholarly Reviewing?

You don't have to look hard to find educational commentators bemoaning the state of training for future scholars. Commonly overlooked in formal curricula—particularly in the United States—are skills related to peer review. The expectation seems to be that students are informally mentored or trained how to assess others' scholarly works, perhaps following an apprenticeship model. Was that the case for you? If so, count yourself lucky, since you actually received some guidance. Why is learning this fundamental skill set so often left to chance—or to trial and error, or to on-the-fly experimentation?

If you have students of your own, consider building formal instruction in the writing of scholarly book reviews into your syllabi. In the so-called book disciplines, you'll find that the skills necessary for reviewing conveniently couple with skills you are already teaching or teaching toward: applying knowledge, forming connections among ideas, appraising ideas, formulating arguments. (Unsurprisingly, these skills align with those at the higher levels of Bloom's Taxonomy of cognitive learning.) Graduate students should be comfortable with the proposition of learning to write scholarly book reviews early in their graduate careers. But these skills—application, analysis, evaluation, and generation—should also be aims of upper-level undergraduate courses. Yes, undergraduate students can learn to write scholarly book reviews. You don't believe me? Let me show you how.

Scholarly Reviewing in the Undergraduate Classroom

Twice I have been invited to teach the art of scholarly book reviewing to upper-level undergraduate history students over the course of a semester. Their professor had prepared them well, so they embraced the challenge. The suggestions below could easily be adapted to any discipline where expecting students to read a scholarly monograph in its entirety seems realistic. Given the commentary arising in the mid-2020s on reluctance or even resistance among undergraduates to read, perhaps due to effects of the pandemic or the advent of generative AI, this project gives students two concrete, achievable goals: first, reading a book (yes, an entire book); second, writing a review of it. If your institution follows the quarter system or another calendar with shorter terms, you could streamline the process by having your students all review the same book, perhaps one that forms a core piece of your curriculum.

Incorporate reading scholarly book reviews into the syllabus. To build familiarity with the genre, assign scholarly book reviews—one or more per week—as readings throughout the term. Select reviews that complement other reading assignments: reviews of works invoked in other assigned readings are ideal. At least once include a pair of contrasting reviews of the same work. Try, also, to select reviews that are models of the form. These reviews will become the exemplary base upon which your students will formulate their understandings of the genre.

Weave mention of the role of scholarly book reviews into your lectures and other presentations throughout the term. You can activate your students' appreciation for the genre of the scholarly book review by emphasizing the role of book reviews in your life as a scholar. If you have written book reviews that are germane to the material for the course, consider including one of your reviews among the weekly readings. Doing so will bring the act of reviewing closer to home. The review will also afford you a shared example to discuss when offering advice and guidelines for the book review you will ask your students to write.

Teach how to read for reviewing. Early in the term, introduce your students to the importance of recording three distinct types of notes when they read scholarly works: direct quotations, summaries of important ideas in their own words, and comments and questions invoked by the text. (See chapter 2.) Share a sample of your notes on a text that the class has already read. Create an assignment that requires students to practice such note-taking on an upcoming assigned reading.

Identify characteristics of scholarly book reviews with your students. A few weeks into the term, after everyone has read several scholarly book reviews, discuss their characteristics as a group. At a minimum, your students will notice that reviews both describe and evaluate. They should notice that reviews identify strengths and weaknesses, emphasize contributions to knowledge, and situate the works within disciplinary traditions or conversations. Explore together how scholarly book reviews differ from the types of reviews commonly posted to social media sites. By discussing these ideas as a group, and by having a shared corpus of reviews from which to draw examples, you will be co-creating, with your students, a strong understanding of the distinctions and objectives of scholarly book reviews.

Provide a list of possible books for reviewing. By curating and offering a list of books you have read, you can identify books that are accessible to your students and with which you are familiar. The works need not be recent releases, since the goal for undergraduate students is not to write a review for publication but rather to gain experience with the genre. You will want to avoid edited collections as well as overly long, dense, or complex works. Controversial works can serve as effective learning opportunities for advanced students. You could allow students to propose other books that align with their interests. Depending on your goals, the review could become the final paper for your course. And depending on your field or the topic of your course, you might allow "crossover" books: scholarly works of nonfiction that are written for audiences of educated nonspecialists.

Ask your students to select a book to read and review, and provide a timeline by which they should read (and take notes on) the book. You should plan periodic check-ins to ensure your students are making sufficient progress and thus to thwart procrastinators. You should also be mindful to reduce your other reading expectations sufficiently during the weeks you would like your students to be focusing on their selected books for review.

A few weeks before the reviews will be due, offer a presentation on writing scholarly book reviews. I invoked sample book reviews and our earlier discussion of their characteristics. I shared copies of Linda Simon's "The Pleasures of Book Reviewing" (from the July 1996 issue of the *Journal of Scholarly Publishing*), highlighting the seven bullet points on page 238 of the article. The bullet points offer a list of questions that reviewers should consider answering—in a form more concise than the material in the appendix to this book.

Share formal instructions for the book review assignment. Consider offering a target range of 3–4 double-spaced pages for the reviews (aligning with 1,000–1,500 words). Be sure to note that only a portion of the review should consist of a summary of the book. The majority of the review should offer a critical analysis. Invite your students to consider:

- discussing the author's main arguments,
- describing the sources the author used,

- evaluating the effectiveness of the methodology the author employed,
- identifying the strengths and weaknesses of the book,
- explaining how the book changed their perceptions of the subject matter, and
- mentioning how well the book addresses its intended audience.

(This list, courtesy of Christopher Mayo of Nagoya Gakuin University, overlaps quite usefully with the bullet points in Linda Simon's essay.)

Make clear that you do not expect your students to be experts on anything other than the books they review. Your students need not situate their selected books in a wider body of related literature. In that sense, these book reviews become more akin to comprehensive response papers: But a good scholarly book review *is* a response to a work. If you are worried that your students will lack sufficient context or disciplinary knowledge with which to frame their reviews, you should relax your expectations on that front. If your students are worried that they won't have anything important to offer, remind them that their responses to the book *are* important. Reviews that address the bullet points listed above can do justice to the works—and can even offer valuable insights.

Proceed with the book review assignment in a manner similar to how you treat other written assignments. If you read and offer comments on drafts, do so here. If your students peer-edit each other's work, have them do so. Demonstrate how the social nature of writing extends to nearly all academic genres.

Consider collecting and distributing copies of the reviews to members of the class at the end of the term. You may need to seek each student's permission before including their work in the collection. But I assume that your classrooms are built on respect, trust, collaboration, and mutual understanding. Explaining your plans for dissemination from the outset would let your students know that they are writing their reviews not only for you but also for their peers.

If time permits, host a symposium where your students present their book reviews to their classmates. Allow them to discuss both their responses to the books they reviewed and what they learned about the skill of scholarly book reviewing.

Include a question about the book review assignment in your end-of-term course evaluations. Not all institutions allow tailoring of these evaluations. If yours does not, capture your students' impressions by asking this open-ended reflective question at another time: *What's one thing you learned by writing your scholarly book review?* You may find that any students considering graduate school especially appreciated the "practicality" of the assignment for its forward-looking preparatory goals.

Use exemplary student-written reviews as aspirational samples the next time you teach scholarly book reviewing. If your students' efforts impress you—and I would be surprised if you were never to receive a review approaching publishable quality—seek permission to share stellar examples with future students. Seeing what another student in a prior term offered in response to the assignment can help clarify your expectations and reinforce to your undergraduates that, yes, they are capable of producing intelligent, reflective reviews of scholarly books.

Scholarly Reviewing in the Graduate Sphere

Graduate students—particularly advanced graduate students—should be quite capable of writing scholarly book reviews of publishable quality. You may choose to mentor graduate students individually or in small groups. You may even invite graduate students to coauthor book reviews with you. If you teach a seminar or recurring workshop, or if you have an opportunity to introduce scholarly book reviewing in a classroom setting, you may adapt the suggestions in the prior section for your graduate students. If the goal you have for your graduate students is to write scholarly book reviews for publication, you will expect your students to situate the books they are reviewing within the related literature. And you will need to cover some additional ground.

Introduce your students to the venues in your field that publish scholarly book reviews. You likely know these venues already. (Chapter 1 of this book can also help.) If your students do not yet know of the primary scholarly associations or the flagship scholarly journals in their field (or fields), you will be filling an important gap in their knowledge.

Show your students how to identify new titles in their areas of interest or specialization. Consider sharing the strategies outlined in chapter 1. You could invite a research librarian to present on identifying venues and potential titles for review. Ideal would be for the students to seek single-authored or coauthored monographs in their areas of specialization, since reviews of such books are the most straightforward.

Work with your students to identify viable target venues and books for review. Offer to review initial email correspondence with book review editors or scholarly publishers. Remind any of your students who may be lacking confidence that they are qualified to review by virtue of their knowledge base, their disciplinary training, and the perspectives that they can offer as members of the intended audience for scholarly books in their field.

Ask your students to collect and read a number of book reviews that have been recently published by their target venue. These reviews will help your students understand the expectations of their target venue in terms of content, tone, and length.

Ensure that your students know how to read and take notes on a scholarly book for review. Consult the material in chapter 2, emphasizing the three types of notes: direct quotations, summaries of important ideas in their own words, and comments and questions invoked by the text. Thorough, attentive reading and note-taking are essential.

Once your students have read and taken notes on the books they are reviewing, explain how to convert reading notes into working notes. Chapter 3 will help here. The goal is for your students to use repeated passes through their reading notes to identify the most important material to mention in their reviews. They will then convert the resultant working notes into preliminary outlines for their reviews.

Work with your students, however you see fit, on drafts of their book reviews. At minimum, you will want to read and offer suggestions on their reviews. If the book is one you happen to have read, you can of course offer additional insights, though you should allow the students' perspectives to take the driver's seat.

Celebrate completion and submission with your students. Modeling such milestones helps to inject positivity into writing for publication, a task that graduate students should relish, not dread. Ask your students to keep you apprised of the disposition of their reviews—and to let you know once they have been published. After publication, make sure to send your students additional notes of congratulations (along with reminders to update their CVs with the publication details).

In lieu of incorporating scholarly book reviewing into a course, you could offer a three-part workshop spread across an academic term:

- Session 1 introduces the genre of the scholarly book review and addresses how to identify venues and books for review. (See chapter 1.)

- Session 2 transpires after the participants (ideally) have books in hand and have identified target venues. At this time you address how to read the book for review. (See chapter 2.)
- Session 3 transpires several weeks later, after the participants have (ideally) read and taken notes on the books they have identified. At this time you address how to write the review. (See chapters 3 and 5.)

Since I have written this book with graduate students in mind, I encourage you to use this book in your curricula. If you do so, I would love to hear from you about your experiences—and about your students' successes in seeing their scholarly book reviews accepted for publication. As their instructor and mentor, you can and should delight in their accomplishments. Congratulations!

ACKNOWLEDGMENTS

I HAVE A CONFESSION. Even though I stress in this book the importance of serial—that is, cover-to-cover, front-to-back—engagement with books, I often read the acknowledgments first, even when they're located in the back matter. By positioning books in the lives of their authors and by emphasizing the community inherent in writing and publishing, acknowledgments personalize the enterprise, orienting me toward greater empathy and generosity in my reviews. And acknowledgments themselves are written with a generous spirit. Who wouldn't want to relish such an appetizer of gratitude prior to partaking of the main course?

The seed for this book, as it turns out, was planted over lunch. Although others had previously told me that I should write a book, Peter Dougherty of Princeton University Press was the first to tell me that I should write a book *for him*. Former press director and founding editor of the Skills for Scholars series, Peter latched onto my commitment to engaged reviewing in summer 2019. After he fully retired, my project, still nascent, passed to the equally encouraging, nurturing hands of associate editor Matt Rohal. Thank you, Peter and Matt, as well as assistant editor Alena Chekanov, assistant production editor Jaden Young, copyeditor Karen Verde, and indexer Elise Hess. Others at the Press have worked behind the scenes to bring this book to you, and they all are overseen by director extraordinaire Christie Henry, who transmits a warmth and generosity of spirit, Midas-like, to all she touches.

Hats off to the three anonymous reviewers of the manuscript of this book. Their pre-publication reviews, eloquent models of the form, were packed with constructive suggestions. When the reviewers "get it": Well, that's one of the most rewarding, encouraging, uplifting feelings. The weaknesses that remain in the text are entirely my responsibility.

At Princeton University, my home from 2017 to 2023, I thank the brilliant Daphne Kalotay for introducing me to some of Princeton's most esteemed creative writers: Jhumpa Lahiri, Yiyun Li, Joyce Carol Oates, Tracy K. Smith. I met John McPhee through his letters of recommendation (miniature masterpieces) and Paul Muldoon over Zoom during the pandemic. For being excellent colleagues within the Office of International Programs, I thank Rebecca Graves-Bayazitoglu, Marisa Benson, Mary Cate Connors, Mariella Diaz, Amanda El-Kadi, Sammi Falvey, Julia Georgiana, Gisella Gisolo, Kimberly Jack, David Jarvis, Nancy Kanach, Scott Leroy, Olga Liamkina, John Luria, Matt Lynn, Barbara MacFarland, Jiyeon McHugh, Michelle McLean, Deirdre Moloney, Kimberly Perez, Ashley Prince, Sebastian Quiroz, Shahreen Rahman, Johanna Rossi Wagner, Manda Ryan, Francesca Schenker, Christine Tizzano, Meaghan Tohill, Michelle Tong, Beth Zawodniak, and Jordan Zilla. Keeping me grounded outside the office were fabulous colleagues Betsy Armstrong, Wendy Laura Belcher, Patrick Caddeau, Gilbert Collins, Kate Coppola, Cole Crittenden, Gabriel Crouch, Mags Dillon, Matthew Hernandez, Stan Katz, Marianne King, Christina Lee, Steve Lestition, Justine Levine, Marianne Ostendorf, Robin Palmer, Seth Perry, Amy Pszczolkowski, Albert Rivera, Alice Señeres, Wright Señeres, Mladenka Tomasevic, James Van Wyck, John Weeren, Matthew Weiner, and Elaine Willey.

Now at the University of Virginia, where I moved in late 2023, I thank colleagues Andrus Ashoo, Lauren Rhodes, Jennifer Schnelle, and Amy Tackitt for their camaraderie and kindness. Bravo to Daniel Sender and Michael Slon for keeping the music alive.

Kudos to Robert Brown, Alex Holzman, and Tom Radko, former editors of the *Journal of Scholarly Publishing*, for which I have written regularly since 2004. Now alongside editor Deborah Poff, I serve as book review editor, a role for which I do my best to help reviewers activate the ideas presented in this book. Over the years, I have learned much from the management and production team at the University of Toronto Press, and I often pass down this knowledge to my students. Thank you, especially, Sylvia Hunter, Mary Lui, Sheree Pell, Antonia Pop, Sandra Shaw, and Aidan Thompson.

You know you're lucky when other authors offer to serve as beta readers of your work. Thank you to fellow Princeton University Press author Laura Portwood-Stacer, who introduced me to the concept of "beta reading" in the first place and offered well-timed reassurance and encouragement. I don't feel out of place also thanking for their inspiration the authors I've cited in this book, many of whom are my writerly role models and, therefore, ideal teachers. Among them, special thanks to fellow Skills for Scholars authors Leonard Cassuto and Helen Sword.

Other friends have been lifelines throughout the consummation to completion of this book. Thank you to Marco Boscolo, Grant Eustice, Jeremy Flood, Jonathan Glade, Koji Matsunobu, and Mark Peltz. Perhaps this project truly originated in 2013, when Christopher Mayo first invited me into his history classroom at Grinnell College to teach scholarly book reviewing to undergraduates. Thank you, Chris. More recently, Matthew Heberger, Michelle Chan, and Gabriel Heberger hosted me in Paris in 2023 and 2024, where we discussed, among other things, the goals of reviewers of all types. Michelle reviews restaurants, and even in cases where a restaurant doesn't resonate with her palate or preferences, she tries to identify who might like it. Book reviewers, remember that point, which is summed up nicely by Jennifer Harris in her "Tips for an Academic Book Review": "Don't dismiss the work of others because it doesn't reflect your interests."

Ultimately, I would not be who I am without the love and support of my parents and brothers, who initially taught me to care about what others have to say. Thank you for being there for me, always.

APPENDIX

Questions for Scholarly Reviewers

HERE YOU WILL FIND a list of questions to consider answering in your scholarly reviews. Don't think for one moment that you would want to address *all* of these questions in a scholarly review. Instead, use these questions as starting points for what to record in your reading notes, as described in chapter 2. Then, when you write your review, as described in chapters 3 through 5, you will have descriptive and reflective material aplenty at your fingertips.

For coauthored books or edited volumes, substitute *author* in what follows with *authors*, *editor*, or *editors*, as appropriate. See also the material in chapter 4 for additional questions specific to other special types of scholarly publications. The questions below assume you are reviewing a print copy. If you are reviewing an electronic publication, you should also feel free to address the reader experience via that format in your review.

Context

Author

- Who is the author?
- What is the author's affiliation?
- What is the author's title? What other positions has the author held or does the author hold?
- For what is the author known?
- What qualifications or expertise does the author bring to the subject at hand?
- What honors or accolades has the author received that are germane to an understanding of this book?
- What other books has the author written? How were they received? Where does this book fit within the author's oeuvre?

Publisher

- Does the publisher of this book have a strong reputation in the field? If not, what are the publisher's disciplinary strengths?
- What audiences does this publisher typically serve?
- What similar titles has this publisher issued? How have those books been received?
- Is this book part of a series? If so, who is the series editor? What are some of the previous and forthcoming books in the series?

Audience

- Who is (or appears to be) the intended audience of the book?
- What does the author take for granted that the readers already know?
- Can you imagine the book being adopted for classroom use? If so, at what level?

Presentation

- Does the title or subtitle of the book suggest the author's thesis? Do section or chapter titles advance this thesis?
- How does the author's use of language reflect the intended audience?
- Are key concepts, terms, and variables appropriately defined and used precisely, consistently?
- What role does theory play in the author's presentation?
- Does the author rely heavily on acronyms? If a large number of acronyms is necessary, does the author provide a list in the front matter?
- Does the text read easily, or is it complex and dense, with overly long paragraphs, sections, or chapters?
- How does the pacing influence the presentation?
- What design elements make the book easy (or difficult) to read?
- Is the quality of the paper, binding, and presentation in line with your expectations for a book at this price point?
- How strong is the copyediting? How distracting are any formatting, language, or other such errors?

Content

Structure

- How many parts, sections, or chapters comprise the book?
- How long is an average chapter? Is the book "balanced" across parts, sections, or chapters?
- What is included in the front matter?
- What is included in the back matter?
- What special features, if any, are included (maps, chronologies, timelines, flowcharts, genealogical or pedigree charts, musical examples, glossaries, color plates, datasets)?
- What types of indexes are included? How thorough and helpful do they seem?

Argument

- What are the author's stated goals? What does the author believe to be the value of the book?
- What is the primary thesis of the book? What are the secondary theses?
- Within what school of thought or upon what theoretical or intellectual foundation does the author stake the primary argument?

Substantiation

- What sources does the author use? Are they suitable? How does the author use them?
- Are tables and figures used effectively? Are legends, headers, and axis labels complete? Are all the tables and figures mentioned in proximal text?

- Would additional special features, such as tables or figures, have helped support or emphasize the argument?
- What sort of referencing system is used? Is it helpful or obtrusive?
- How extensive are the references? Are they current? Are they appropriate to the subject and to the author's goals?
- Which references were surprising or unexpected? What references did you expect to see that the author did not include?
- Are the appendixes (if any) necessary and helpful to substantiating or furthering the author's claims?
- What additional information, mentioned in the text, would have been helpful to have presented in an appendix?

Consequence

Associations

- How is this work distinct from any similar works with which you are familiar?
- Can the argument be extended to be relevant to other cases or contexts? If so, to what cases or contexts?
- What questions have been raised by this book that you wish would be addressed in future scholarship?
- Does the book introduce a new framework? Does it extend or challenge paradigms?
- Would readers from other disciplines benefit from this work? If so, which disciplines?
- What is something that surprised you—something you were not expecting to encounter in this book—that you continue to think about?

Assessment

- How well does the author accomplish the stated goals of the book?
- Based on the author's stated goals, does the book at least meet your expectations? Why or why not?
- Are you persuaded by the arguments presented by the author?
- What significant knowledge does the book contribute or advance?
- How valuable are the core contributions of this work to the field?
- How effective is the author's prose?
- How well does the work flow? Do the chapters seem logically ordered and organized?
- Do you ultimately trust the author? Does the author project a command of the material?
- Who would benefit from reading this book?
- Is the work too long? Too short? Just right?
- Was the time you invested in reading this book time well spent?
- In what ways has reading this book altered your understanding of the subject?
- Now that you've read this book, how do you see your field—and the world—differently?

NOTES

1: Getting Started as a Scholarly Book Reviewer

1. Milardo, *Crafting Scholarship*, 64. Some things never seem to change. Consider this assessment by Bruce MacPhail from thirty-five years prior: "Book reviews are generally not appreciated as fully as they deserve to be." MacPhail, "Book Reviews," 55.

2. On scholarly book reviews as a genre, see Hartley, "Reading and Writing."

3. For example, you may know of journals that publish *book review articles, state-of-the-art papers, bibliometric reviews*, and other types of reviews. For discussions of these subgenres, see, for example, Hallinger and Kovačević, "Applying Bibliometric Review Methods"; and Hyland and Diani, *Academic Evaluation*.

4. I have also seen the term *omnibus review* refer to what I am here calling a *review essay*.

5. As Lynn Z. Bloom explains, "By the time a book is published it has survived the scrutiny of a multitude of gatekeepers." Bloom, "How to Talk," 8.

6. Halpenny, "Responsibilities of Scholarly Publishers," 223.

7. Pool, "Point of View."

8. S. Stephenson Smith rightly notes that book reviews "must concentrate meaning into small compass." Smith, *Craft of the Critic*, 45.

9. Ylva Lindholm-Romantschuk finds that "the reviewing process in the humanities tends to be somewhat more delayed than in the social sciences." Lindholm-Romantschuk, *Scholarly Book Reviewing*, 132. And William Germano notes that "your second book may be published before the reviews are all in for your first." Germano, *Getting It Published*, 232.

10. East, "Scholarly Book Review."

11. What about blogs and other online venues that skew toward more specialized audiences? Some of these venues publish reviews of scholarly books, have high

profiles within their fields, and even include layers of editorial vetting. For scholars of higher education, for example, the practitioner-oriented *Chronicle of Higher Education* is one such venue. I would generally qualify reviews published in such outlets as "journalistic" reviews. Compared with reviews published in scholarly outlets, journalistic reviews more often have shorter paragraphs, fewer quotations, clear connections to contemporary discussions and events, and obvious applications or takeaways.

12. McCanse, *Art of the Book Review*, 4.

13. Baker, *U and I*, 64. See Belcher, *Writing Your Journal Article*, 169–70.

14. Beer, "In Defence."

15. Beer, "In Defence."

16. Donovan, "Long and the Short," 36. Donovan is also a paleontologist who writes frequently about scholarly writing and publishing.

17. He is also not alone. See also, among many others, arguments offered by Addis, "Academic Book Reviews"; Eastman, "In Defense"; Gibbs et al., "On the Potential of Book Reviews"; and O'Neill, "Necessity of Book Reviews."

18. See Vinyard and Colvin, *Demystifying Scholarly Metrics*, 88; Krieger, *Scholar's Survival Manual*, 280.

19. Stahl, "So What."

20. William Germano explains that academic authors commonly make more money from these "consequences of a publication" than from royalties on sales. Germano, *Getting It Published*, 125.

21. Deutsch, *In Praise of Good Bookstores*, 56 (original emphasis).

22. McCanse, *Art of the Book Review*, 5.

23. Wulf, "Efficient Reading."

24. See, for example, Felber, "Book Review"; McKinzie, "Noble Art of Reviewing"; Simon, "Pleasures of Book Reviewing"; Worsham, "Endangered Scholarly Book Review."

25. Gibbs et al., "On the Potential of Book Reviews."

26. French, "Academic Writing."

27. "Writing [a book review] for one of the top journals in your field means that those whom you respect and admire will see your work and, you hope, respect and admire it. Being in good company is always appealing." Toor, "Why Bother." And John East, in an excellent survey of the book review in the humanities, notes that writing a book review offers "a means of getting published in a prestigious journal with less effort than is needed to write a full-scale research article." East, "Scholarly Book Review," 58.

28. Rich Furman and Julie Kinn agree that book reviews are a "good way to gain confidence and to begin to build experience and a track record of publications." As a result, "they are often scholars' first publications." Furman and Kinn, *Practical Tips*, 56.

29. According to Wayne Journell, book reviews "are often easy ways to get into top-tier journals, so they are particularly useful for doctoral students and early-career faculty who want to start building reputations in their fields of study." Journell, *Becoming*, 29. See also Burgess, "Learning to Be"; Childress, *PhDictionary*, 30; De Costa, "Opening the Gates"; Habibie, "Gatekeeping and Gateopening"; Toor, "Why Bother."

30. Leahy, "(Selfish) Power," 48.

31. See May, *Write Crowd*.

32. Ross, "Fondling the Lemur's Tail," 17.

33. Brienza, "Why You (Yes, You!) Should Write." Françoise Salager-Meyer and Beverly Lewin concur, explaining that "scholars are dependent on other scholars, and this close dependency is fundamental to the advancement of knowledge." Salager-Meyer and Lewin, "Introduction," 12.

34. Haggerty and Doyle, *57 Ways*, 91.

35. Jensen, *Write No Matter What*, 117.

36. Stevens, *Write More, Publish More*, 126. To Beth Luey, book "reviewing is a relatively quick and painless way to publish." And to Robert Lussier, a book review "is a fairly quick and easy non-refereed publication. . . . If you already read the book, all you have to do is write the review." To me, "all you have to do" invokes activities requiring little thought or intentionality—not intellectual activities like writing scholarly book reviews. Luey, *Handbook for Academic Authors*, 36; Lussier, *Publish Don't Perish*, 163.

37. If you're interested and qualified, don't count yourself out. For example, was I delighted to work with a high school teacher with twenty years of experience (and a relevant doctoral degree) on a review for the *Journal of Scholarly Publishing*? Of course!

38. Karen Kelsky warns new faculty members (or those aspiring to such positions) against writing too many book reviews, given that they "count for little on your CV." She continues: "A book review does show that you are considered legitimate enough to review a significant book for an established journal—that is, that you have some degree of reputation and visibility in your field. So it will not harm your record, as long as it is accompanied by peer-reviewed publications, and as long as you don't have more than about three [reviews]. . . . Be aware that a preponderance

of book reviews on the record of a junior candidate (say, more than five or so) will cast doubt on your understanding of publishing for tenure." Kelsky, *Professor Is In*, 105. Wendy Laura Belcher offers a similar warning: "Depending on your discipline, you must publish six to ten book reviews before you have something equivalent in weight to a research article. In some fields or departments, book reviews never add up, counting for nothing." Belcher, *Writing Your Journal Article*, 39.

39. Explains Rachel Toor, "there's no such thing as a free book: The commitment to write a review is much greater than just the time you spend reading the book." Toor, "Why Bother."

40. Fish, *Is There a Text*.

41. As Jennifer Harris aptly and succinctly writes, ideal reviewers "will read books generously, thoughtfully, and with an understanding of the field." Harris, "Tips."

42. If you can parse the double negative, the following sentence could reassure: "Young and hungry beginners or near-beginners are not infrequently as much on top of their fields as are august eminences." Hoge and West, "Academic Book Reviewing," 37.

43. Such was the case for Matthew Deroo, whose doctoral adviser at Michigan State University served as an ideal mentor regarding writing for scholarly publication. See Deroo, "Writing with, Learning from, and Paying Forward."

44. Perry, "Who Do You Think You Are?"

45. Van Viegen, "Writing Belonging," 53.

46. See, for example, Gump, "Writing Successful Covering Letters"; Gump, "Recovering the Covering Letter." For the latest and greatest evolution of my perspectives, see Gump, "Reimagining the Covering Letter."

47. Brienza, "Writing Academic Book Reviews."

48. For example, *Metascience*, a review journal, annually publishes between 100 and 120 reviews of books in the history and philosophy of science and in science and technology studies. A November 2022 editorial helpfully details the review types, solicitation policies, and stylistic expectations. See Wray, Nash, and Simon, "What We Publish." And the *Journal of Teaching in Physical Education* published an editorial in 2024 indicating the addition of a book review section. See Hemphill, "Scholarly Book Reviews."

49. Wray, Nash, and Simon, "What We Publish," 295.

50. Contemplate the following, adjusting the pronouns as necessary: "One can often tell more about a [job] candidate's scholarly standards by reading his reviews than by reading his articles." Hoge and West, "Academic Book Reviewing," 36. And,

in the words of Bruce Mazlish: "A book reviews the reviewer as much as the reviewer reviews the book." Mazlish, "Art of Reviewing."

51. Henige, "Reviewing Reviewing," 24.

52. Prior to the advent of electronic books, publishers routinely mailed hard copies to key journals, hopeful that a review would ensue.

53. See https://cshm-schm.ca/en/journal/books-for-review.

54. See https://www.food-culture.org.

55. I wish it could go without saying that you should always follow through when you *offer* to review a book, as well. Unfortunately, some potential reviewers aren't especially conscientious. See, for example, Barkan, "On the Art of Reviewing."

56. Rich Furman and Julie Kinn refer to this exercise as "wandering through the stacks." Furman and Kinn, *Practical Tips*, 59.

57. Trubek, *So You Want to Publish a Book?*, 107. I once shared this quotation with a librarian; she was not amused.

58. In doing so myself, I learned in September 2022 that Cornell University Press has discontinued its seasonal catalogs in favor of more creative approaches to marketing its books, including highlighting seasonal "collections" on the press's website.

59. Lynn Z. Bloom offers an excellent overview of the subject, addressing the importance of disciplinary expertise, fairness, and the avoidance of conflicts of interest. Bloom, "How to Talk." See also Ashley, "Ethics of Academic Book Reviewing"; other articles in the Spring 2002 issue of the *Journal of Information Ethics* (a special issue on "Ethical Aspects of Book Reviewing"); and Gump, "Ethics of Scholarly Book Reviewing."

60. See, for example, Batten, "'Thankless Task'?" Some journals, such as *American Historical Review*, have different policies regarding a reviewer's prior involvement with a published work. Always check with your target venue before proceeding.

61. If you would be content with an electronic copy, your institutional library may have an arrangement that allows you to download one for no charge. I have also purchased copies of books I have reviewed, as well. Sometimes publishers never respond to requests for review copies, and sometimes I just love a book that much and wish to have a copy for my personal library. I've found that the contents of books I don't own are more easily forgotten than the contents of books I own.

62. Some couriers require phone numbers for package deliveries.

63. On another occasion, an editor received reviews of the same book just days apart and elected to publish both of them in the same issue, thus creating an unplanned omnibus review.

64. James Hoge and James West note the capacity that securing review copies has "for stalling the entire operation." Hoge and West, "Academic Book Reviewing," 37.

2: Reading for Reviewing

1. Anderson, *Scholarly Communication*, 233. Rick Anderson should be pleased to know that I unearthed this sentence not by mining his book for a relevant quotation but by attentively reading it for the purposes of writing a review for the *Journal of Scholarly Publishing*. William Germano invokes a similar distinction between scholars who *read* a text and those who use the text, instrumentally, to *look for* particular information. Germano, *Getting It Published*, 214. And Anthony Grafton describes the *looking for* phenomenon as "a particularly postmodern way of approaching texts: rapid, superficial, appropriative, individualistic." Grafton, *Codex in Crisis*, 56.

2. And you would be in good company. Roland Barthes apparently preferred readers who write in books, for they give "life to an otherwise mute text." See Williams, "Shelf Life." And to essayist and bibliophile Anne Fadiman and her family, "it was no sacrilege to treat them [books] as wantonly as desire and pragmatism dictated. Hard use was a sign not of disrespect but of intimacy." Fadiman, "Never Do That," 38.

3. Pyne notes that "writing, after all, begins as a verb." Pyne, *Voice and Vision*, 4.

4. Places of publication are less commonly being required in bibliographic entries, with major style guides dropping the requirement in 2016 (Modern Language Association), 2019 (American Psychological Association), 2020 (American Medical Association), and 2024 (University of Chicago Press).

5. According to Jeffrey Williams, "Sometimes there is a kind of book karma. That is, writers correct the mistakes of their last book in their next." Williams, "Book Angst." And as William Germano puts it, "The next book is always an opportunity to write a book better than your last." Germano, *Getting It Published*, 234.

6. In the humanities and book-oriented social sciences, dissertations, when done well (and when written by individuals aspiring to academic careers), are often revised into "first books"—a term I've always found to be charmingly optimistic: The term presumes that the author will someday complete at least one subsequent book. If you happen to be a dissertator in one of these fields, you won't want to

miss William Germano's *From Dissertation to Book* or Katelyn Knox and Allison Van Deventer's *Dissertation-to-Book Workbook*.

7. Germano, *Getting It Published*, 230.

8. Realize, of course, that most production details are beyond the control of the author.

9. Price, *What We Talk About*, 110–17.

10. Gump, review of *Inside the Critics' Circle*, 300.

11. For one example of especially effective—I'd venture even *elegant*—titling, William Germano gives away his thesis in the subtitle of his *On Revision: The Only Writing That Counts*. For another example of a thesis embedded in a title, consider Leonard Cassuto's *Academic Writing as if Readers Matter*. (That *as if*!)

12. Chenail, "How to Read and Review," 1637.

13. Zachary Shore, in *Grad School Essentials*, explains such a process quite clearly in two chapters on "How to Read." See also Wulf, "Efficient Reading."

14. You might sense an irony here, since you'll be extracting material from the book to serve your review. But the difference is that, to find this material, you're engaging deeply with the text in the first place.

15. Either coincidentally or due to effective (and lasting) training, these three types of notes directly parallel the types of notes differentiated by Kate Turabian: "Be sure to clearly distinguish what you quote from a source, what you paraphrase or summarize from a source, and your own thoughts." Turabian et al., *Student's Guide*, 68.

16. The bracketing suggestion comes straight from Turabian et al., *Student's Guide*, 70.

17. Pyne, *Voice and Vision*, 19.

18. Embedded herein is one point that differentiates most scholarly books from dissertations. Dissertators, especially ethnographic researchers, often use quotations to present and advance their arguments.

19. Just be aware that these verbs can operate as metalinguistic smokescreens in scholarly texts. (On their obfuscatory use, see Tan, "Problem.") One of your jobs as a reviewer is to sniff out empty signaling.

20. I repeat this point here because the confidence behind your positioning underscores the reception of your review. Be certain you are not a "mere reader" (ouch!) with but a "running acquaintance" of a field: "To review a book when one is a mere reader of its area and has a running acquaintance of it is to do a great disservice to the author, her or his work and area of study." Orteza y Miranda, "On Book Reviewing," 201.

21. Haag, *Revise*, 91.

22. See Gump, review of *Writing for Publication*. Others have noticed the same phenomenon. For one: "Often left over or copied straight from the author's book proposal, the highly conventional introductory section that describes the upcoming chapters at length is usually one of the most boring things in the universe." Hayot, *Elements of Academic Style*, 100.

23. Germano, *On Revision*, 145. Notes James Richardson: "Only half of writing is saying what you mean. The other half is preventing people from reading what they expected you to mean." Richardson, *Vectors*, 99.

24. If the sociolinguistics behind such assessment intrigues you, consult Julia Molinari's *What Makes Writing Academic*.

25. Hayot, *Elements of Academic Style*, 49.

26. Wait! The book I'm reviewing doesn't have an index! If you believe an index would improve the usability and usefulness of the book, you are welcome to note this point in your review. (Indexes may unfortunately be omitted for financial, temporal, or other logistical reasons.)

27. Germano, *On Revision*, 182. (I'm not oblivious to how you could be feeling at this point. That's why I've placed this apt quotation so close to the end of this chapter.)

28. Harris, "Tips."

3: Writing a Scholarly Book Review

1. Gail Pool writes that "independent judgment is the only worthwhile judgment." Your impressions are worthwhile and important. Pool, *Faint Praise*, 138.

2. Ah, but what about Artificial Intelligence? Anything I write about the matter now—in summer 2024—will be outdated by the time you read this text. Balázs Kovács, of Yale University, has conducted groundbreaking research on online restaurant reviews, discovering that AI-generated reviews tricked (human) readers into believing they were not fake approximately half the time. "Fake Yelp reviews are only the tip of the iceberg," according to Kovács, in a profile by Aimee Levitt. The implications for scholarly book reviewing are yet to be seen. See Kovács, "Turing Test"; Levitt, "AI Can Write."

3. Wheelan, *Write for Your Life*, 46.

4. In a fittingly meta move, one generous peer reviewer of this manuscript—before acceptance for publication—provided a fully annotated reading of the original draft of this book, offering nearly one hundred questions, suggestions, reflections, and other considerations, all of which helped me improve the text.

5. Reviewers who contribute such reviews are typically invited by the review editors, who often seek perspectives that they presume will differ.

6. Gard, *Book Reviewing*, 37. Gard's book was published in a year—1927—when, according to the foreword, the average American spent $1.10 per year on books. (Adjusted for inflation, the figure is $19.94 in 2024 dollars. *Quiz*: How many books have you bought so far this year that cost more than that inflation-adjusted amount *apiece*?)

7. Gard, *Book Reviewing*, 47.

8. Give this image from a work of prizewinning fiction a moment of reflection: "Books diverge and radiate, as fluid as finches on isolated islands." Powers, *Overstory*, 382.

9. If you must have a seven-paragraph organizational structure for your review—not exactly a template, but close—consult Brienza, "Writing Academic Book Reviews."

10. Tobin, "Commensality," 49.

11. According to Carol Fisher Saller, "Discriminating readers look for reasons to trust a writer and reasons not to. Inelegant expression and carelessness in the details are two reasons not to." Saller, *Subversive Copy Editor*, 11.

12. Ashley, "Ethics of Academic Book Reviewing," 47.

13. In the wise words of Beth Luey, "nitpicking is neither useful nor appreciated." Luey, *Handbook for Academic Authors*, 37. Yet Mark Wilson writes that "it is necessary to nitpick, no matter how good the book is, in order to retain credibility as a reviewer." Untrue. Credibility in reviewing comes from demonstrating relevant disciplinary knowledge, describing the contents of the book accurately and fairly, and signaling that the book was read carefully and conscientiously. Wilson, review of *Reassembling Scholarly Communications*, 191.

14. Writes David Weissman: "Accurately reporting ideas and arguments doesn't require liking them." Weissman, "Some Thoughts," 716.

15. Fussell, "Vanity in Review," 69.

16. Cortada, "Five Ways," 35.

17. Mishan, "Life of James Beard." In the same key, Ronald Tobin concludes that "A bad review is one produced by a writer's notion of what he or she would have liked to see rather than what was actually composed." Tobin, "Commensality," 48.

18. This point marks another of Cortada's "sins" of book reviewing. Cortada, "Five Ways," 36.

19. Although the context is that of a critical book manuscript and not a book review, see Kaiser, "Peer Review."

20. Germano, *Getting It Published*, 132.

21. Frank Swinnerton implores reviewers to "find the vital speck" in a work—and not "to dwell meaninglessly upon the difficulty of the search." Swinnerton, *Reviewing and Criticism*, 41.

22. Wolper, "On Academic Reviewing," 270.

23. Simon, "Pleasures of Book Reviewing," 238.

24. Klemp, "Reviewing Academic Books," 138.

25. Chong, *Inside the Critics' Circle*, 85.

26. Simon, "Pleasures of Book Reviewing," 238. Jeffrey Kahan concurs, writing that, in a review, "you might want to go easier on an assistant professor, just as a matter of professional courtesy." Kahan, *Getting Published*, 35.

27. Felber, "Book Review," 169.

28. Smith, *Craft of the Critic*, 47.

29. Quindlen, *Write for Your Life*, 110.

30. Haag, *Revise*, 85.

31. Shatz, "Odd Case," 40.

32. See American Psychological Association, *Publication Manual*, section 4.12.

33. McCloskey, *Economical Writing*, 44. See also Haag, *Revise*, 57; Tan, "Problem."

34. Germano, *Getting It Published*, ix (original emphases).

35. But what if the venue for your review asks for chapter-by-chapter summaries? If you don't feel emboldened to challenge the directions, keep the summaries brief, and ensure that your review includes thematic synthesis and analysis, as well.

36. Here is a more comprehensive list of "empty" adjectives that I share with my students: *admirable, amazing, awesome, captivating, challenging, difficult, engaging, enjoyable, excellent, exciting, eye-opening, fabulous, fascinating, ideal, incredible, inspiring, interesting, intriguing, meaningful, overwhelming, powerful, remarkable, revelatory, rewarding, rigorous, stimulating, strenuous, surprising, transformative, tremendous, unique, wonderful*. You are likely aware of others. When such adjectives work their way into your prose, do avoid having them stand alone, unelaborated, where their emptiness is most obvious and meaning is most open to interpretation. Why would what's interesting to you necessarily be interesting to me?

37. King, *On Writing*, 125.

38. Sword, *Writer's Diet*, 43.

39. As James Hoge and James West note: "Academic journals which forbid footnotes in reviews are much mistaken," since reviewers must be permitted to support their criticisms. Hoge and West, "Academic Book Reviewing," 38.

40. Wolper, "On Academic Reviewing," 274.

41. Milardo, *Crafting Scholarship*, 75.

42. Benade, Stewart, and Devine, "Writing for Various Academic Purposes," 11.

43. Swinnerton, *Reviewing and Criticism*, 22.

44. Gump, review of *What They Didn't Teach You*. The quotation appeared on the cover of Gray and Drew, *What They Didn't Teach You*. Quotations appearing on the back cover are more common. For example, a sentence from my January 2010 *Journal of Scholarly Publishing* review of the first edition of Wendy Laura Belcher's *Writing Your Journal Article in Twelve Weeks: A Guide to Academic Publishing Success* (SAGE, 2009) appears on the back cover of the second edition (University of Chicago Press, 2019).

45. Pool, "Point of View."

46. McCanse, *Art of the Book Review*, 9. Likewise, Jennifer Harris offers a list of excellent questions for reviewers to consider. She notes: "A good book review need not address all of these or even the majority; but the attentive reading required to produce a decent review does mean that the reviewer should have a handle on them." Harris, "Tips."

47. Chenail, "How to Read and Review," 1638.

48. Updike, *Hugging the Shore*, 851.

49. Hoge and West, "Academic Book Reviewing," 39.

4: Considering Special Cases

1. Reference books, by contrast, are more likely to be reviewed in specialist publications for librarians and other information professionals. For a survey of that literature prior to the advent of the internet, see Walford, "Reference Books."

2. Outside the scope of this book—but not outside the realm of possibility for scholarly reviews—are other materials of scholarly or professional interest. Depending on your field, these materials could include films, audio recordings, websites, podcasts, archives, document collections, museums and other historical sites, and other media genres of interest to scholars.

3. Kelsky, *Professor Is In*, 57.

4. Furstenberg, *Behind the Academic Curtain*, 95.

5. Increasing pressures to publish on the part of scholars and evolving economies of scale on the part of publishers have together created an environment of relentless productivity. Digitally published edited volumes, even when complemented by hard-copy editions (now likely printed on demand), allow the possibility for the purchase of individual chapters, sacrificing the whole for its parts while

cultivating platforms for "breakout scholarship" that can feed the publisher's bottom line. The more edited volumes that are published, the greater the possibility for such breakout scholarship. Publishers seem willing, as well, to allow for a more substantial shift of editorial responsibilities onto the scholars who propose (or who agree to curate) such volumes, saving overhead and other costs related to the preparation of manuscripts for publication. (Publishers refer to the scholars who spearhead edited collections as "authors," but I refer to them as "editors" in this section.)

6. For more sanguine views on the potentials of edited collections, see Ambrosio, review of *The Aesthetics of Science*; Peters, Jandrić, and Hayes, "Revisiting the Concept"; and Webster, *Edited Collection*.

7. Germano, *Getting It Published*, 108.

8. On the ethics of respecting language variations, see Sotejeff-Wilson and Lehtinen, "Language Professionals."

9. Jonathan Jansen agrees that edited volumes that lack concluding chapters—most such volumes, unfortunately—have missed a key opportunity to offer generative syntheses. To Jansen, these final chapters separate "a world-class edited book from just another compilation of other people's research ideas." Jansen, "Editing a Scholarly Book," 166.

10. Baverstock, "Introduction."

11. Gump, review of *Contemporary Publishing*.

12. Gump, review of *How Writing Faculty Write*.

13. For example, see Immler, review of *Literary Reviewing*.

14. Gump, review of *Scholarly Publication Trajectories*.

15. Previously unpublished works are occasionally included in books referred to as anthologies. In such cases, you will want to describe the new material and its merits.

16. Pierazzo, *Digital Scholarly Editing*, 149.

17. Dahlhaus, "'New Grove,'" 249.

18. Encyclopedias and other encyclopedic volumes can be veritable minefields, once you start looking. (The reason? The contributors—who may easily number in the scores—are almost always expected to check their own facts.) Some factual errors persist from edition to edition in certain works (I keep my own errata), making me long for a straightforward method for submitting corrections for future editions. I was delighted to learn that Guilford Press, for one, provides a solution: a dedicated errata@guilford.com email address that signals not that Guilford Press books must contain errors (what books don't?) but that the press values accuracy.

19. Gump, review of *Food and Culture*, 609.

20. Shrock, *Choral Repertoire*, v.

21. Shrock, *Choral Repertoire*, 2nd ed., vii.

22. Gump, review of *Manual for Writers*.

23. In fact, scholars of rhetoric and composition Lynée Lewis Gaillet and Letizia Guglielmo contend that a "review essay 'counts' as a scholarly article in the tallying of publications for hiring and promotion purposes and should be included in the 'articles and essays' section of your CV." Gaillet and Guglielmo, *Scholarly Publication*, 38. Yes, disciplines weigh and rank different scholarly genres in different ways. Always check with a trusted mentor if you are unsure where to include different types of scholarly reviews on your CV.

24. Gump, review of *Murōji*. (According to WorldCat, a third English-language monograph with *rearranging* in its title was published in Sweden in 2005; it addresses pedestrian movement within cities—urban pilgrimages, by a stretch.)

25. Gump, review of *Writing on the Job*.

26. Gump, review of *On Revision*.

27. On the helpfulness of disciplinary focus for review essays, see Brown, "Reasons for Publishing," 23–24.

28. Bloom, "How to Talk," 13.

29. I unapologetically perpetuate, in the words of critic Louis Menand, "the general sentiment that reading is somehow superior to viewing." Menand, "Remainders," 70.

30. According to Michael Adams, "A good book review is not a freely ranging essay; the book in question is not merely the review's point of departure, but its persistent focus." (Adams might question whether essays by the likes of Adam Gopnik or Jill Lepore are thus truly *reviews*.) Adams, "In the Profession," 203.

31. Gump, review of *Very Short Book*.

32. Cortada, "Five Ways," 35.

33. Bardsley, "Liza Dalby's *Geisha*."

34. Lane, "High Crimes," 64.

35. For an excellent primer that illuminates the benefits and challenges of collaborative scholarly writing, see Thomson and Kamler, *Writing for Peer Reviewed Journals*, chapter 8.

36. Alford, McFadyen, and Nozue, "Collaborating in Writing," 99.

37. Silvia, *Write It Up*, 71.

38. Seth Schwartz contrasts "passive coauthoring" (making marginal comments about what should be done to a text) with "active coauthoring" (actually making the proposed revisions to the text itself). You likely won't know which approach

suits you better—or which approach you'd like your coauthor to take—until you've been through the process of coauthoring. In the end, the choice is a matter of how much control you'd like to have over the text yourself. Schwartz, *Savvy Academic*, 425.

39. Gump and Gump, review of *Getting Your Research Paper Published*.

5: Improving the Craft and Context of Reviewing

1. Wolper, "World of Fleas," 228.

2. Child, Bertholle, and Beck, *Mastering the Art*, 126–38. Readers are even challenged, on p. 127, to develop their "own personal omelette style." As a youth, I idolized Julia Child. My wish with this book is that you are inspired to develop your own scholarly book reviewing style.

3. For an excellent argument in favor of the scholarly review as art, see Nord, "Reviewing Scholarly Books." Others, such as Bilhartz ("In 500 Words"), take for granted that scholarly book reviewing is an art.

4. I have borrowed the concept of connoisseurship from the work of Elliot Eisner, who argues that scholars should seek to develop rich appreciations of their fields and then make their knowledge public. See, for example, Eisner, "Roots of Connoisseurship."

5. Renkl, "I Reread a Book."

6. In language typical of the mid-twentieth century, John Drewry explains that "when one thinks enough about a book to do a review—with all that the review implies—he is making that book a part of him—his thinking and memory processes." Drewry, *Book Reviewing*, 4. Taking a step toward existentialism, Pierre Bayard writes that "we *are* the sum of these accumulated books" that populate our "inner libraries." Bayard, *How to Talk*, 73 (original emphasis).

7. Childress, *PhDictionary*, 30.

8. Dettmar, *How to Chair*, 182.

9. Sturm, "Critical Gift," 450.

10. Chinnery, "Editorial," 418.

11. Strunk and White, *Elements of Style*, 17.

12. Leahy, "(Selfish) Power," 49.

13. May, *Write Crowd*, 72.

14. Conover, *Immersion*, 126.

15. McCanse, *Art of the Book Review*, 16.

16. Adams, "In the Profession," 203.

17. McCanse, *Art of the Book Review*, 16.

18. Cited in Sword, *Air & Light & Time & Space*, 120. For more of Sword's ideas on stylishness and wit in scholarly writing, see her *Stylish Academic Writing*.

19. Toor, "Becoming."

20. Zinsser, *On Writing Well*, chapter 19.

21. Pyne, *Style and Story*, 79.

22. Sword, *Stylish Academic Writing*, chapter 5. See also Sword, *Writer's Diet*.

23. And if these ideas aren't radical enough for you, consult the even more creative possibilities outlined by Sean Sturm in Sturm, "Critical Gift," 453.

24. Schwartz, *Savvy Academic*, 200.

25. Klinkenborg, *Several Short Sentences*. For additional inspiration, check out the works of writer and poet Sarah Manguso.

26. Hayot, *Elements of Academic Style*, 171.

27. Haag, *Revise*, 268. The whole of Haag's chapter 10, on fine-tuning figurative language, offers excellent advice about metaphors in scholarly writing.

28. Wright, "Rethinking the Literary Review," 140.

29. Zinsser, "Unexpected Visitors," 123.

30. Lane, "Taming Nature," 75. For an anthology of Lane's writings, see Lane, *Nobody's Perfect*.

31. In an April 21, 1968, letter to fellow writer Tom Wolfe, Thompson wrote: "Every now and then I stumble on a word-jewel; they have a special dimension, like penetrating oil." Thompson, *Fear and Loathing*, 54.

32. In chapter 1 of this book, you may have noticed my use of the word *freudenfreude* (being happy for others' successes): proof that writerly style and voice cross-fertilize genres.

33. For example, *trouvaille* is a genuine "lucky find" that is courtesy of Nicholson Baker, *U and I*, 40. And I learned *éclaircissement* from Roger Rosenblatt; the term appears in his *The Story I Am*, 173. Elsewhere Rosenblatt explains his approach: "I enjoy dropping in exotic words from time to time. Either they put off readers or drive them to the dictionary. I do it anyway." Rosenblatt, *Unless It Moves*, 62.

34. See https://phrontistery.info/index.html.

35. Vendler, *Art of Shakespeare's Sonnets*.

36. Gump, review of *Publishing from Your Doctoral Research*.

37. Gump, review of *Inside the Critics' Circle*.

38. Gump, review of *Voice and Vision*; Gump, review of *Style and Story*.

39. Gump, review of *Economical Writing*. McCloskey is far from alone. I could list several other writers on writing who discourage use of the semicolon.

McCloskey points out that colons, too, are overused in academic writing. McCloskey, *Economical Writing*, 75.

40. Chong, *Inside the Critics' Circle*, 64.

41. Hayot, *Elements of Academic Style*, 80. Before throwing down the gauntlet, Hayot offers this context: "The best writing is the best because it upends standards in some way, either by enacting them with opalescent, devastating skill (at the limit, the truest violation) or by carving new paths through the shady woods that separate what the reader understands from what the writer means." Wow.

42. Coincidentally, Rudolf Flesch sets an average of thirty words per sentence as the tipping point between a "difficult" and "very difficult" text in his *The Art of Readable Writing*. If you've heard of either the Flesch reading-ease score or the Flesch–Kinkaid Grade Level, you've previously encountered the name—and the concept of sentence length contributing to complexity.

43. Sword, *Stylish Academic Writing*, 8.

44. Nord, "Reviewing Scholarly Books," 199.

45. Pushman, *How to Read*, 3.

46. Thanks to Justin Chang for the concept of "tucking art into the margins." Chang, "Screams from a Marriage," 87.

47. With respect to writing in general, that message is, fittingly, a central theme in Helen Sword's *Writing with Pleasure*.

48. Eastman, "In Defense."

49. Germano, *Getting It Published*, ix (original emphases).

50. Hayot, *Elements of Academic Style*, 218.

51. As Jean-Pierre Hérubel notes, specifically with respect to the context of scholarly book reviews: "Cross-fertilization from one academic discipline to another offers fresh insights, new approaches, including critical techniques, theoretical perspectives, and methodologies, not always employed in a given discipline." Hérubel, "Disciplinary Fluidity," 418.

52. Gump, "Special Section," 5.

53. Woodcock, "Critic as Mediator," 208.

54. Jeffrey Wasserstrom, a historian of modern China and former editor of the *Journal of Asian Studies*, agrees. For a compelling take on the importance of reading diverse types of reviews, see his "Why Read Book Reviews?"

55. Williams, "Introduction."

56. Wray, Nash, and Simon, "What We Publish," 294.

57. Glasberg, "Jhumpa Lahiri Returns to Barnard."

58. Hayot, *Elements of Academic Style*, 40.

59. Lahiri, *Translating Myself and Others*, 7.

60. Sword, *Air & Light & Time & Space*, 132.

61. Nord, "Reviewing Scholarly Books," 201.

62. Adams, "In the Profession," 204.

63. With respect to advisers writing with doctoral students, Pat Thomson and Barbara Kamler explain that "writing together is hands-on learning about writing for publication per se. It's not talking about writing for publication as an idea—it's the reality." Thomson and Kamler, *Writing for Peer Reviewed Journals*, 160.

64. For a view from academic librarians on developing students' skills as scholarly reviewers, see Rowland, Knapp, and Fargo, "Collaborative Book Review"; and Rowland, Knapp, and Fargo, "Learning."

65. I wish more such conference sessions would take on afterlives instead of being confined to one-off events. Occasionally such events are summarized for posterity. See, for example, Aveyard, "Academic Book Reviewing"; Berryhill, "Instructing Theological Students."

66. Perry, "Who Do You Think You Are?," 13 (original emphasis).

67. See, for example, Batten, "'Thankless Task'?"; Chibnik, *Scholarship, Money, and Prose*; Oinas and Leppälä, "Views on Book Reviews"; Wolper, "World of Fleas."

68. Zeruvabel, *Clockwork Muse*, 33.

69. I'll let my records tell the story. (I did not keep such robust notes about my writing processes twenty years ago, alas.) The hundredth review involved a 345-page edited volume that I read between May 30 and June 2, 2022. I wrote the review within the following week, let it sit, revised it, and submitted the 2,100-word (a generous allocation) review on June 15. The writing and revising of the review, including the multiple passes through my reading notes, likely required between eight and ten hours. The review was published in record time in October 2022. See Gump, review of *Scholarly Publication Trajectories*.

WORKS CITED

Adams, Michael. "In the Profession: Re-viewing the Academic Book Review." *Journal of English Linguistics* 35, no. 2 (June 2007): 202–5. https://doi.org/10.1177/0075424207302347.

Addis, Victoria. "Academic Book Reviews Deserve Some Respect." *Inside Higher Ed*, October 2, 2019. https://www.insidehighered.com/advice/2019/10/03/why-reviewing-books-good-avenue-scholarly-engagement-opinion.

Alford, L. Maurice, Emma McFadyen, and Akiko Nozue. "Collaborating in Writing: Crossing the Threshold." In Stewart, Devine, and Benade, *Writing for Publication*, 97–109.

Ambrosio, Chiara. Review of *The Aesthetics of Science: Beauty, Imagination and Understanding*, edited by Milena Ivanova and Steven French. *British Journal for the History of Science* 57, no. 1 (March 2024): 125–27. https://doi.org/10.1017/S0007087423001024.

American Psychological Association. *Publication Manual of the American Psychological Association*. 7th ed. Washington, DC: American Psychological Association, 2020.

Anderson, Rick. *Scholarly Communication: What Everyone Needs to Know*. New York: Oxford University Press, 2018.

Ashley, Leonard R. N. "The Ethics of Academic Book Reviewing." *Journal of Information Ethics* 11, no. 1 (2002): 37–51.

Aveyard, Karina. "Academic Book Reviewing." *Media International Australia* 166, no. 1 (February 2018): 81–84. https://doi.org/10.1177/1329878X17744703.

Baker, Nicholson. *U and I: A True Story*. New York: Random House, 1991.

Bardsley, Jan. "Liza Dalby's *Geisha*: The View Twenty-five Years Later." *Southeast Review of Asian Studies* 31 (2009): 309–23.

Barkan, Elliott R. "On the Art of Reviewing." *Perspectives on History* 39, no. 3 (March 2001). https://www.historians.org/perspectives-article/on-the-art-of-reviewing-march-2001.

Batten, Bruce L. "A 'Thankless Task'? My Work as a Book Review Editor." *Journal of Scholarly Publishing* 53, no. 2 (January 2022): 63–74. https://doi.org/10.3138/jsp.53.2.01.

Baverstock, Alison. "Introduction." In *Contemporary Publishing and the Culture of Books*, edited by Alison Baverstock, Richard Bradford, and Madelena Gonzalez, 1–21. London: Routledge, 2020.

Bayard, Pierre. *How to Talk About Books You Haven't Read*. Translated by Jeffrey Mehlman. New York: Bloomsbury, 2007.

Beer, David. "In Defence of Writing Book Reviews." *Times Higher Education*, April 7, 2016. https://www.timeshighereducation.com/blog/defence-writing-book-reviews.

Belcher, Wendy Laura. *Writing Your Journal Article in Twelve Weeks: A Guide to Academic Publishing Success*. 2nd ed. Chicago: University of Chicago Press, 2019.

Benade, Leon, Georgina Tuari Stewart, and Nesta Devine. "Writing for Various Academic Purposes and Genres." In Stewart, Devine, and Benade, *Writing for Publication*, 1–15.

Berryhill, Carisse Mickey. "Instructing Theological Students in Book Reviewing." *ATLA Summary of Proceedings* 49 (1995): 161–64.

Bilhartz, Terry D. "In 500 Words or Less: Academic Book Reviewing in American History." *The History Teacher* 17, no. 4 (August 1984): 525–36.

Bloom, Lynn Z. "How to Talk About Heartbreaking Works of Staggering Genius—and Those That Are Not: A Guide to Ethics in Book Reviewing." *Journal of Information Ethics* 11, no. 1 (Spring 2002): 7–18.

Brienza, Casey. "Why You (Yes, You!) Should Write Book Reviews." *Inside Higher Ed*, December 4, 2014. https://www.insidehighered.com/advice/2014/12/05/essay-argues-young-academics-should-write-book-reviews.

Brienza, Casey. "Writing Academic Book Reviews." *Inside Higher Ed*, March 26, 2015. https://www.insidehighered.com/advice/2015/03/27/essay-writing-academic-book-reviews.

Brown, Robert. "Reasons for Publishing Scholarly Book Reviews from a Journal Editor's Perspective." *Journal of Scholarly Publishing* 50, no. 1 (October 2018): 21–25. https://doi.org/10.3138/jsp.50.1.05.

Burgess, Sally. "Learning to Be a Non-native Speaker: A Retrospective Autoethnographic Account of an Early-Career Researcher's Publishing Trajectory." In

Habibie and Burgess, *Scholarly Publication Trajectories*, 113–29. https://doi.org/10.1007/978-3-030-85784-4_7.

Cassuto, Leonard. *Academic Writing as if Readers Matter*. Princeton, NJ: Princeton University Press, 2024.

Chang, Justin. "Screams from a Marriage." *New Yorker*, September 16, 2024, 86–87.

Chenail, Ronald J. "How to Read and Review a Book Like a Qualitative Researcher." *Qualitative Report* 15, no. 6 (November 2010): 1635–42. https://doi.org/10.46743/2160-3715/2010.1369.

Chibnik, Michael. *Scholarship, Money, and Prose: Behind the Scenes at an Academic Journal*. Philadelphia: University of Pennsylvania Press, 2020.

Child, Julia, Louisette Bertholle, and Simone Beck. *Mastering the Art of French Cooking*. New York: Knopf, 1961.

Childress, Herb. *The PhDictionary: A Glossary of Things You Don't Know (but Should) about Doctoral and Faculty Life*. Chicago: University of Chicago Press, 2016.

Chinnery, Ann. "Editorial: Reviews and Rejoinders in *Studies in Philosophy and Education*." *Studies in Philosophy and Education* 29, no. 5 (September 2010): 417–19. https://doi.org/10.1007/s11217-010-9192-9.

Chong, Phillipa K. *Inside the Critics' Circle: Book Reviewing in Uncertain Times*. Princeton, NJ: Princeton University Press, 2020.

Chrisomalis, Stephen. *The Phrontistery* (website). https://phrontistery.info/index.html.

Conover, Ted. *Immersion: A Writer's Guide to Going Deep*. Chicago: University of Chicago Press, 2016.

Cortada, James W. "Five Ways to Be a Terrible Book Reviewer." *Journal of Scholarly Publishing* 30, no. 1 (October 1998): 34–37.

Dahlhaus, Carl. "'The New Grove.'" *Music & Letters* 62, no. 3/4 (July–October 1981): 249–60.

De Costa, Peter I. "Opening the Gates for the Next Generation of Scholars." In Habibie and Hultgren, *Inner World of Gatekeeping*, 83–98. https://doi.org/10.1007/978-3-031-06519-4_6.

Deroo, Matthew R. "Writing with, Learning from, and Paying Forward Mentorship from Early-Career Scholars: My Scholarly Formation into Academic Writing." In Habibie and Burgess, *Scholarly Publication Trajectories*, 59–75. https://doi.org/10.1007/978-3-030-85784-4_4.

Dettmar, Kevin. *How to Chair a Department*. Baltimore, MD: Johns Hopkins University Press, 2022.

Deutsch, Jeff. *In Praise of Good Bookstores*. Princeton, NJ: Princeton University Press, 2022.

Donovan, Stephen K. "The Long and the Short and the Tall." *Journal of Scholarly Publishing* 38, no. 1 (October 2006): 36–40. https://doi.org/10.3138/jsp.38.1.36.

Drewry, John E. *Book Reviewing*. Boston: The Writer, 1945.

East, John W. "The Scholarly Book Review in the Humanities: An Academic Cinderella?" *Journal of Scholarly Publishing* 43, no. 1 (October 2011): 52–67. https://doi.org/10.3138/jsp.43.1.52.

Eastman, Carolyn. "In Defense of the Beleaguered Academic Book Review." *Chronicle of Higher Education*, September 21, 2023.

Eisner, Elliot W. "The Roots of Connoisseurship and Criticism: A Personal Journey." In *Evaluation Roots: Tracing Theorists' Views and Influences*, edited by Marvin C. Alkin, 196–202. Thousand Oaks, CA: SAGE, 2004.

Fadiman, Anne. "Never Do That to a Book." In *Ex Libris: Confessions of a Common Reader*, 37–44. New York: Farrar, Straus & Giroux, 1998.

Felber, Lynette. "The Book Review: Scholarly and Editorial Responsibility." *Journal of Scholarly Publishing* 33, no. 3 (April 2002): 166–72. https://doi.org/10.3138/jsp.33.3.166.

Fish, Stanley. *Is There a Text in This Class? The Authority of Interpretive Communities*. Cambridge, MA: Harvard University Press, 1980.

Flesch, Rudolf. *The Art of Readable Writing*. New York: Harper and Brothers, 1949.

French, Amanda. "Academic Writing as Identity-Work in Higher Education: Forming a 'Professional Writing in Higher Education Habitus.'" *Studies in Higher Education* 45, no. 8 (August 2020): 1605–17. https://doi.org/10.1080/03075079.2019.1572735.

Furman, Rich, and Julie T. Kinn. *Practical Tips for Publishing Scholarly Articles: Writing and Publishing in the Helping Professions*. 2nd ed. Chicago: Lyceum, 2012.

Furstenberg, Frank F. *Behind the Academic Curtain: How to Find Success and Happiness with a PhD*. Chicago: University of Chicago Press, 2013.

Fussell, Paul. "Vanity in Review." *Harper's*, February 1982, 68–73.

Gaillet, Lynée Lewis, and Letizia Guglielmo. *Scholarly Publication in a Changing Academic Landscape: Models for Success*. New York: Palgrave Macmillan, 2014.

Gard, Wayne. *Book Reviewing*. New York: Knopf, 1927.

Germano, William. *From Dissertation to Book*. 2nd ed. Chicago: University of Chicago Press, 2013.

Germano, William. *Getting It Published: A Guide for Scholars and Anyone Else Serious about Serious Books.* 3rd ed. Chicago: University of Chicago Press, 2016.

Germano, William. *On Revision: The Only Writing That Counts.* Chicago: University of Chicago Press, 2021.

Gibbs, Gary G., Karen F. Harris, Whitney A. M. Leeson, and James M. Ogier. "On the Potential of Book Reviews: Building a More Inclusive and Cohesive Community." *Perspectives on History* 62, no. 1 (January 2024). https://www.historians.org/perspectives-article/on-the-potential-of-book-reviews-building-a-more-inclusive-and-cohesive-community-january-2024.

Glasberg, Eve. "Jhumpa Lahiri Returns to Barnard as a Professor." *Columbia News*, August 29, 2023. https://news.columbia.edu/news/jhumpa-lahiri-returns-barnard-professor.

Grafton, Anthony. *Codex in Crisis.* 2nd ed. New York: Crumpled Press, 2008.

Gray, Paul, and David E. Drew. *What They Didn't Teach You in Graduate School, 2.0: 299 Helpful Hints for Success in Your Academic Career.* Sterling, VA: Stylus, 2012.

Gump, Steven E. "The Ethics of Scholarly Book Reviewing." *Journal of Scholarly Publishing* 55, no. 3 (July 2024): 385–403. https://doi.org/10.3138/jsp-2023-0073.

Gump, Steven E. "Recovering the Covering Letter: Submitting Manuscripts to Scholarly Journals in the Twenty-First Century." *Journal of Scholarly Publishing* 45, no. 2 (January 2014): 172–85. https://doi.org/10.3138/jsp.45.2.004.

Gump, Steven E. "Reimagining the Covering Letter: Why, When, and How to Communicate with Journal Editors before Manuscript Submission." *Journal of Scholarly Publishing* 55, no. 1 (January 2024): 84–100. https://doi.org/10.3138/jsp-2023-0047.

Gump, Steven E. Review of *Contemporary Publishing and the Culture of Books*, edited by Alison Baverstock, Richard Bradford, and Madelena Gonzalez. *Journal of Scholarly Publishing* 52, no. 3 (April 2021): 192–97. https://doi.org/10.3138/jsp.52.3.06.

Gump, Steven E. Review of *Economical Writing: Thirty-Five Rules for Clear and Persuasive Prose*, 3rd ed., by Deirdre Nansen McCloskey. *Journal of Scholarly Publishing* 51, no. 2 (January 2020): 155–58. https://doi.org/10.3138/jsp.51.2.04.

Gump, Steven E. Review of *The Food and Culture around the World Handbook*, edited by Helen C. Brittin. *Food, Culture & Society* 14, no. 4 (December 2011): 607–10. https://doi.org/10.2752/175174411X13046092851190.

Gump, Steven E. Review of *How Writing Faculty Write: Strategies for Process, Product, and Productivity*, by Christine E. Tulley. *Journal of Scholarly Publishing* 50, no. 2 (January 2019): 152–57. https://doi.org/10.3138/jsp.50.2.08.

Gump, Steven E. Review of *Inside the Critics' Circle: Book Reviewing in Uncertain Times*, by Phillipa K. Chong; *Why Writing Matters*, by Nicholas Delbanco; *Every Day I Write the Book: Notes on Style*, by Amitava Kumar; *What We Talk About When We Talk About Books: The History and Future of Reading*, by Leah Price; and *The Story I Am: Mad about the Writing Life*, by Roger Rosenblatt. *Journal of Scholarly Publishing* 52, no. 4 (July 2021): 294–303. https://doi.org/10.3138/jsp.52.4.06.

Gump, Steven E. Review of *A Manual for Writers of Research Papers, Theses, and Dissertations: Chicago Style for Students and Researchers*, 9th ed., by Kate L. Turabian et al. *Journal of Scholarly Publishing* 51, no. 1 (October 2019): 99–104. https://doi.org/10.3138/jsp.51.1.06.

Gump, Steven E. Review of *Murōji: Rearranging Art and History at a Japanese Buddhist Temple*, by Sherry D. Fowler; and *Rearranging the Landscape of the Gods: The Politics of a Pilgrimage Site in Japan, 1573–1912*, by Sarah Thal. *Southeast Review of Asian Studies* 29 (2007): 264–69.

Gump, Steven E. Review of *On Revision: The Only Writing That Counts*, by William Germano; and *Revise: The Scholar-Writer's Essential Guide to Tweaking, Editing, and Perfecting Your Manuscript*, by Pamela Haag. *Journal of Scholarly Publishing* 54, no. 1 (January 2023): 152–57. https://doi.org/10.3138/jsp-2022-0011.

Gump, Steven E. Review of *Publishing from Your Doctoral Research: Create and Use a Publication Strategy*, by Janet Salmons and Helen Kara. *Journal of Scholarly Publishing* 52, no. 1 (October 2020): 61–66. https://doi.org/10.3138/jsp.52.1.07.

Gump, Steven E. Review of *Scholarly Publication Trajectories of Early-Career Scholars: Insider Perspectives*, edited by Pejman Habibie and Sally Burgess. *Journal of Scholarly Publishing* 53, no. 4 (October 2022): 294–300. https://doi.org/10.3138/jsp-2022-0042.

Gump, Steven E. Review of *Style and Story: Literary Methods for Writing Nonfiction*, by Stephen J. Pyne. *Journal of Scholarly Publishing* 50, no. 4 (July 2019): 279–83. https://doi.org/10.3138/jsp.50.4.04.

Gump, Steven E. Review of *A Very Short Book about Writing*, by Jonathan G. Davies; *Letters to an Aspiring Scholar: Embracing Creativity for Doctoral Scholarship and Overcoming Obstacles in Everyday Life*, by Christopher M. Strickland; and *Productivity and Publishing: Writing Processes for New Scholars*, by Margaret-Mary Sulentic Dowell, Leah Katherine Saal, Cynthia F. DiCarlo, and Tynisha D. Willingham. *Journal of Scholarly Publishing* 53, no. 4 (October 2022): 275–82. https://doi.org/10.3138/jsp-2022-0052.

Gump, Steven E. Review of *Voice and Vision: A Guide to Writing History and Other Serious Nonfiction*, by Stephen J. Pyne. *Journal of Scholarly Publishing* 41, no. 3 (April 2010): 379–84. https://doi.org/10.3138/jsp.41.3.379.

Gump, Steven E. Review of *What They Didn't Teach You in Graduate School: 199 Helpful Hints for Success in Your Academic Career*, by Paul Gray and David E. Drew. *Journal of Scholarly Publishing* 40, no. 3 (April 2009): 323–28. https://doi.org/10.3138/jsp.40.3.314.

Gump, Steven E. Review of *Writing for Publication: Transitions and Tools That Support Scholar's Success*, by Mary Renck Jalongo and Olivia N. Saracho. *Journal of Scholarly Publishing* 49, no. 4 (July 2018): 494–99. https://doi.org/10.3138/jsp.49.4.10.

Gump, Steven E. Review of *Writing on the Job: Best Practices for Communicating in the Digital Age*, by Martha B. Coven; *Writing with Sweet Clarity*, by John E. Eck; *Write for Your Life*, by Anna Quindlen; and *Write for Your Life: A Guide to Clear and Purposeful Writing (and Presentations)*, by Charles Wheelan. *Journal of Scholarly Publishing* 54, no. 1 (January 2023): 167–72. https://doi.org/10.3138/jsp-2022-0057.

Gump, Steven E. Review of *Writing Your Journal Article in 12 Weeks: A Guide to Academic Publishing Success*, by Wendy Laura Belcher. *Journal of Scholarly Publishing* 41, no. 2 (January 2010): 246–52. https://doi.org/10.3138/jsp.41.2.246.

Gump, Steven E. "Special Section on the Value of Scholarly Book Reviews." *Journal of Scholarly Publishing* 50, no. 1 (October 2018): 1–7. https://doi.org/10.3138/jsp.50.1.01.

Gump, Steven E. "Writing Successful Covering Letters for Unsolicited Submissions to Academic Journals." *Journal of Scholarly Publishing* 35, no. 2 (January 2004): 92–102. https://doi.org/10.3138/jsp.35.2.92.

Gump, Steven E., and William C. Gump. Review of *Getting Your Research Paper Published: A Surgical Perspective*, edited by Mohit Bhandari and Anders Joensson; and *Anatomy of Writing for Publication for Nurses*, by Cynthia Saver. *Journal of Scholarly Publishing* 44, no. 2 (January 2013): 174–81. https://doi.org/10.3138/jsp.44.2.170.

Haag, Pamela. *Revise: The Scholar-Writer's Essential Guide to Tweaking, Editing, and Perfecting Your Manuscript*. New Haven, CT: Yale University Press, 2021.

Habibie, Pejman. "Gatekeeping and Gateopening: A Narrative of Becoming." In Habibie and Hultgren, *Inner World of Gatekeeping*, 27–44. https://doi.org/10.1007/978-3-031-06519-4_3.

Habibie, Pejman, and Sally Burgess, eds. *Scholarly Publication Trajectories of Early-Career Scholars: Insider Perspectives*. Cham, Switzerland: Palgrave Macmillan, 2021.

Habibe, Pejman, and Anna Kristina Hultgren, eds. *The Inner World of Gatekeeping in Scholarly Publication*. Cham, Switzerland: Palgrave Macmillan, 2022.

Haggerty, Kevin D., and Aaron Doyle. *57 Ways to Screw Up in Grad School: Perverse Professional Lessons for Graduate Students*. Chicago: University of Chicago Press, 2015.

Hallinger, Philip, and Jasna Kovačević. "Applying Bibliometric Review Methods in Education: Rationale, Definitions, Analytical Techniques, and Illustrations." In *International Encyclopedia of Education*, 4th ed., edited by Robert J. Tierney, Fazal Rizvi, and Kadriye Ercikan, 546–56. Amsterdam: Elsevier Science, 2023. https://doi.org/10.1016/B978-0-12-818630-5.05070-3.

Halpenny, Francess G. "Responsibilities of Scholarly Publishers." *Scholarly Publishing* 24, no. 4 (July 1993): 223–31.

Harris, Jennifer. "Tips for an Academic Book Review." *Words in Place*, August 20, 2018. https://englishatwaterloo.wordpress.com/2018/08/20/tips-for-an-academic-book-review.

Hartley, James. "Reading and Writing Book Reviews Across the Disciplines." *Journal of the American Society for Information Science and Technology* 57, no. 9 (July 2006): 1194–1207.

Hayot, Eric. *The Elements of Academic Style: Writing for the Humanities*. New York: Columbia University Press, 2014.

Hemphill, Michael A. "Scholarly Book Reviews in the *Journal of Teaching in Physical Education*." *Journal of Teaching in Physical Education* 43, no. 2 (April 2024): 197–98.

Henige, David. "Reviewing Reviewing." *Journal of Scholarly Publishing* 33, no. 1 (October 2001): 23–36. https://doi.org/10.3138/jsp.33.1.23.

Hérubel, Jean-Pierre V. M. 2021. "Disciplinary Fluidity: Academic Journals, Book Reviewing, Information and Knowledge Flow." *Publishing Research Quarterly* 37, no. 3 (September 2021): 407–19. https://doi.org/10.1007/s12109-021-09824-7.

Hoge, James O., and James L. W. West III. "Academic Book Reviewing: Some Problems and Suggestions." *Scholarly Publishing* 11, no. 1 (October 1979): 35–41.

Hyland, Ken, and Giuliana Diani, eds. *Academic Evaluation: Review Genres in University Settings*. Houndmills, UK: Palgrave Macmillan, 2009.

Immler, Frank. Review of *Literary Reviewing*, edited by James O. Hoge. *College & Research Librarians* 50, no. 3 (May 1989): 367–71. https://doi.org/10.5860/crl_50_03_367.

Jansen, Jonathan. "Editing a Scholarly Book." In *On Becoming a Scholar: What Every New Academic Needs to Know*, edited by Jonathan Jansen and Daniel Visser, 160–69. Cape Town, South Africa: African Minds, 2022.

Jensen, Joli. *Write No Matter What: Advice for Academics*. Chicago: University of Chicago Press, 2017.

Journell, Wayne. *Becoming a Scholarly Journal Editor: Practical Advice for Editors and Tips for Authors*. Lanham, MD: Rowman & Littlefield, 2023.

Kahan, Jeffrey. *Getting Published in the Humanities: What to Know, Where to Aim, How to Succeed*. Jefferson, NC: McFarland, 2012.

Kaiser, Alan. "Peer Review: What Doesn't Kill You Makes You Stronger." In *Writing Anthropology: Essays on Craft & Commitment*, edited by Carole McGranahan, 158–62. Durham, NC: Duke University Press, 2020.

Kelsky, Karen. *The Professor Is In: The Essential Guide to Turning Your Ph.D. into a Job*. New York: Three Rivers Press, 2015.

King, Stephen. *On Writing: A Memoir of the Craft*. New York: Scribner, 2000.

Klemp, P. J. "Reviewing Academic Books: Some Ideas for Beginners." *Scholarly Publishing* 12, no. 2 (January 1981): 135–39.

Klinkenborg, Verlyn. *Several Short Sentences about Writing*. New York: Knopf, 2012.

Knox, Katelyn E., and Allison Van Deventer. *The Dissertation-to-Book Workbook: Exercises for Developing and Revising Your Book Manuscript*. Chicago: University of Chicago Press, 2023.

Kovács, Balázs. "The Turing Test of Online Reviews: Can We Tell the Difference between Human-Written and GPT-4-Written Online Reviews?" *Marketing Letters* (April 2024). https://doi.org/10.1007/s11002-024-09729-3.

Krieger, Martin H. *The Scholar's Survival Manual: A Road Map for Students, Faculty, and Administrators*. Bloomington: Indiana University Press, 2013.

Kumar, Amitava. *Every Day I Write the Book: Notes on Style*. Durham, NC: Duke University Press, 2020.

Lahiri, Jhumpa. *Translating Myself and Others*. Princeton, NJ: Princeton University Press, 2022.

Lane, Anthony. "High Crimes." *New Yorker*, June 18, 2018, 64–69.

Lane, Anthony. *Nobody's Perfect: Writings from "The New Yorker."* New York: Knopf, 2002.

Lane, Anthony. "Taming Nature." *New Yorker*, July 29, 2019, 75.

Leahy, Anna. "The (Selfish) Power of Book Reviews: Reading, Citizenship, and Platform." In *Creative Writing Scholars on the Publishing Trade: Practice, Praxis, Print*, edited by Sam Meekings and Marshall Moore, 48–58. London: Routledge, 2022.

Levitt, Aimee. "AI Can Write a More Believable Restaurant Review Than a Human Can." *Yale Insights*, May 28, 2024. https://insights.som.yale.edu/insights/ai-can-write-more-believable-restaurant-review-than-human-can.

Lindholm-Romantschuk, Ylva. *Scholarly Book Reviewing in the Social Sciences and Humanities: The Flow of Ideas Within and Among Disciplines*. Westport, CT: Greenwood, 1998.

Luey, Beth. *Handbook for Academic Authors*. 6th ed. Cambridge: Cambridge University Press, 2022.

Lussier, Robert N. *Publish Don't Perish: 100 Tips That Improve Your Ability to Get Published*. Charlotte, NC: Information Age, 2010.

MacPhail, Bruce D. "Book Reviews and the Scholarly Publisher." *Scholarly Publishing* 12, no. 1 (October 1980): 55–63.

May, Lori A. *The Write Crowd: Literary Citizenship and the Writing Life*. New York: Bloomsbury Academic, 2015.

Mazlish, Bruce. "The Art of Reviewing." *Perspectives on History* 39, no. 2 (February 2001). https://www.historians.org/perspectives-article/the-art-of-reviewing-february-2001.

McCanse, Ralph Alan. *The Art of the Book Review: A Comprehensive Working Outline*. Madison: University of Wisconsin Extension Division, 1963.

McCloskey, Deirdre Nansen. *Economical Writing: Thirty-Five Rules for Clear and Persuasive Prose*. 3rd ed. Chicago: University of Chicago Press, 2019.

McKinzie, Steve. "The Noble Art of Reviewing: Challenges, Rewards, and Tricks of the Trade." *College & Undergraduate Libraries* 3, no. 2 (1996): 91–99. https://dx.doi.org/10.1300/J106v03n02_10.

Menand, Louis. "Remainders." *New Yorker*, August 26, 2024, 68–72.

Milardo, Robert M. *Crafting Scholarship in the Behavioral and Social Sciences: Writing, Reviewing, and Editing*. New York: Routledge, 2015.

Mishan, Ligaya. "A Life of James Beard Stocked with Tasty Morsels." Review of *The Man Who Ate Too Much: The Life of James Beard*, by John Birdsall. *New York Times*, October 9, 2020. https://www.nytimes.com/2020/10/09/books/review/the-man-who-ate-too-much-john-birdsall.html.

Molinari, Julia. *What Makes Writing Academic: Rethinking Theory for Practice*. London: Bloomsbury Academic, 2022.

Nord, Walter. "Reviewing Scholarly Books." In *Winning Reviews: A Guide for Evaluating Scholarly Writing*, edited by Yehuda Baruch, Sherry E. Sullivan, and Hazlon N. Schepmyer, 196–202. Houndmills, UK: Palgrave Macmillan, 2006.

Oinas, Päivi, and Samuli Leppälä. "Views on Book Reviews." *Regional Studies* 47, no. 10 (2013): 1785–89. https://doi.org/10.1080/00343404.2013.856530.

O'Neill, Jill. "The Necessity of Book Reviews." *Scholarly Kitchen*, November 17, 2023. https://scholarlykitchen.sspnet.org/2023/11/17/the-necessity-of-book-reviews.

Orteza y Miranda, Evelina. "On Book Reviewing." *Journal of Educational Thought* 30, no. 2 (August 1996): 191–202.

Perry, Seth. "Who Do You Think You Are? Reading, Authority, and Book Reviewing." *Journal of Scholarly Publishing* 50, no. 1 (October 2018): 12–15. https://doi.org/10.3138/jsp.50.1.03.

Peters, Michael A., Petar Jandrić, and Sarah Hayes. "Revisiting the Concept of the Edited Collection: *Bioinformational Philosophy and Postdigital Knowledge Ecologies.*" *Postdigital Science and Education* 3, no. 2 (April 2021): 283–93. https://doi.org/10.1007/s42438-021-00216-w.

Pierazzo, Elena. *Digital Scholarly Editing: Theories, Models and Methods.* London: Routledge, 2015.

Pool, Gail. *Faint Praise: The Plight of Book Reviewing in America.* Columbia: University of Missouri Press, 2007.

Pool, Gail. "Point of View: Too Many Reviews of Scholarly Books Are Puffy, Nasty, or Poorly Written." *Chronicle of Higher Education,* July 20, 1988.

Powers, Richard. *The Overstory: A Novel.* New York: Norton, 2018.

Price, Leah. *What We Talk About When We Talk About Books: The History and Future of Reading.* New York: Basic Books, 2019.

Pushman, Erin M. *How to Read Like a Writer: 10 Lessons to Elevate Your Reading and Writing Practice.* London: Bloomsbury Academic, 2022.

Pyne, Stephen J. *Style and Story: Literary Methods for Writing Nonfiction.* Tucson: University of Arizona Press, 2018.

Pyne, Stephen J. *Voice and Vision: A Guide to Writing History and Other Serious Nonfiction.* Cambridge, MA: Harvard University Press, 2009.

Quindlen, Anna. *Write for Your Life.* New York: Random House, 2022.

Renkl, Margaret. "I Reread a Book That Changed My Life, but I'd Changed, Too." *New York Times,* June 3, 2024. https://www.nytimes.com/2024/06/03/opinion/rereading-beloved-books.html.

Richardson, James. *Vectors: Aphorisms & Ten-Second Essays.* Keene, NY: Ausable Press, 2001.

Rosenblatt, Roger. *The Story I Am: Mad about the Writing Life.* Brooklyn, NY: Turtle Point Press, 2020.

Rosenblatt, Roger. *Unless It Moves the Human Heart: The Craft and Art of Writing.* New York: Ecco, 2011.

Ross, David A. "Fondling the Lemur's Tail: A Discussion of Book Reviewing in Which Lemurs Figure Only Metaphorically." *Journal of Scholarly Publishing* 50, no. 1 (October 2018): 16–20. https://doi.org/10.3138/jsp.50.1.04.

Rowland, Nicholas J., Jeffrey A. Knapp, and Hailley Fargo. "The Collaborative Book Review as an Opportunity for Undergraduate Research Skill Development." *Higher Education Research & Development* 39, no. 3 (2020): 577–90. https://doi.org/10.1080/07294360.2019.1680614.

Rowland, Nicholas J., Jeffrey A. Knapp, and Hailley Fargo. "Learning 'Scholarship as Conversation' by Writing Book Reviews." *Scholarship and Practice of Undergraduate Research* 2, no. 3 (Spring 2019): 20–27. https://doi.org/10.18833/spur/2/3/6.

Salager-Meyer, Françoise, and Beverly A. Lewin. "Introduction." In *Crossed Words: Criticism in Scholarly Writing*, edited by Françoise Salager-Meyer and Beverly A. Lewin, 11–19. Bern, Switzerland: Peter Lang, 2011.

Saller, Carol Fisher. *The Subversive Copy Editor: Advice from Chicago (or, How to Negotiate Good Relationships with Your Writers, Your Colleagues, and Yourself).* 2nd ed. Chicago: University of Chicago Press, 2016.

Schwartz, Seth J. *The Savvy Academic: Publishing in the Social and Health Sciences.* New York: Oxford University Press, 2022.

Shatz, David. "The Odd Case of Book Reviews." *Against the Grain* 21, no. 3 (June 2009): 40–42. https://doi.org/10.7771/2380-176X.2308.

Shore, Zachary. *Grad School Essentials: A Crash Course in Scholarly Skills.* Oakland: University of California Press, 2016.

Shrock, Dennis. *Choral Repertoire.* Oxford: Oxford University Press, 2009.

Shrock, Dennis. *Choral Repertoire.* 2nd ed. Oxford: Oxford University Press, 2023.

Silvia, Paul J. *Write It Up: Practical Strategies for Writing and Publishing Journal Articles.* Washington, DC: American Psychological Association, 2015.

Simon, Linda. "The Pleasures of Book Reviewing." *Journal of Scholarly Publishing* 27, no. 4 (July 1996): 237–41.

Smith, S. Stephenson. *The Craft of the Critic.* New York: Thomas Y. Crowell, 1931.

Sotejeff-Wilson, Kate, and Alice Lehtinen. "Language Professionals as Cultural Mediators: Whose Style Matters?" In *Proofreading and Editing in Student and Research Publication Contexts: International Perspectives*, edited by Nigel Harwood, 179–97. London: Routledge, 2024. https://doi.org/10.4324/9781003334446-13.

Stahl, Levi. "So What If It's Not the *New York Times*: Why One University Press Seeks Book Reviews in Scholarly Journals." *Journal of Scholarly Publishing* 50, no. 1 (October 2018): 8–11. https://doi.org/10.3138/jsp.50.1.02.

Stevens, Dannelle D. *Write More, Publish More, Stress Less! Five Key Principles for a Creative and Sustainable Scholarly Practice.* Sterling, VA: Stylus, 2019.

Stewart, Georgina Tuari, Nesta Devine, and Leon Benade, eds. *Writing for Publication: Liminal Reflections for Academics.* Singapore: Springer Nature Singapore, 2021. https://doi.org/10.1007/978-981-33-4439-6.

Strunk, William, Jr., and E. B. White. *The Elements of Style.* New York: Macmillan, 1959.

Sturm, Sean. "The Critical Gift: Revaluing Book Reviews in *Educational Philosophy and Theory*." *Educational Philosophy and Theory* 54, no. 5 (2022): 450–56. https://doi.org/10.1080/00131857.2020.1741335.

Swinnerton, Frank. *The Reviewing and Criticism of Books.* The Ninth Dent Memorial Lecture. London: J. M. Dent & Sons, 1939.

Sword, Helen. *Air & Light & Time & Space: How Successful Academics Write.* Cambridge, MA: Harvard University Press, 2017.

Sword, Helen. *Stylish Academic Writing.* Cambridge, MA: Harvard University Press, 2012.

Sword, Helen. *The Writer's Diet: A Guide to Fit Prose.* Chicago: University of Chicago Press, 2016.

Sword, Helen. *Writing with Pleasure.* Princeton, NJ: Princeton University Press, 2023.

Tan, Jenny. "The Problem with 'I Argue That. . . .'" *Feeding the Elephant: A Forum for Scholarly Communications*, July 28, 2021. https://networks.h-net.org/node/1883/discussions/7982424/problem-i-argue.

Thompson, Hunter S. *Fear and Loathing in America: The Brutal Odyssey of an Outlaw Journalist, 1968–1976.* New York: Simon & Schuster, 2000.

Thomson, Pat, and Barbara Kamler. *Writing for Peer Reviewed Journals: Strategies for Getting Published.* London: Routledge, 2013.

Tobin, Ronald W. "The Commensality of Book Reviewing." *Journal of Scholarly Publishing* 35, no. 1 (October 2003): 47–51. https://doi.org/10.3138/jsp.35.1.47.

Toor, Rachel. "Becoming a 'Stylish' Writer." *Chronicle of Higher Education*, July 2, 2012.

Toor, Rachel. "Why Bother Writing Book Reviews?" *Chronicle of Higher Education*, April 2, 2012.

Trubek, Anne. *So You Want to Publish a Book?* Cleveland, OH: Belt Publishing, 2020.

Turabian, Kate L., with Gregory G. Colomb, Joseph M. Williams, Joseph Bizup, William T. FitzGerald, and the University of Chicago Press Editorial Staff. *Student's Guide to Writing College Papers*. 5th ed. Chicago: University of Chicago Press, 2019.

Updike, John. *Hugging the Shore: Essays and Criticism*. New York: Knopf, 1983.

Van Viegen, Saskia. "Writing Belonging with Critical Autoethnography." In Habibie and Burgess, *Scholarly Publication Trajectories*, 41–57. https://doi.org/10.1007/978-3-030-85784-4_3.

Vendler, Helen. *The Art of Shakespeare's Sonnets*. Cambridge, MA: Harvard University Press, 1997.

Vinyard, Marc W., and Jaimie Beth Colvin. *Demystifying Scholarly Metrics: A Practical Guide*. Santa Barbara, CA: Libraries Unlimited, 2022.

Walford, A. J. "Reference Books." In *Reviewers and Reviewing: A Guide*, edited by A. J. Walford, 27–36. London: Mansell, 1986.

Wasserstrom, Jeffrey N. "Why Read Book Reviews?" *Chronicle of Higher Education*, September 4, 2011.

Webster, Peter. *The Edited Collection: Pasts, Present and Futures*. Cambridge: Cambridge University Press, 2020. https://doi.org/10.1017/9781108683647.

Weissman, David. "Some Thoughts about the Requirements for Reviewing Books." *Metaphilosophy* 41, no. 5 (October 2010): 715–16. https://doi.org/10.1111/j.1467-9973.2010.01656.x.

Wheelan, Charles. *Write for Your Life: A Guide to Clear and Purposeful Writing (and Presentations)*. New York: Norton, 2022.

Williams, Jeffrey J. "Book Angst." *Chronicle of Higher Education*, May 22, 2012.

Williams, Jeffrey J. "Introduction: Criticism without Footnotes." In *How to Be an Intellectual: Essays on Criticism, Culture, and the University*, 1–8. New York: Fordham University Press, 2014.

Williams, Jeffrey J. "Shelf Life." *Chronicle of Higher Education*, January 6, 2006.

Wilson, Mark C. Review of *Reassembling Scholarly Communications: Histories, Infrastructures, and Global Politics of Open Access*, edited by Martin Paul Eve and Jonathan Gray. *Journal of Scholarly Publishing* 52, no. 3 (April 2021): 190–92. https://doi.org/10.3138/jsp.52.3.05.

Wolper, Roy S. "On Academic Reviewing: Ten Common Errors." *Scholarly Publishing* 16, no. 3 (April 1985): 269–75.

Wolper, Roy S. "The World of Fleas: Publishing in a Review Journal." *Journal of Scholarly Publishing* 20, no. 4 (July 1989): 227–32. https://doi.org/10.3138/JSP-020-04-227.

Woodcock, George. "The Critic as Mediator." *Scholarly Publishing* 4, no. 3 (April 1972): 201–9.

Worsham, Lynn. "The Endangered Scholarly Book Review." *Chronicle of Higher Education*, April 1, 2012.

Wray, K. Brad, Lori Nash, and Jonathan Simon. "What We Publish in *Metascience*." *Metascience* 31, no. 3 (November 2022): 293–96. https://doi.org/10.1007/s11016-022-00819-4.

Wright, Charlotte M. "Rethinking the Literary Review." *Western American Literature* 24, no. 2 (Summer 1989): 137–46. https://doi.org/10.1353/wal.1989.0103.

Wulf, Karin. "Efficient Reading." *Karin Wulf* (blog), January 31, 2018. https://karinwulf.com/trove/efficient-reading.

Zerubavel, Eviatar. *The Clockwork Muse*. Cambridge, MA: Harvard University Press, 1999.

Zinsser, William. *On Writing Well: The Classic Guide to Writing Nonfiction*. 30th anniversary ed. New York: Harper Perennial, 2016.

Zinsser, William K. "Unexpected Visitors: Why *Voodoo* Is Preferable to *Adumbrate*." In *The Writer Who Stayed*, 123–25. Philadelphia: Paul Dry Books, 2012.

INDEX

Academia.edu, 30, 123
accuracy, 112, 113, 139–40
acronyms, 74
acrostics, 175
active coauthoring, 221–22n38.
  See also coauthoring reviews
Adams, Michael, 170, 184, 221n30
adjectives, empty, 112, 172, 218n36
advance reader's copy, 47
adverbs, 112, 172
advisers, 29, 212n43
almanacs, review of, 139–42
Amazon.com, 37–38
American Historical Review (journal), 32
American Psychological Association, 106
analogies, 174–75
Anderson, Rick, 54, 65, 214n1
Andrews, Debby, 27
anthologies, review of, 137–38
argument, 70–73, 206
Art of Shakespeare's Sonnets, The (Vendler), 177
Art of the Book Review, The (McCanse), 15
Artificial Intelligence (AI), 102, 216n2
Ashley, Leonard, 97

assessment, 12–13, 51, 208
Association for the Study of Food and Society, 35
associations, questions regarding, 207
asynchronous cowriting, 155–56.
  See also coauthoring reviews
A-time and B-time, 186–87
attentiveness, in reviewing, 167
audience: identification of, in review, 116; lack of understanding of, 87–88; questions regarding, 205; of reference works, 140; of scholarly book reviews, 13–14; of scholarly books, 71; use of language for, 73
authority, in writing, 174
authors: alerting of, to scholarly book review, 124; alternate publications of, 60–61; boldness of, 77; conflict of interest regarding, 40–41; criticism of, 98, 113; of edited collections, 135–36; enemies of, 40–41; epistemology of, 72; language use by, 73; personal attacks on, 99–100; personal changes of, 119–20; questions regarding, 204; response to reviews by, 90; scholarly book reviews as serving, 16–17; source

243

244 INDEX

authors (*continued*)
use by, 71–72; stated goals of, 71, 76; trust in, 77, 217n11; understanding origins of, 60–61; voice of, transferred to review, 177–78

back matter, considerations regarding, 78
back-burner projects, 22
back-door approach, for review venue identification, 30
Baker, Nicholson, 15–16, 55
Bardsley, Jan, 151
Barthes, Roland, 214n2
Baverstock, Alison, 133
Bayard, Pierre, 222n6
Beer, David, 16
Belcher, Wendy Laura, 15, 168, 212n38
bias, reviewing without, 50
bibliography, of scholarly books, 62
binge-reading, 146
biographies, in edited volumes, 129
blogs, reviews in, 209–10n11
Bloom, Harold, 16
Bloom, Lynn Z., 209n5, 213n59
book karma, 214n5
book note, defined, 10
book review/book review essay, 10, 143, 192–93
book symposium, 11
books. *See* scholarly books
Bottom Line Up Front (BLUF), 82, 106
Bradford, Richard, 133
breakout scholarship, 220n5
Brienza, Casey, 20–21, 28
"buddy log" metaphor, 22, 186
Business Communication Quarterly (journal), 27, 121

Cambridge University Press, 17
Canadian Journal of Health History (journal), 35
Canadian Society for the History of Medicine, 35
capsule review, 10, 182
categorizing, of scholarly book reviews, 10–11
Chang, Justin, 4, 175
Chenail, Ronald, 64
Child, Julia, 164, 222n2
Chinnery, Ann, 169
Chong, Phillipa, 102, 177
Choral Repertoire (Shrock), 141
Chrisomalis, Stephen, 176
Chronicle of Higher Education (journal), 210n11
clichés, 175
coauthoring reviews: asynchronous cowriting in, 155–56; celebration of, 157; compromise in, 156; diminishing returns in, 156; discussion for, 154; drafting process for, 154–55; final version of, 156; first draft of, 155–56; identifying colleague for, 153; lessons regarding, 158; meeting for, 154; passive *versus* active, 221–22n38; pitching idea for, 153; presenting a process for, 152–57; of retrospective essay, 157; review copy for, 153–54; of review essay, 157; revision in, 156; synchronous cowriting in, 156
colons, 224n39
commentators, reviewers as, 161
communication skills, improvement of, 167–68
comparative review, 10, 126
completion, celebrating, 119–24, 196

composing the scholarly book review: addressing weaknesses in, 100–102; assessing the text in, 96–103; conclusion in, 115–17; direct quotation review in, 92; distilling your reading notes in, 86–96; of edited collections, 134–37; filling out your review in, 111–15; identifying weaknesses in, 97–100; introduction in, 106; lessons for, 117–18; overview of, 85–86, 103–8; plagiarizing in, 100; presenting assessment in, 103–17; quoting from the text in, 108–11; reflection in, 92; review venue policy considerations in, 93; singing praises in, 103; sorting and organizing of notes in, 94–96; strength highlighting in, 101–2; writing your way into, 108. *See also* reviewing, scholarly
compromise, in coauthoring reviews, 156
computer, for note-taking, 58
concision, in scholarly reviewing, 105, 169
conclusion, 115–17
concordances, review of, 139–42
conference proposals, review of, 162–63
confidence, 211n28, 215n20
conflicts of interest, 40–41, 213n59
connoisseurship, 4, 165, 222n4
Conover, Ted, 169
consequence, questions regarding, 207–8
consistency, in scholarly reviews, 50
content, consideration of, 70–73, 206–7
contextualization, 51, 127–28, 142–45

cooling off period, 119
copyediting, 122
copyright protocols, 121–22, 123
Cornell University Press, 213n58
Cortada, James, 99, 149
cover letters, 120
cracking a project, 119
creativity, in scholarly book reviews, 171–79
critical review, 3, 113
cross-fertilization, 224n51
cross-referencing, in edited volumes, 131
curiosity, 181
CVs, 23, 30, 123, 160–61

Dahlhaus, Carl, 139
Dalby, Liza, 151
dashes, 178
declarative sentences, 106
definitions, clarity in, 73–74
Deroo, Matthew, 212n43
description, in scholarly book reviews, 12–13
descriptive metadata, 58
design, virtue of, 62–63
Dettmar, Kevin, 168
Deutsch, Jeff, 17
dictionaries, review of, 139–42
digital books, advantages of, 56. *See also* scholarly books
digital technology, as outlet for scholarly book reviews, 15
diminishing returns, in coauthoring reviews, 156
disciplinary journals, as outlet for scholarly book reviews, 15
dissemination, of scholarly book reviews, 33
dissertations, 22–23, 60, 215n18

diversity, in scholarly book reviews, 50
Donovan, Stephen, 16
Doyle, Aaron, 21
Drewry, John, 222n6
Dubinsky, Jim, 27

East, John, 210n27
Eastman, Carolyn, 179
Economical Writing (McCloskey), 177
Economist (magazine), 175, 176
Edelweiss+, 39, 59
edited collections/volumes: benefits of, 128; biographies in, 129, 136; challenges of, 128; chapters in conversation in, 131; contextualizing, 127–28; cross-referencing in, 131; diversity of contributors in, 135–36; editor role in, 131, 136; emphasizing themes, approaches, and ideas in notes for, 130–31; examples of, 127; imbalance in, 133; inconsistencies of presentational matters in, 132; introduction of, 132–33; justifications in introduction in, 129–30; monographs as compared to, 130; organization and coherence of, 131–32; outliers in, 131; overall impression of, 130; pointers regarding, 137; protocols for, 136; reading and evaluating individual chapters of, 130; reviewer as emcee for, 137; selectivity in, 135, 158; standout chapters of, 137; success of, 137; taking notes on, 128–34; unevenness of, 135; writing reviews of, 134–37
editing, virtue of, 62–63

editors: asking for review copy from, 44; background sharing with, 44; comments from, 120; communication with, 120, 167–68; confirmation from, 121; copyediting processes of, 122; of edited volumes, 131, 136; encouraging to publish book reviews, 185; feedback from, 121; first impressions of, 43; impressing, 168; intervention of, 162; reaching out to, 27–28, 40–46; responses of, 45; of review essays, 144; role of, 105; of scholarly journals, 160–61, 162; transparency with, 46; viewpoint of, 105; volunteering as, 185
Eisner, Elliot, 222n4
Elements of Academic Style (Hayot), 177–78
encyclopedias, review of, 139–42, 220n18
enlivening your reviews, 171–79
essay notes, 147–48
ethics, 40, 99, 213n59, 220n8
evaluations, of teaching for scholarly book reviewing, 194
excerptible sentence, function of, 114
experimentation, in writing, 178
extended review, 182

Fadiman, Anne, 214n2
fatal flaws, 99–100
feedback, 119, 121
Felber, Lynette, 102
figures, 62, 74
figures of speech, 174–75
"first books," defined, 214–15n6
Fish, Stanley, 24
Fisher Saller, Carol, 217n11
Flesch, Rudolf, 224n42

focusing, in scholarly book reviewing, 19, 169
Food, Culture & Society (journal), 35
footnotes, 218n39
foregrounding, 99
foreshadowing, in the introduction, 78
Furman, Rich, 211n28, 213n56
Fussell, Paul, 98

Gaillet, Lynée Lewis, 221n23
Gard, Wayne, 94
Geisha (Dalby), 151
generosity, in scholarly book reviews, 101, 102
Germano, William, 62–63, 73, 79, 108, 128, 209n9, 214n1
Gonzalez, Madelena, 133
Goodreads, 15
Gopnik, Adam, 143, 148
grace, in scholarly book reviews, 102
gracious note, 182
graduate students: celebration of, 196; mentoring, 184; note-taking by, 196; as readers, 187; requesting scholarly book copy by, 47–48; requirements of, 25–26; as reviewers, 20, 25–26, 194–97; teaching of scholarly reviewing to, 189; time of, 26
grandstanding, 99, 149
grant proposals, review of, 162–63
Guglielmo, Letizia, 221n23
Guilford Press, 220n18

Haag, Pamela, 72, 105, 175
habits, correcting, 178
Haggerty, Kevin, 21
Halpenny, Francess, 13
handbooks, review of, 139–42

Harris, Jennifer, 79, 202, 212n41, 219n46
Hayot, Eric, 77, 174–75, 177–78, 180, 183
hedge words, 174
Henige, David, 34
Hérubel, Jean-Pierre, 224n51
H-Net (Humanities and Social Sciences Online), 33
Hoge, James, 214n64, 218n39
honesty, in scholarly reviewing, 42
hooks, defined, 81
How to Be an Intellectual (Williams), 182
humanities, review process in, 209n9
humor, writing with, 172

ideas, differentiation of, 112
imaginary book, critiquing, 99
improvement, striving for, 179–87
inconsistencies, in edited volumes, 132
index, function of, 216n26
integrated book review, 11
intellectual work, practicing of, 166
interrelated words, use of, 176–77
introduction, 78, 106, 129–30, 132–33
I-want-to-try-that list, 179

Jansen, Jonathan, 220n9
jargon, defined, 13
Jensen, Joli, 22, 26, 186
journal articles, visibility of, 127
journals. *See* scholarly journals
Journell, Wayne, 211n29
judgment, in scholarship, 7–8
jump-right-in approach, 81
justifications, in introduction, 129–30

Kahan, Jeffrey, 218n26
kaizen, 122–23, 180

Kakutani, Michiko, 177
Kamler, Barbara, 225n63
Kelsky, Karen, 211n38
King, Stephen, 112
Kinn, Julie, 211n28, 213n56
Klemp, P. J., 101
Klinkenborg, Verlyn, 174
Kumar, Amitava, 173

Lahiri, Jhumpa, 183
Lane, Anthony, 152, 175–76
language, use of, 73
laptop, for note-taking, 58
Leahy, Anna, 20, 169
lectures, roles of scholarly book reviews in, 190–91
length, of scholarly book reviews, 14, 95, 104, 105, 126, 136
Lepore, Jill, 143, 148
Levitt, Aimee, 216n2
levity, writing with, 172
Lewin, Beverly, 211n33
library, for scholarly book identification recent acquisitions shelf at, 36–37
LibraryThing, 15
Lindholm-Romantschuk, Ylva, 209n9
linearly, reading, 64–65, 87
linguistic skills, 182–83
list price, locating, 58–59
literary book review, 3–4, 108–9
log-burning metaphor, 22, 186
Los Angeles Review of Books, 109
Luey, Beth, 211n36, 217n13
Lussier, Robert, 211n36

MacPhail, Bruce, 209n1
Manual for Writers of Research Papers, Theses, and Dissertations (Turabian), 141–42

Mastering the Art of French Cooking (Child), 164
Mayo, Christopher, 193, 201
Mazlish, Bruce, 213n50
McCanse, Ralph Alan, 15, 19, 115, 170, 172
McCloskey, Deirdre Nansen, 108, 177
Menand, Louis, 221n29
mentoring, 29, 184
metadata, verification of, 119
metaphors, 174–75
Metascience (journal), 32, 182–83, 212n48
Milardo, Robert, 10, 114
Mishan, Ligaya, 99
modifiers, 112
monographs, 129, 130, 134
Monumenta Nipponica (journal), 32

National Book Critics Circle, 3
needless words, omission of, 169
networking, 29–30, 39–40
New Yorker (magazine), 109, 175, 182
nitpicking, 78, 98, 217n13
Nona Balakian Citation for Excellence in Reviewing, 3
noncommittal language, 174
nonfaculty academics, as reviewers, 23
Nord, Walter, 179, 184
notes/note-taking: acknowledging bias and ingrained habit in, 56–57; attentiveness in, 167; back matter consideration in, 78; beginning, 57–59; bulletproofing, 66–67; colors in, 66; commentary in, 65, 66; compression of, 88; descriptive metadata in, 58; direct, factual descriptive matter in, 65–66; direct quotations in, 65, 66; discerning

noteworthy material in, 68–74; distilling of, 86–96; for edited volumes, 128–34; essay, 147; filling out your review with, 111–15; for graduate students, 196; lectures regarding, 191; length of, 68, 88; length of book considerations in, 79; lessons for, 117–18; line numbering of, 89; of monographs, 129; outlining of, 89; personal feelings in, 79; plagiarizing in, 65; preliminary walkthrough for, 59–64; printing of, 88–89; progressions in, 87; quotations in, 66–67, 92; reading and rereading of, 88; reflection in, 92, 147; rereading introduction in, 78; for review essays, 145–47; selectivity in, 88; sorting and organizing of, 94–96; textual emphases in, 67; themes and resources for review essay in, 147; title reconsideration in, 78; transcription in, 67, 68; types of, 57, 58, 65–66, 191, 214n2; understanding approaches to careful, 64–67; understanding changes in, 79; winnowing and focusing in, 86–93; wrapping up, 77–80

noteworthy material, discerning, 68–74

nouns, concrete, 172–73

offprints, 123
omission, as intentional, 113
omnibus review, 11, 209n4
on spec, reviewing a book as, 41–42
online journals, as outlet for scholarly book reviews, 15. *See also* scholarly journals

online review sites, as outlet for scholarly book reviews, 15
outliers, in edited volumes, 131
outline, for review essays, 147–48
outside knowledge, usage of, 112
Oxford University Press, 17

Pan, Yuling, 27
paragraphs, variation to, 175
passive coauthoring, 221–22n38. *See also* coauthoring reviews
passive voice, 112
past tense, 106
patience, in scholarly book review, 101, 102
Peanuts (cartoon strip), 46
peer review: anonymity of, 41; of edited volumes, 127; lack of skills in, 189; post-publication, 12, 97, 160–61; pre-publication, 12, 159–62; scholarly books in, 12; transferring your skills to, 159–63
Perry, Seth, 26, 119, 184, 187
personal attacks, on the author, 99–100
perspectival diversity, 136, 153
Pierazzo, Elena, 138
Pinker, Steven, 172
plagiarizing, 65, 100
"The Pleasures of Book Reviewing" (Simon), 192
Pool, Gail, 13, 115, 216n1
post-publication peer review, 97, 160–63. *See also* peer review
precision, 112
preconceptions, reviewing without, 50
prefatory matter, considerations regarding, 139
preparation, for scholarly book reviewing, 10–17

pre-publication peer review, 12, 159–62. *See also* peer review
present perfect tense, 106
present tense, 106
presenting the scholarly book review: conclusion in, 115–17; crafting in, 103–8; filling out your review in, 111–15; questions regarding, 205; quoting from the text in, 108–11; symposium for, 194; on writing scholarly book reviews, 192; writing your way in to, 108
Price, Leah, 63
print journals, as outlet for scholarly book reviews, 15
Professional Communication in International Settings (Pan, Scollon and Scollon), 27
professional organizations, 29, 162–63
professional social network, for scholarly book identification, 39–40
program evaluation, 162
pronouns, 172
ProQuest Dissertations & Theses Global database, 60
publishers/publishing: advance reader's copy from, 47; book review guidelines in, 34; communication with, 167–68; copyediting processes of, 122; copyright protocols of, 121–22, 123; editor role in, 27–28; eligibility determination of, 32; formats for scholarly book reviews in, 33; landscape of, 27–28; management of book reviews in, 34; marketing by, 49; overview of, 14–15; pressures in, 219–20n5; processes of, 21; questions regarding, 204; recommendations for review of scholarly books by, 34–35; requesting review copy from, 46–48, 153–54; rereading in, 122–23; reviewing for insights into world of, 21; for scholarly book identification, 38–39; scholarly book reviews as serving, 16–17; stand-alone sentences or phrases for, 148; timing of, 33; understanding origins of, 61. *See also* review venues; *specific outlets*
Pulitzer Prizes in Criticism, 3–4
puns, 175–76
Pushman, Erin, 179
Pyne, Stephen, 57, 69, 172, 177

Quindlen, Anna, 104
quotations: as claims support, 69; considerations regarding, 92; on cover, 219n44; in dissertations, 215n18; function of, 69–70; guidelines for, 69; in note-taking, 66–67; overview of, 108–11; review of, 119; transcription of, 67

readers, researchers as compared to, 54
reading for reviewing: associating in, 55; boredom in, 76; confusion in, 76; considering content in, 70–73; curiosity in, 181; dialoguing with the text in, 75–77; discerning noteworthy material in, 68–74; engagement with text in, 74–80; expectations of book in, 75; getting granular in, 73–74; lessons for, 80; linearly, 64–65, 87; note-taking in, 56–67; of other reviews, 180–82; overview of, 54–56; questions

arising in, 75; seeing the bigger picture in, 68–70; teaching, 191; theories in, 76; understanding in, 55; verbs for, 71, 111–12
reading notes, 65–80, 86–96, 103–4, 115, 117, 145–47, 154
recent acquisitions shelf, for scholarly book identification, 36–37
reference works, review of, 139–42, 219n1
reflection, 19, 92, 147
Renkl, Margaret, 166
reprints, 123
research librarian, for review venue identification, 30, 195
researchers, readers as compared to, 54, 214n1
ResearchGate, 30, 123
retention, improving with figures of speech, 174–75
retrospective review essay, 11, 150–52, 157, 158
reverse-engineering, for review venue identification, 30–31
review copy, 46–48, 153–54
review essay: adding books to, 148–49; argument in, 149–50; arranging themes and resonances for, 147; binge-reading for, 146; as bringing full circle, 150; coauthoring of, 157; comparative dimensions of, 148; comparison in, 146; constructing, 145–50; contextualizing, 142–45; defined, 10, 126; length of, 144; lessons regarding, 158; note-taking for, 145–47; outline for, 147–48; praise in, 148; retrospective, 150–52; reviewer role in, 142; scaling in, 144–45; as scholarly article, 221n23; stand-alone sentences or phrases in, 148; styles of, 148; themes and resources for, 147, 148
review forum, 11
The Review of Higher Education (journal), 32
review roundtable, 11
review venues: asking for review copy from, 44; background sharing with, 44; confirmation from, 121; copyediting processes of, 122; copyright protocols of, 121–22, 123; distinction of, 35; expectations of, 31–36; forthcoming themed issue of, 45; for graduate students, 195; identifying, 28–31; networking for identification of, 29–30; policies of, 93, 104, 116–17; publishing landscape and, 27–28; reaching out to editor of, 43–46; requirements of, 51; responses of, 45; for review essays, 144; submission portal of, 120. *See also* publishers/publishing
reviewers, scholarly: analysis of other, 181–82; background sharing of, 44; characteristics of, 13; conflicts of interest of, 40–41, 213n59; contextualization by, 51; as critic, 52–53; development of, 19–20; eligibility determination of, 32; as emcee, 137; expertise of, 19, 25, 89, 138; goal of, 42, 97–98, 102, 104–5, 114; gracious note to, 182; improving as, 179–87; influences to, 86; in interpretive communities, 24; journal requests to, 35–36; as keeping in touch with field developments, 18–19; knowledge of, 13–14; lessons regarding, 188; of literary works, 143; as model

reviewers, scholarly (*continued*)
academic citizens, 20; motivations of, 50; positioning as viable, 17–26; post-publication, as commentators, 161; preparation by, 52–53; pre-publication, power of, 161; presence and belonging of, 20; purposes of, 18–26, 86, 89–90; qualifications for, 24–26; questions for, 192, 203–8, 219n46; reviewers, pre-publication, as gatekeepers, 161; as scholar, 19–20; selectivity by, 135, 139, 158; stature of, 28; as striving for greater impact, 180–85; thinking like, 49–53; visibility of, 28, 210n27, 211–12n38; as writer, 19–20

reviewing, scholarly: as academic service, 20; as act of good will, 120; for adding titles to personal library, 23–24; analogy of, 164; approaches for, 101; for attentiveness, 167; authority in, 174; benefits of, 170–71, 188, 211n36; challenges in, 49; cliches in, 171–72; for communication skills improvement, 167–68; compaction in, 105; concision in, 105, 169; concrete nouns and active verbs in, 172–73; for connection in field, 166–67; for contributions to scholarly ecosystem, 20–21; creativity in, 171–79; credibility in, 217n13; for CV development, 23; for developing relationships in your field, 168; as drawing attention to works, 18; of edited collections, 134–37; embracing challenge of, 170–71; embracing work of, 170–71; encouraging others in, 183–84; focus in, 19, 169; in graduate studies, 194–97; honesty in, 42; improvement in, 179–87; insights from, 21; involving others in process of, 183; jump-right-in approach in, 81; for keeping in touch with field developments, 18–19; lessons regarding, 188; making room for, 185–87; mentoring others for, 184; as nitpicking, 217n13; by nonfaculty academics, 23; personal benefits of, 166–69; for practicing intellectual work, 166; presence and belonging through, 20; process of, 27, 68, 95, 225n69; as propelling larger projects, 21–22; qualifications for, 24–26; as reactive, 104; selectivity in, 135; by senior scholars, 23; as service to your field, 168–69; sharing talents in, 168–69; something-else approach in, 81–82; on spec, 41–42; stylishness in, 172; surprise in, 82; teaching, 189–97; as thinking work, 19; thrill in, 49; timeline for, 185–87, 192; time-management and, 22–23; in the undergraduate classroom, 190–94; value of, 166–71; warning regarding, 211–12n38; wit in, 172; without bias, 50; without preconceptions, 50; workmanlike approach to, 171; workshop for, 196–97; for writing improvement, 169. *See also* composing the scholarly book review; notes/note-taking

Richardson, James, 216n23
Rosenblatt, Roger, 223n33
Ross, David, 20
Rothfeld, Becca, 3

Salager-Meyer, Françoise, 211n33
Saller, Carol Fisher, 217n11
sample reviews, 51–52, 81–82, 84, 107–8, 194
scaling, in review essays, 144–45
scholarly book reviews: as annunciative, 13; of books in foreign languages, 182–83; categorizing, 10–11; characteristics of, 11–17, 170, 171, 191; consistency in, 50; as corrective to a peccadillo, 178; creativity in, 171–79; as describing and assessing, 12–13; digital copies of, 213n61; diminished value of, 3; dissemination of, 33; as distinctive, 94–95; diversity of, 50; as effective or successful, 4; embodiment in, 178–79; as enjoyable, 4–5; enlivening, 171–79; as evaluative, 3; fatal flaws of, 99–100; as form of criticism, 4; goals of, 53; grandstanding in, 99; guidelines for, 34; hooks in, 81; illustrious past of, 16; as influencers, 55; introduction in, 106; judgment in, 7–8; length of, 14, 95, 104, 105, 126, 136; literary book review as compared to, 3, 108–9; materialization of, 14; as negative, 98, 100–102; objectivity of, 117; patience and generosity in, 101; as positive, 103, 114; preparing for the task of, 9–17; printing of, 123; publication formats for, 33; publishing outlets for, 14–15; purpose of, 14, 16–17; questions about, 51; readers of, 13–14; reading aloud of, 120; reading of other, 180–81; requesting copy of, 46–48; rereading of, 122–23; reviewing, 51–52; roles of, 17–24, 190–91; special cases in, 125–26; as time-savers, 15–16; tone of, 105–6; as unengaging, 2; value of, 13; verbs for, 71, 111–12

scholarly books: acquiring copy of, 42; advance reader's copy of, 47; approach to, 54–55; assessment of, 51; audience of, 71; author's stated goals regarding, 71; back matter of, 78; bibliography of, 62; characteristics of, 51; complexity of, 74; consequence questions regarding, 207–8; content questions regarding, 206–7; as databases, 65; descriptive metadata of, 58; design and layout of, 62–63; dialoguing with, 75–77; as digital, 56; distancing from, 86–87; engagement with, 54–55, 63, 74–80; goals of, 76; for graduate student review, 195; identifying, for review, 36–40; identifying weaknesses of, 97–100; imbalance in, 62; intellectual processing of, 86–87; introduction of, 78; knowledge contributions of, 77; length considerations regarding, 79; linearly reading of, 64–65, 87; list prices of, 58–59; logic regarding, 64; as mines or quarries, 54; organization of, 72–73; pacing influence of, 74; in peer review, 12; personal feelings regarding, 79; preliminary walkthrough of, 59–64; pricing of, 217n6; as print copy, 56–57; providing list of, in teaching, 191–92; purpose of, 64; questions regarding, 205; recommendations for review of, 34–35; sources for, 71–72; structures of, 72–73;

scholarly books (*continued*)
  subjectivity regarding, 75; tables and figures in, 62, 74; theoretical perspectives in, 72; title appropriateness of, 78; types of, 12; understanding changes in, 79; understanding organization of, 61–62; understanding origins of, 60–61; understanding substantiation of, 62; users of, 12; uses for, 12
scholarly editions, review of, 137–38
scholarly journals: book review publishing policies of, 31–32; books received at, 39; footnotes in, 218n39; instructions for review of, 161; as outlet for scholarly book reviews, 14–15; peer review of, 160–61; recommendations for review of scholarly books in, 34–35; requests of, 35–36; reviews, sharing draft of, 162; types of reviews in, 209n3. *See also specific journals*
scholarly organizations, books received at, 39
scholarly reviewers. *See* reviewers, scholarly
scholarly reviewing. *See* reviewing, scholarly
Schulz, Charles M., 46
Schwartz, Seth, 221n38
Scollon, Ron, 27
Scollon, Suzanne Wong, 27
The Scriblerian (journal), 164
selectivity, 135, 139, 158
self-censorship, 102
semicolons, 177, 178, 223n39
senior scholars, as reviewers, 23
sentence length, 173–74, 224n42
series, understanding origins of, 61

Shatz, David, 105
Shrock, Dennis, 141
Silvia, Paul, 155
Simon, Linda, 101, 192
skills, reviewing, 164–65, 167–68, 169, 182–83
Smith, S. Stephenson, 103, 209n8
snarkiness, 117
soapbox, in review essay, 149
social media, for scholarly book identification, 39
social sciences, review process in, 209n9
something-else approach, 81–82
special cases, of scholarly book reviewing: anthologies as, 137–38; coauthoring reviews as, 152–57; edited volumes as, 127–42; lessons regarding, 157–58; overview of, 125–26; reference works as, 139–42; review essays as, 142–52; scholarly editions as, 137–38
structure, of scholarly book review, 173–79, 206. *See also* composing the scholarly book review
Strunk, William, Jr., 169
Sturm, Sean, 168–69
subheadings, 72
submission, celebration of, 119–24, 157, 196
substantiation, 70–73, 206–7
summary, defined, 12
Swinnerton, Frank, 218n21
Sword, Helen, 112, 172–73, 178, 179, 183
syllabus, reading scholarly book reviews in, 190
symposium, for scholarly book review presentation, 194
synchronous cowriting, 156. *See also* coauthoring reviews

tables, 62, 74
teaching, scholarly reviewing, 189–97
tear sheets, 123
templates, 94–95, 107, 172, 217n9
textual emphases, care regarding, 67
thematic words, use of, 176–77
thesis, 70–73, 215n11
Thompson, Hunter S., 176
Thomson, Pat, 225n63
time management, 185–87
Times Literary Supplement, 109
titling, 116–17, 215n11
Tobin, Ronald, 217n17
Toor, Rachel, 172, 210n27, 212n39
transferring your skills, 159–63
transformation, by the book, 114
translations, reviewing, 42
trenchant efficiency, in review essays, 145
Trubek, Anne, 37
trust: in authors, 77, 217n11; in reviewers, 13, 112
Turabian, Kate, 141–42, 215n15

undergraduate classroom, scholarly reviewing in, 190–94
university press, for scholarly book identification, 38–39
unsolicited submissions, risks regarding, 27–28
Updike, John, 117
utility, in review of reference works, 140–42

value, of scholarly book reviewing, 166–71
Van Viegen, Saskia, 26
Vendler, Helen, 176–77
verbs, 71, 111–12, 172–73
vetting, for reviews, 15
vocabulary, imaginative, 176
volunteering, 184, 185

weaknesses, in text, 97–102
West, James, 214n64, 218n39
Wheelan, Charles, 87–88
White, E. B., 169
Williams, Jeffrey, 182, 214n5
Wilson, Mark, 217n13
Wolper, Roy, 101, 112, 164, 174
Wong Scollon, Suzanne, 27
Woodcock, George, 181
word play, 175–76
word-jewel, 176, 223n31
working notes, 95–96, 104–5, 108, 111, 117–18, 146–47, 154
workshop, for scholarly reviewing, 196–97
WorldCat.org, 37
Wright, Charlotte, 175
writerly reading, 169
writing habits, correcting, 178, 188
Wulf, Karin, 19

Zerubavel, Eviatar, 186
Zinsser, William, 172, 175

A NOTE ON THE TYPE

This book has been composed in Arno, an Old-style serif typeface in the classic Venetian tradition, designed by Robert Slimbach at Adobe.

GPSR Authorized Representative: Easy Access System Europe - Mustamäe tee 50, 10621 Tallinn, Estonia, gpsr.requests@easproject.com

www.ingramcontent.com/pod-product-compliance
Lightning Source LLC
Chambersburg PA
CBHW020049170426
43199CB00009B/227